P38?

LONDON BOROUGH OF ENFIELD
LIBRARY SERVICES

This book to be RETURNED on or before the latest date stamped unless a renewal has been obtained by personal call, post or telephone, quoting the above number and the date due for return.

THE BRITISH CAMPAIGN IN IRELAND

1919–1921

THE DEVELOPMENT OF POLITICAL AND MILITARY POLICIES

BY

CHARLES TOWNSHEND

OXFORD UNIVERSITY PRESS
1975

Oxford University Press, Ely House, London W.1

GLASGOW NEW YORK TORONTO MELBOURNE WELLINGTON
CAPE TOWN IBADAN NAIROBI DAR ES SALAAM LUSAKA ADDIS ABABA
DELHI BOMBAY CALCUTTA MADRAS KARACHI LAHORE DACCA
KUALA LUMPUR SINGAPORE HONG KONG TOKYO

ISBN 0 19 821863 X

© OXFORD UNIVERSITY PRESS 1975

PRINTED IN GREAT BRITAIN
BY EBENEZER BAYLIS AND SON LIMITED
THE TRINITY PRESS, WORCESTER, AND LONDON

To my mother and father

PREFACE

The primary aim of this work is the simple one of providing a comprehensive account of the British employment of military and paramilitary forces in Ireland as a response to the guerrilla situation created by the Irish Republican movement from 1919 to 1921. The fact that no such account has previously been produced is remarkable, for the conflict had importance not only in itself but also in the example it set.[1] The lesson of Ireland, as Elizabeth Monroe, for example, remarked in the context of Middle East history, was not lost on 'abroad'.[2] In many colonial areas it was a direct inspiration. The British themselves perhaps drew their conclusions more warily. (It is not clear, for instance, how far the British Army regarded its Irish experience as a likely paradigm of its involvement in future colonial situations.) None the less, few people could doubt that a significant failure of modern state power had somehow occurred.

The author would not like to claim that he has fully achieved even the simple object of furnishing a complete description of this process. One obstacle which has stood in the way of earlier works on or around the subject, the sheer difficulty of obtaining reliable evidence, has by no means yet been fully demolished. The major documentary sources which have made this book possible, such as the official papers in the Public Record Office, and private papers, most notably in the Beaverbrook collection, have only become available in recent years; and approximatly one-third of the Irish records in the War Office papers in the P.R.O. remain under closure of 100 years. It will presumably be necessary to make many revisions in the year 2022. In less distant perspective, it is likely that other important sources may appear at any time, for there are many gaps as yet unfilled. However, it is hoped that the present work is sufficiently coherent and comprehensive to justify publication, and that, to take one small point only, it will no longer be necessary for writers on Irish history to regard the number of troops and police employed in the conflict as a matter of uncertainty.

There are, of course, dimensions to this study beyond that of simple description and narration. Of particular interest to the author have been the balance of political and military influences in the formulation of policy, and still more the relationship of civil and military authorities in the processes of administrative decision-making and execution. The structure of what was then called the Irish Government, and the

---

[1] For a note on literature on the conflict see R. Higham (ed.), *A Guide to the Sources of British Military History* (London, 1972), p. 460.

[2] E. Monroe, *Britain's Moment in the Middle East* (London, 1963).

interaction of government, army, and police, are thus primary focuses of this analysis. They are, however, treated as far as possible within a cogent—it is hoped—and chronological narrative form.

In the process of preparing this book I have amassed a number of undischargeable debts. The foremost of these is to Professor Norman Gibbs, whose encouragement and constructive criticism sustained my work from inception to completion. For invaluable critical and other help I am also most indebted to Dr. George Boyce, Dr. Ronan Fanning, Mr. Martin Gilbert, Dr. Cameron Hazlehurst, Mr. A. J. P. Taylor, and Dr. Gunter Treitel. Amongst the many generous providers of assistance and advice at research institutions I should like to thank especially Dr. Philip Bull of the Department of Western Manuscripts, Bodleian Library, Oxford; Dr. Stephen Inwood of the Imperial War Museum; Mr. Padraig O Maidin of the Cork County Library; and Mr. Breandan Mac Giolla Choille of the State Paper Office, Dublin.

For permission to utilize documents to which copyright attaches I am grateful to the First Beaverbrook Foundation, Major James Percival, and Major Cyril Wilson. Transcripts of Crown copyright records in the Public Record Office appear by permission of the Controller of H.M. Stationery Office. I hope that anyone whose copyright my work unwittingly infringes will accept my sincere apologies.

My special thanks to my colleague, Malcolm Crook, who assisted with the proofs, and to Carolyn Busfield, who made the index possible. To Frances Jameson I cannot adequately express what I owe.

University of Keele   C.J.N.T.
October 1973

CONTENTS

LIST OF TABLES, GRAPH AND MAPS

LIST OF ABBREVIATIONS

A. PERSONAL AND ORGANIZATIONAL TITLES, ETC.

A.D.R.I.C.	Auxilliary Division, Royal Irish Constabulary
A.U.S.	Assistant Under Secretary, Chief Secretary's Office
C.I.	County Inspector, Royal Irish Constabulary
C.I.G.S.	Chief of the Imperial General Staff
C.S.I.	Chief Secretary for Ireland, in Cabinet
C.S.O.	Chief Secretary's Office (Dublin Castle administration)
D.A.G.	Deputy Adjutant General
D.C.	Divisional Commissioner, Royal Irish Constabulary
D.I.	District Inspector (1st, 2nd and 3rd classes), Royal Irish Constabulary
D.M.O.	Director of Military Operations, War Office
D.M.P.	Dublin Metropolitan Police
D.O.R.A.	Defence of the Realm Acts
D.O.R.R.	Defence of the Realm Regulations
G.O.C.	General Officer Commanding (brigade and above)
G.O.C.-in-C.	General Officer Commanding-in-Chief
G.S.O.	General Staff Officer
I.G. R.I.C.	Inspector-General, Royal Irish Constabulary
I.O.	Intelligence Officer
I.R.A.	Irish Republican Army
I.R.B.	Irish Republican Brotherhood
I.V.	Irish Volunteers (later IRA)
J A.G.	Judge Advocate General
Ld.Lt.	Lord Lieutenant (Viceroy) of Ireland
M.I.	Military Intelligence
M.L.A.	Martial Law Area
R.I.C.	Royal Irish Constabulary
R.O.I.A.	Restoration of Order in Ireland Act
R.O.I.R.	Restoration of Order in Ireland Regulations
U.S.	Under Secretary, Chief Secretary's Office (head of Dublin administration)

B. SOURCES CITED

Callwell, *Wilson*: C. E. Callwell, *Sir Henry Wilson; His Life and Diaries.* See bibliography.

C.S.I. Weekly Surveys: Weekly Surveys of the State of Ireland by the Chief Secretary; circulated to the Cabinet Irish Situation Committee from July 1920, and to the Cabinet from January 1921.

C.S.O. R.P.: Index of Registered Papers of the Chief Secretary's Office. Suffix 'R. O.' indicates that only the note of a document in the register, not the document itself, now exists. See note p. 7.

G.H.Q. Ireland, *Record*: General Staff, Irish Command, *Record of the Rebellion in Ireland in 1920–21*. 2 vols.

G.O.C.-in-C. W.S.R.: Weekly Situation Reports by G.O.C.-in-C. Irish Command, circulated as C.S.I. Weekly Surveys.

Hist. 5th Div.: General Staff, 5th Division (?), *History of the 5th Division in Ireland 1919–1921*.

Macready, *Annals*: General Sir Nevil Macready, *Annals of an Active Life*. See Bibliography.

M.C.I.: Military Courts of Inquiry in Lieu of Inquest on Civilians, proceedings in W.O. 35 146–61A.

Rev. Org.: Cabinet, Home Office Weekly Reports on Revolutionary Organizations in the United Kingdom.

R.I.C. Reports: Monthly Confidential Reports of Inspector-General (I.G.) and County Inspectors (C.I.)., R.I.C., in C.O. 904.

S.I.C.: Cabinet, Irish Situation Committee minutes and memoranda.

Map 1: Ireland (showing places mentioned in the text)

I

THE CHALLENGE OF SINN FEIN

'It is a fair and square fight between the Irish Government and Sinn Fein as to who is going to govern the country.'

Walter Long, December 1918

1. THE SHAPING OF THE CONFLICT (1916–1918)

The aftermath of the 1916 Rising

THE apathy of the Irish public towards the Easter Rising, and the rapid disappearance of any military threat, encouraged the British Government's inclination to believe that it was an isolated outbreak. 'Physical force' as an element in Irish politics seemed once more to have been discredited. Lloyd George's attempt to bring off a settlement later in the year foundered on the familiar shoals of Ulster, unconnected with the recent drama.

But a new and revolutionary political force was soon to arise from the fertile ruins of the Rising. It is significant that it was immediately christened the 'Sinn Féin Rebellion', although Sinn Féin was a party which aimed only at securing autonomy, by means of civil resistance such as it was believed had been used by the Hungarians in 1867. Its founder and leader, Arthur Griffith,[1] detested violence and bloodshed, and was prepared to accept the nominal sovereignty of the British Crown over Ireland. The principles of Sinn Féin differed noticeably from those which had taken the Irish Volunteers into the Dublin streets to fight for an independent Republic. Yet, in the two years following the Rising, the Sinn Féin banner became the rallying-point for nearly every nationalist group, whether moderate or extremist, peaceful or violent. In the process there was an inexorable tendency for the majority to be borne along or driven by the active extremists, until at last the whole nationalist movement stood behind the Irish Volunteers in their final armed confrontation with Britain.

This transformation owed much to the British Government. While lethargically seeking a formula for eventual constitutional settlement, it continued to administer Ireland on the basis of mild coercion—repression too weak to root out opposition, but provocative enough to nurture it. Despite much criticism, the structure of the Irish Government (or Executive) was not altered after 1916. It was headed

---

[1] Arthur Griffith, 1872–1922. Founder and editor of *Sinn Féin*, 1906, of *Nationality*, 1916; Sinn Féin MP, 1918–22; Minister of Home Affairs and Acting President, Irish Republic, 1919; President of Provisional Government, Irish Free State, 1922.

nominally by a Lord Lieutenant, effectively by a Chief Secretary for
Ireland, who was a Cabinet Minister; its main body was the civil
administration, largely in the hands of an Under Secretary and Assistant
Under Secretary at Dublin Castle;[2] and its strongest limbs were the
police forces—the Dublin Metropolitan Police (D.M.P.) in the capital
and the Royal Irish Constabulary (R.I.C.) outside it.

The only changes which followed the Rising were in personnel: a
new Chief Secretary, H. E. Duke,[3] a new Under Secretary, W. P.
Byrne,[4] and a new Inspector General of the R.I.C., Brigadier-General
J. A. Byrne,[5] were appointed. These officers were not particularly
happy with the organizations they found. A composite memorandum
assembled by Duke in August 1916 indicated several inadequacies,
especially in the vital sphere of political intelligence. Byrne wrote that
'to have Dublin under the supervision of one secret service special
crimes system (i.e. that of the D.M.P.) and the remainder of the country
under another (the R.I.C.) cannot be considered sound policy'.[6] There
were, indeed, no less than seven intelligence systems in Ireland, varying
in effectiveness but all independent.[7] The Royal Commission which
sat during May and June 1916 to investigate the causes of the Rising
also laid blame on the division of the police forces, and on the weakness
and confusion of the administration generally. 'If the Irish system of
government be regarded as a whole', it said, 'it is anomalous in quiet
times and almost unworkable in times of crisis.'[8]

The Government does not appear to have been disturbed by this
advice. In fact by 1919 the structure of the Irish Executive was to
become perhaps more confused than it had been before the Rising. The
prime reason for this was the traditional British lack of 'touch' in Irish
affairs. The real effect of the Rising was not understood, and most
political efforts in 1917 centred on the abortive Irish Convention.[9]
(The Irish Nationalist party itself had lost touch with popular feeling,
and had become almost Anglicized in its outlook.) Moreover, since
Home Rule in some form was accepted as inevitable, there seemed to

    [2] In the following footnotes the holders of these posts are abbreviated as, respectively,
Ld.Lt., C.S.I., U.S., and A.U.S.
    [3] Henry Edward Duke, 1855–1939. Barrister; Conservative M.P., 1900–6, 1910–18;
C.S.I., 1916–18; Judge, 1919; President, P.D. & A. Division, 1919–33; Baron, 1925
(Merrivale).
    [4] William Patrick Byrne, 1855–1935. Barrister; Chairman, Board of Control, Home
Office, 1913–19; U.S., Ireland, 1916–18.
    [5] Joseph Aloysius Byrne, 1874–1942. Brig.-Gen. and D.A.G. Irish Command, 1916;
I.G. R.I.C., 1916–20; Barrister, 1921; Governor of the Seychelles, 1922–7, of Sierra
Leone, 1927–31; Governor and C.-in-C., Kenya, 1931–7.
    [6] Memo by I.G. R.I.C., in memo by C.S.I., August 1916. C.A.B.37 154/1.
    [7] See the illuminating survey in B. Mac Giolla Choille, *Intelligence Notes 1913–1916*
(Dublin, 1966), p. xxii.
    [8] Royal Commission on the Rebellion in Ireland, 1916. 79/Irish/195, W.O. 32 4307.
Cf. L. Ó. Broin, *Dublin Castle and the 1916 Rising* (London 1970,), pp. 153–61.
    [9] Cf. R. B. McDowell, *The Irish Convention 1917–1918* (London, 1970), pp. 43f.

be little need to strengthen the Executive. It was not anticipated that Sinn Féin would cut the ground from the concept of Home Rule itself, and bring forward instead its own, far more radical demands.

The recovery of Republicanism

As early as 11 June 1916 the Commander-in-Chief in Ireland, Sir John Maxwell,[10] informed Asquith that a change in public feeling was noticeable: there was now 'a disposition to demonstrate on every possible occasion in favour of Sinn Feinism or republicanism'. He thought that its manifestations so far were trivial, 'but if permitted will shortly embarrass the police'.[11] Such foresight was not common, however, least of all among the intelligence services. In October 1916 the military Intelligence Officer for the Midland and Connaught District[12] declared that

Any marked disloyalty can be put down to
(1) the younger sons of farmers who in ordinary times would emigrate to the USA and who now cannot do so. They have nothing to do at home, will not enlist in the Army, and spend their time hatching mischief or brooding over old wrongs which their forefathers suffered under English rule;
(2) shopkeepers' assistants, who are employed in large numbers in country towns, and who, to save themselves from serving their country or the terrors of conscription, meet together and join any political society that is anti-English.[13]

Although this officer had served in the R.I.C., he added with sweeping oversimplification that 'the real reason for any unrest is the fear of being taken from comfortable homes to fight under any flag'; two months later, in the same vein, he recommended the immediate enforcement of conscription, which would, he said, 'eventually tend to settle the Irish question'.[14]

The intelligence reports misdiagnosed, but they did not conceal the facts of Sinn Féin's advance. While Nationalists and Unionists wrangled in the Convention, the separatists were initiating their revolution. In February 1917 the Roscommon by-election was won by an independent, who declined, in accordance with Griffith's policy, to take up his seat at Westminster. In May the first outright Sinn Féiner was elected for Longford. Military intelligence wrote of this election that

[10] John Grenfell Maxwell, 1859–1929. Lt. Gen., G.O.C. Forces in Egypt, 1908–12, 1914–15; G.O.C.-in-C. Irish Command, April–November 1916; G.O.C.-in-C. Northern Command, 1916–19.
[11] G.O.C.-in-C. Ireland to Prime Minister, 11 June 1916 (Hol.). 79/Irish/195, W.O. 32 4307.
[12] Until 1919 Irish Command had three divisions, Northern, Midland and Connaught, and Southern, referred to here as N.D., M.C.D., and S.D. The Military Intelligence Reports for 1916–18, in C.O. 904 157, were regarded as useful sources by Dublin Castle.
[13] Military Intelligence (M.I.) Report, M.C.D., October 1916. C.O. 904 157.
[14] Ibid., December 1916.

The Sinn Fein party are ably organized and are making a most determined effort to capture this seat. Organizers from Dublin and other parts of Ireland are brought in and money seems plentiful.[15]

Meanwhile at Easter the Irish Volunteers had organized parades, including one down the Falls Road in Belfast. Sinn Féin publicity made strides, and the I.O. of Southern District reported in February that

A determined effort is being made to spread extremist ideas by means of so-called newspapers, containing no current news, which circulate largely throughout the district. . . . Papers of this kind . . . do an immense amount of harm amongst the semi-educated people who are their readers, and who notice the Government do not interfere with them or contradict their mis-statements.[16]

This disparity between the strength of Sinn Féin and Government propaganda was to be a major feature of the conflict.

Other future developments were clearly adumbrated at this stage. By July 1917, when Eamon de Valera[17] won a resounding election victory in East Clare, it had become, in the south, 'almost hopeless to expect a conviction, no matter how conclusive the evidence, from an ordinary petty sessions bench'.[18] Special Courts of two Resident Magistrates, as provided for in the 1887 Crimes Act, were re-established. In Clare, Limerick, and Kerry, there were unmistakable signs of a campaign to boycott the R.I.C., both economically and socially.[19] Intimidation was mounting, and in August detachments of troops had to be provided to 'strengthen' the police even in the midlands.[20]

British reactions

The Government had no formula for repression. Martial law had been imposed during the Rising, and maintained for a few months afterwards, but General Maxwell's attempts to make it effective had been thwarted by the Chief Secretary,[21] and Maxwell himself was recalled in November 1916. Extensive powers still remained under the Defence of the Realm Act (D.O.R.A.); indeed, one military I.O. thought that martial law was still in force in March 1917.[22] But these powers were not applied consistently, and an old tendency reappeared of ignoring

[15] M.I. Report, M.C.D., April 1917. C.O. 904 157.
[16] M.I. Report, S.D., February 1917.
[17] Eamon de Valera, 1882–1974. Commandant, Irish Volunteers, at Boland's Mill in Easter Rising; Sinn Féin M.P., and President of Sinn Féin and Irish Volunteers, 1917; President, Irish Republic, 1919–22; Prime Minister, Irish Free State, 1932–48, Irish Republic, 1951–4, 1957–9; President, 1959–73.
[18] M.P. Report, S.D., July 1917, C.O. 904 157.
[19] Ibid., and Minute by C.I. R.I.C., Tralee, 14 August 1917. C.O. 904 157.
[20] M.I. Report, M.C.D., August 1917.
[21] W. Alison Phillips, *The Revolution in Ireland* (London, 1923), p. 113.
[22] M.I. Report, M.C.D., March 1917, and Note by Judicial Division, C.S.O. C.O. 904 157.

illegal activities where the police were unable to prevent them. During the summer of 1917, as F. S. L. Lyons has succinctly put it, the Government 'with almost inconceivable foolhardiness . . . resorted to the old policy of pin-pricking coercion'.[23] A number of Volunteers were arrested and imprisoned, where they went on hunger-strike to obtain 'political' treatment. On 25 September a famous young leader, Thomas Ashe,[24] died in Mountjoy Gaol after forcible feeding: yet another potent martyr for the Republican cause. The Government weakened, and thereby, as it often did later, endangered the morale of its own forces. A military I.O. wrote bitterly next month that

As it is now evident to the parties concerned that they have only to hunger-strike for a couple of days in order to get out of gaol, whether convicted or untried, it is really very little use arresting them.[25]

Particularly dubious was the spirit of the Irish police, where, as in Britain, trade unionism was making some headway.[26] This was peculiarly anomalous in the case of the R.I.C., which was an armed force, often labelled 'paramilitary' by both its opponents and its members; though beyond the fact that it was under centralized control, and that constables were not stationed in their own counties (to minimize intimidation of relatives), it bore little resemblance to the 'army of occupation' portrayed in Sinn Féin propaganda. Its personnel were all Irish, and up till now the career of a policeman had been a secure and widely respected one. By 1917, however, a numerical deficiency of some 1,400 (from an establishment of 10,715)[27] aggravated its organizational problems, and it has been suggested, on the basis of entries in the *Constabulary Gazette* of the period, that morale had become 'chronically bad'.[28] Although this verdict seems to go beyond the evidence, there can be no doubt that attention should have been paid to the problem early on. As it was, the expected imminence of Home Rule discouraged reform,[29] and a commission of inquiry was not appointed until 1919.

The status of the R.I.C. was also peculiar. General Maxwell had pointed out that, as an armed force governed by their own regulations and 'in no sense' under the Army Act, they were unique in the British Empire.[30] The 1916 crisis, he said, had

[23] F. S. L. Lyons, *Ireland Since the Famine* (London, 1971), p. 386.
[24] Who had carried out the only notable guerrilla action of 1916, and was now President of the Supreme Council of the I.R.B. See S. Ó Lúing, *I Die in a Good Cause* (Dublin, 1970).
[25] M.I. Report, S.D., November 1917. C.O. 904 157.
[26] Memo by C.S.I., 30 October 1916. CAB.1 20/33.
[27] R.I.C. Nominal Rolls, 1916–18. H.O. 184 58–60.
[28] See R. Hawkins, 'Dublin Castle and the R.I.C.', in D. Williams (ed.), *The Irish Struggle* (London, 1966), pp. 174–6.
[29] Cf. Report of the Proceedings of the Irish Convention, Cmd. 9019 x, 697, App. XV, A, p. 125 (evidence of Sir Joseph Byrne).
[30] Memo No. 11 by G.O.C.-in-C. Ireland, in memo by C.S.I., August 1916. CAB.37 154/1.

clearly shown ... that the necessity exists for power to bring this force under the direct orders of the GOC-in-C should rebellion or invasion occur, and when so employed be under military law.[31]

Such a fusion was never permitted, and the independence of the R.I.C. was to be a major feature of the final crisis.

The Army itself envisaged this crisis only in terms of another open rebellion. The military performance during the 1916 Rising was viewed with satisfaction, and if one considers the weakness and inexperience of the troops employed (some of whom had never fired a rifle before) and the advantages of the defence in street fighting, it had been something of a success to root out 1,500 men in the space of a week.[32] But much of it was due to the rebel dispositions, and little military thought seems to have been given to what might have happened if the rebels had also operated against British communications. In the provinces, the rebels had risen openly and been rapidly crushed: only one guerrilla operation, that mounted by Thomas Ashe, had shown what they might have done.[33] When 59th Division carried out exercises in Ireland four months after the Rising, the scenario was another open rebellion, but this time with German support (which produced the evocative order, 'Any German troops south of the Liffey are to be vigorously attacked').[34] The military outlook at this time was well expressed by the Intelligence Officer for the midlands:

The presence of the military and the rapid dispersal of all armed bodies in the past rebellion have put an end to all hope of success by armed opposition in the future and the extremists recognize this.[35]

A year later his view remained substantially unchanged:

The Sinn Fein party has not yet sufficient arms of military value, or stores, has no artillery, and, therefore, without aid from Germany, can never raise an armed force that cannot be dealt with at once by the troops already in this country.[36]

The assumptions implied by the words 'all hope' and 'never' were those of a dangerous complacency.

The march of Sinn Féin

Yet the growing strength of the republican movement was unmistakable. At the end of 1917 Sinn Féin and the Irish Volunteers held con-

[31] Ibid.

[32] G.O.C.-in-C. Ireland to C.-in-C. Home Forces, 30 April 1916. 79/Irish/195. For a recent military assessment see Col. P. J. Hally, 'The Easter 1916 Rising in Dublin: the Military Aspects', Irish Sword, vii–viii. Nos. 29–30 (1966–7).

[33] Operation Reports, Cos. Meath, Clare, Galway, Wexford, and Wicklow, 27 April–3 May 1916. W.O. 35 69/1. Ashe's battalion, in northern Co. Dublin, chose the R.I.C. as its main target.   [34] 59th Division Orders, September 1916. W.O. 35 69/1.

[35] M.I. Report, M.C.D., October 1916. C.O. 904 157.

[36] Ibid., October 1917.

ventions in Dublin, and, though tension was developing between the
exponents of 'moral force' and those of 'physical force', they achieved
nominal unity by electing de Valera president of both bodies (after
Griffith had stood down from the leadership of Sinn Féin). Even the
midland I.O. now admitted that

The whole Sinn Féin movement is peculiarly well disciplined, having regard to
similar political organizations in the past. The results of its indoor meetings are
very hard to obtain. Drunkenness is almost unknown amongst those deeply
implicated, and is apparently severely dealt with. This is . . . foreign to the
usual state of things in similar movements.[37]

The military, or 'physical force', section became still more prominent
in 1918, and this was realized by the compilers of Dublin Castle's
annual intelligence summary.[38] The organizational structure of the
Volunteers was known to the authorities by late March 1918.[39] It was,
however, so imitative of regular military formations that it probably
reinforced the Army's confidence, and there was no rebellion in 1918—
only an upsurge of general lawlessness.

By March a 'bitter and aggressive feeling' was 'gradually and
generally being manifested towards the police' in the midlands as well
as the south,[40] while in Clare, until April

a state of utter lawlessness existed amounting to anarchy. Cattle-driving was
general. Large crowds, numbering from 300 to . . . 900 persons, assembled to
carry out a well-organized raid, utterly regardless of the presence of the few
police available.[41]

The helplessness evident in the style of this report (taken from that of
the Inspector General of the R.I.C.) seems to have been repeated across
the country. Raids for arms by the Volunteers were common, though
one fertile source was at last stopped when arrangements were made to
store the rifles of soldiers returning to Ireland on leave.[42] In February
1918, under the terms of Regulation 29B of the Defence of the Realm
Act (D.O.R.R. 29B), Clare was proclaimed a Special Military Area,
under the command of a brigadier-general, with extra troops and

[37] M.I. Report, December 1917.
[38] C.S.O. Intelligence Notes, 1918, p. 25 (Co. Tipperary S.R.). C.O. 903 19/4. For the
compilation of the Notes see Mac Giolla Choille, *Intelligence Notes 1913–1916*,
pp. xxviii f.
[39] I.G. R.I.C. to U.S., 28 March 1918. W.O. 35 69/8. This is a very full analysis and
contradicts later military assertions that the R.I.C. had done nothing to establish the
order of battle of the I.R.A.
[40] M.I. Report, M.C.D., March 1918. C.O. 904 157.
[41] C.S.O. Intelligence Notes, 1918, p. 14 (Co. Clare). C.O. 903 19/4.
[42] C.S.O. R.P. 1161(18), 11 January; R.P. 1543(18), 16 January 1918. R.O. (Register
only—note of document, not document itself, in C.S.O. register, Dublin).

powers to impose extensive restrictions.[43] Kerry went the same way in June, and West Cork in September.

Military restrictions, such as curfews and the prohibition of markets, had a noticeable effect on these areas,[44] but the number of troops required meant that they could hardly be applied if disorder became widespread. In January 1918, 65th Division was withdrawn from Ireland and replaced by two-and-a-half cyclist brigades. The military authorities told Dublin Castle that although the number of effective infantry had been reduced,

it is not considered, in view of the increased mobility of the fresh troops, that the military strength of the Garrison in Ireland will be adversely affected, and the GOC-in-C is satisfied that a sufficient force is available to deal with any contingency that is likely to arise.[45]

But the Army would have much to learn both about likely contingencies and about the value of mobility in Ireland. And when Ludendorff's great offensive opened against the British 5th Army on the western front late in March, only Lord French's personal request kept even these troops in the country.[46]

Lord French and the arrests of 1918

The situation in France led the Government to announce, on 9 April, that conscription would at last be applied to Ireland. Instantly Sinn Féin's national leadership became undisputed; even moderates and the Catholic hierarchy stood behind the republicans in their resistance to this 'oppressive and inhuman law'.[47] Displays by the Volunteers, including the carrying of arms, became more reckless. Duke, the Chief Secretary, was worried, and he did not share the Army's outlook on the Volunteers' prospects: a rising, he thought, was less likely than a campaign of civil obstruction and subversion of the police. He was equally perceptive in suggesting that, in spite of the unprecedented opposition to conscription, a well-judged voluntary recruitment campaign might still succeed.[48]

The Government, however, was definitely moving towards coercion. The tone was set by the appointment of a new Lord Lieutenant, Field-Marshal Viscount French.[49] On 8 May the Cabinet

[43] M.I. Report, S.D., February 1918. C.O. 904 157.
[44] C.S.I. to Cabinet, 27 February 1918. W.C. 355, CAB.23 5; M.I. Report, S.D., June 1918.
[45] Gen. Stanton, G.H.Q., to U.S., 6 February 1918. C.O. 904 187.
[46] War Cabinet, 29 March 1918. W.C. 377, CAB.23 5.
[47] These words being from the public statement of the Irish bishops at Maynooth on 18 April. D. Macardle, *The Irish Republic*, new edn. (London, 1968), p. 234.
[48] Memo by C.S.I., 21 April 1918. G.T. 4326, CAB.24 48.
[49] John Denton Pinkstone French, 1852–1925. C.I.G.S., 1912–14; Field-Marshal, 1913; C.-in-C. B.E.F., 1914–15, and Home Forces, 1915–18; Viscount, 1916 (French of Ypres) : Ld. Lt., Ireland, 1918–21 (in Cabinet Oct. 1919–Apr. 1921); Earl, 1922 (of Ypres).

instructed him to concentrate on suppressing seditious speeches and on investigating Sinn Féin intrigues with the Germans, as well, of course, as preparing to enforce conscription. (Characteristically, it warned him that 'to hold a meeting to organize resistance to a prospective law was not treason'.) Otherwise he had a free hand in administrative matters.[50] At the same time two further appointments were made: Edward Shortt,[51] who had come to Lloyd George's attention as an administrator of conscription, became Chief Secretary; and Lieutenant-General Sir Frederick Shaw[52] became G.O.C.-in-C.

French acted swiftly. Eschewing the pomp and ceremony of the Viceroyalty, he set up a small headquarters in the Viceregal Lodge, and drew up plans to police the country with air power.[53] On 15 May the Cabinet accepted his proposal to arrest the leaders of Sinn Féin on grounds of association with the enemy (necessary for trial under the Defence of the Realm Act), though it was less amenable to his 'firm conviction that Ireland should be at once put under complete martial law' with pure military government for at least two months.[54] Mass arrests were carried out on the night of 17 May, and the majority of the Sinn Féin leaders were taken: the significant exceptions were Cathal Brugha and Michael Collins,[55] both extremists and physical force men, whose influence now grew in the absence of the moderates. But the police regarded the arrests as 'a severe shock to the extremists, who really thought the Government would not dare to arrest their leaders', and a blow to Sinn Féin prestige.[56] Military intelligence agreed, and French wrote confidently to Lloyd George that the lack of public protest showed that 'the people are not really "in" with the Sinn Fein' [sic].[57]

Conscription was not enforced, however, despite French's original determination. Instead the Cabinet accepted Shortt's proposal of a voluntary recruiting campaign (suggested earlier by Duke).[58] But other

[50] War Cabinet, 8 May 1918. W.C. 4.7, CAB.23 5.
[51] Edward Shortt, 1862–1935. Barrister; Liberal M.P., 1910–22; Chairman, Select Cttee. on Administration of Military Service Acts, 1917; C.S.I., 1918; Home Secretary, 1919–22.
[52] Frederick Charles Shaw, 1861–1942. Director, Home Defence, War Office, 1915; C.G.S., Home Forces, 1916–18; K.C.B., 1917; G.O.C.-in-C. Irish Command, 1918–20; Lt. Gen., 1919.
[53] See below, p. 170.
[54] War Cabinet, 15 May 1918. W.C. 412, CAB.23 14. Cf. French to Prime Minister, 19 May 1918. Lloyd George papers, F/48/6/8.
[55] Michael Collins, 1890–1922. Director of Organization, Irish Volunteers, 1917; President, Supreme Council, I.R.B., ?1917; Minister for Finance, Dáil Eireann, 1919, and Director of Intelligence, I.R.A.; Chairman of Cabinet, Provisional Government, Irish Free State, 1922; killed in ambush, 1922.
[56] Report of I.G. R.I.C., in Report of Ld. Lt., 2 August 1918. G.T. 5289, CAB.24 59. There is no official note of the number of Sinn Féin leaders arrested; Macardle (The Irish Republic, p. 236) states that 73 were 'deported to England immediately', and others later.
[57] French to Prime Minister, 19 May 1918. Lloyd George papers, F/48/6/12.
[58] War Cabinet, 10 and 15 May 1918. W.C. 408, 412, CAB.23 14.

strong measures were in train. On 21 May a system of controls on entry into Ireland, which had been in preparation for two months, was put into effect, to keep out undesirables.[59] French then proceeded, on 14 June, to issue proclamations in fourteen counties,[60] declaring Sections 3 and 4 of the 1887 Crimes Act to be in force. Under this Act he could now issue Special Proclamations naming certain organizations in these counties as 'dangerous associations'; the final step would be to issue Orders declaring them illegal.[61]

Dublin Castle was not in favour of this course. The Under Secretary, Byrne, wrote to Shortt insisting that what was needed was a real clampdown on seditious speeches. So far, he said, the Government had balked at prosecution, but it was now taking the much less effective and less desirable step of trying to prevent meetings. 'Proclamation' he thought useless.

> The present state of parts of Ireland does not seem to me to be the result of the machinations of any secret unlawful association . . . but a fairly wide estrangement of the people from law and order, and a contempt of authority. . . .[62]

This contempt he blamed on the Government's weakness in hoping that, if left alone, Sinn Féin would 'spend itself'.

Special Military Areas
Although taking a different line from that recommended by Byrne, Lord French was certainly not leaving Sinn Féin alone. On 3 July he proclaimed as dangerous associations not only the Irish Volunteers but also the whole Sinn Féin organization (including the Sinn Féin clubs, by this time over a thousand in number and with some 100,000 members), together with the women's organization Cumann na mBan, and, for good measure, the Gaelic League.[63] The military authorities issued proclamations under D.O.R.R. 9AA prohibiting meetings and fairs except by permit, though the Government lawyers feared that the inclusion of fairs 'overstrained' the Regulation, and Orders in Council were hastily drawn up to insert '(including fairs and markets)' after the word 'assemblies' in the Regulation.[64]

The ban on meetings, as the Under Secretary had said, could never

---

[59] Instructions by IG RIC, 1 April 1918. C.O. 904 169/4.

[60] Clare, Cork, Galway, Kerry, King's, Limerick, Longford, Mayo, Queen's, Roscommon, Sligo, Tipperary, Tyrone, and Westmeath.

[61] Cf. Criminal Law and Procedure (Ireland) Act, 50 Victoria Sess. 2, Chap. 20. *Law Reports*, 1887, pp. 53–4. The best historical account of this Act is L. P. Curtis, *Conciliation and Coercion in Ireland 1880–1892* (Princeton, N.J., 1963), pp. 179–210.

[62] U.S. to C.S.I., 15 June 1918, C.O. 904 169/2.

[63] Criminal Law and Procedure (Ireland) Act: List of Proclamations and Orders in Force, 1919. W.O. 35 66. The number of Sinn Féin Clubs reported at the end of 1918 was 1,354, with 112,080 members. C.S.O. Intelligence Notes, 1918. C.O. 903 19/4.

[64] Attorney-General's Opinion, 16 July; Orders in Council, 19 July; Solicitor-General to Attorney-General, 20 July 1918. C.O. 904 169/2.

be fully enforced by the police, and the refusal of Sinn Féin to apply for permits only meant that the R.I.C. lost one of its main sources of information. Henceforth republican meetings took place in secret, while hostility to the police grew more overt. On 10 July two constables were actually attacked near Ballingeary, Co. Cork, an assault which was, in the words of the County Inspector, 'calculated to shake to its foundations all sense of public security'.[65] There followed further attacks in West Cork, 'clearly organized from one source' in the opinion of the R.I.C.[66] After the most serious of them, at Donnemark on 24 September, subsequent police enquiries encountered 'the greatest reticence' on the part of the public, and the Inspector General decided that 'the time has come when drastic steps are necessary to put an end to this lawless state of affairs'.[67]

On 28 September, West Cork was made a Special Military Area: troop strength was increased to two battalions, centred on Bantry and Macroom, with companies at Dunmanway, Skibbereen, Bandon, and Millstreet. Fairs and markets were prohibited without military permit, public houses were closed at 7 p.m., and a curfew was imposed on the very lawless town of Eyeries.[68] In spite of this assistance, the local police were hard pressed throughout October 1918, and called for a reinforcement of 40 men (the West Cork R.I.C., some 250 strong, were 50 short of 'fixed strength' and 20 short of 'working strength').[69] By mid-November, however, attacks on them had ceased, the number of outrages—the R.I.C.'s term for 'political' as against 'ordinary' crimes—had decreased, and morale was recovering. District Inspector Greer, the Acting County Inspector for West Cork, was enthusiastic:

The effect [of the Special Military Area] on the Riding force has been very encouraging. They know that the Commandant is here on the spot to deal with any attacks on them and that in the performance of their duty they can rely on his support and that of the military.[70]

So far there had been no fatal casualties, and at the end of December military intelligence was able to report that during the period of the Special Military Area there had been only one attack on the police and one threatening letter, as against 6 attacks, 55 raids for arms, 8 threatening letters, and 12 malicious injuries in the preceding months of 1918.

The inhabitants are now behaving themselves because the disloyal element are

[65] Report of C.I. R.I.C., Cork W.R., 10 July 1918. C.O. 904 169/2.
[66] C.S.O. Intelligence Notes, 1918, p. 18 (Cork W.R.). C.O. 903 19/4.
[67] I.G. R.I.C. to U.S., 26 September 1918. C.O. 904 169/3.
[68] Acting C.I. R.I.C., Cork W.R., to I.G. R.I.C., 7 October, 19 November 1918. C.O. 904 169/3.
[69] Ibid., 7 October 1918; R.I.C. Nominal Roll, 1919. H.O. 184 61.
[70] Acting C.I. R.I.C., Cork W.R., to I.G. R.I.C., 19 November 1918.

fully aware that if they don't, further restrictions will be imposed which will mean pecuniary loss.[71]

Dublin Castle added that the Military Area seemed 'a remarkable instance of the effect which a mild system of military control can have on a community'.[72] What no one pointed out, however, was that this success depended on the fact that the moderate majority could still control the men who were taking to the gun as the final answer to the Irish question: the imminent reversal of this situation would once again change things utterly.

European peace, Irish war

Towards the end of 1918 the lines of the new Irish conflict became clearly drawn. By October it was evident that repressive policy had not succeeded in reducing disaffection.[73] The attempt to link conscription and home rule had been a failure, and Walter Long,[74] whose influence with the Conservative back benches allowed him great weight in Irish policy, now advised that they should both be dropped, and that the Government should wait until obedience to law prevailed before taking any decisive step.[75] This rationalization of inaction was certainly welcome to the Cabinet, for the ending of the Great War on 11 November posed its own problems. Wartime administration was essentially simple, there being only one political norm—maximum effort. Postwar retrenchment, the attempt to reset the old norms of society, was far more complicated.

Problems of retrenchment—especially demobilization—were of immediate relevance to the Irish Executive. Restoring 'obedience to law' was by now a task which the police alone could not hope to accomplish. Yet the Army could hardly be strengthened. In August 1918 there had been 111,222 troops in Ireland, of which 52,572 were being trained as drafts for overseas. Many of the rest were convalescents. Only 9,919 were specifically available for internal security work—and this total included engineer and artillery units.[76] After the armistice, Lt. Gen. Shaw put his minimum requirements at 15 full-strength battalions (each 800) and 24 cyclist units of 450 each.[77] In fact, however,

[71] Col. Owens to I. Branch, G.H.Q. Ireland, 28 December 1918. C.O. 904 169/3.

[72] C.S.O. Intelligence Notes, 1918, p. 18 (Cork W.R.). C.O. 903 19/4.

[73] Monthly Confidential Reports of Inspector General and County Inspectors, R.I.C.; Report of I.G., October 1918. C.O. 904 107. These reports, the fullest R.I.C. records now extant, are here referred to as R.I.C. Reports, I.G., etc.

[74] Walter Hume Long, 1854–1924. Conservative M.P., 1880–1921; C.S.I., 1905; Leader of Irish Unionists, 1907; Colonial Secretary, 1916; 1st Ld. of the Admiralty, 1919–21; Viscount, 1921 (Long of Wraxall). Responsible for Irish affairs, Cabinet, from 10 May 1918.

[75] Memo by Sec. of State for the Colonies, 9 October 1918. G.T. 5926, CAB.24 66.

[76] Report of G.O.C.-in-C. Ireland, in Report of Ld. Lt., 30 August 1918. G.T. 5570, CAB.24 62.

[77] Ibid., 16 December 1918. CAB.24 72/1.

Irish Command was not supplied with this number of effective infantry until the summer of 1920.

The European peace also increased the Cabinet's reluctance to employ 'martial' measures in Ireland, and consequently—since it was not yet prepared to implement home rule either—its propensity towards half-measures. One of the most promising steps to have been taken in 1918 was the introduction of a permit system for passage from Britain to Ireland, and the reduction in the number of permitted routes to 12.[78] This carefully prepared scheme involved liaison between the R.I.C., whose County Inspectors were responsible for vetting applications for entry visas, and three British permit offices, in London, Liverpool, and Glasgow. Despite some inconveniences, it appears to have worked, and might have provided the basis for more comprehensive passport and identity controls, whose absence proved to be a severe handicap as the conflict developed. Instead, shortly after the armistice, the Government decided, for reasons which can hardly have been connected with the Irish situation, that 'it is no longer necessary to maintain the Permit System'; from 21 November 'British subjects and alien friends will be able to proceed to Ireland without a permit and by any route'.[79]

Lord French was also finding that his 'free hand' in administrative matters was shackled. As Sinn Féin activity spread, he became concinced that the civil administration was incapable of coping with it. He clashed repeatedly with the Chief Secretary, and in October he complained to Lloyd George that

Not only has he [Shortt] placed views which he knew to be opposed to mine before the War Cabinet without any reference to me, but he has displayed a most tactless and ill-advised judgment in endeavouring to thwart measures which I have insisted upon carrying through, for no other reason, so far as I can make out, than those of personal expediency in connection with the Irish Vote at a General Election.[80]

From the start French had been frustrated by the inefficiency of the Castle organization, especially the bottleneck caused by the Assistant Under Secretary, Sir John Taylor,[81] who kept all work in his own hands. French looked to swift, strong measures to end the crisis, and warned the Cabinet in November that 'any relaxation of D.O.R.A. at this time would make it impossible to govern Ireland', as would any reduction in the military garrison.[82] By December he had decided

---

[78] J. F. Moylan, Home Office, to U.S., 10 April 1918. C.O. 904 169/4.

[79] U.S., Home Office, to Chief Constable, 20 November 1918. C.O. 904 169/4; see also *Irish Times*, 20 November 1918.

[80] Ld. Lt. to Prime Minister, 12 October 1918. Lloyd George papers, F/48/6/20.

[81] John James Taylor, 1859–1945. P.S. to C.S.I. (Long), 1905; Principal Clerk, C.S.O., 1911–18; Clerk to Privy Council and A.U.S., Ireland, 1918–20; K.C.B., 1919.

[82] War Cabinet, 21 November 1918. W.C. 505, CAB.23 11.

that the Castle must be temporarily replaced by an executive body which could bring the emergency to an end.[83]

Events were to vindicate his analysis, but for the time being the Cabinet ignored it, even though the magnitude of the problem was spectacularly advertised at the General Election of December 1918. While in Britain the 'coupon election' returned Lloyd George's coalition to power, in Ireland Sinn Féin won a landslide victory comparable to that of the Nationalists under Parnell.[84] Unlike the old Nationalist party, however, Sinn Féin now had within it a 'physical force' wing which was independent, organized, and determined. The Inspector General of the R.I.C. recognized that although this wing could not take on the Army openly, it could 'make government impossible' if the Army were weakened.[85] French, drawing the Cabinet's attention to 'the continued increase in the strength of the Irish Volunteers', said that they had now become a republican secret society 'in the worst and most dangerous sense'.[86] And Long, in a memorandum on the last day of 1918, presented a striking analysis of the confrontation which had now begun.

I have watched the rise and fall of every political party in Ireland for the last forty years, and I think that the present movement is much the most difficult and dangerous of any the Government have had to deal with and for this reason.

Their leaders are brave and fanatical and do not fear imprisonment or death; they are not to be influenced by private negotiations with Bishops or Priests, or captured by getting the patronage of appointments, which has been the favourite instrument of the Irish Government since 1905. Neither do they care a straw for the press.

It is a fair and square fight between the Irish Government and Sinn Féin as to who is going to govern the country.[87]

2. REPUBLIC AND REACTION (January–July 1919)

The first Dáil Government

The newly-elected Sinn Féin M.P.s not only refused to take up their seats at Westminster, but proceeded to establish themselves as an independent legislative assembly, Dáil Eireann. On 21 January 1919 those of them who were not in prison[88] met in the Dublin Mansion House

[83] Report of Ld. Lt., 16 December 1918. G.T. 6540, CAB.24 72/1.
[84] It won 73 seats, and reduced the Nationalist party to 6; the Unionists took the remaining 26 seats. Macardle, The Irish Republic, p. 247.
[85] R.I.C. Reports, I.G., November 1918. C.O. 904 107.
[86] Report of Ld. Lt., 16 December 1918. G.T. 6540, CAB.24 72/1.
[87] Memo by Sec. of State for the Colonies, 31 December 1918. G.T. 6574, CAB.24 72/1.
[88] Of the 69 names on the roll, the answer 'Fe ghlas ag Gallaibh'—imprisoned by the foreign enemy—was given to 36. Macardle, The Irish Republic, p. 252.

and adopted three foundation deeds: a Declaration of Independence, an Address to the Free Nations of the World, which announced that a state of war existed which could never end 'until Ireland is definitely evacuated by the armed forces of England', and a Democratic Programme, which declared that every citizen had a right to an 'adequate share of the produce of the Nation's labour', but which steered clear of any real commitment to socialist theory.[89] Pure nationalism was the basis of republican unity.

The president and vice-president of the new republic, de Valera and Griffith, were both in prison, though both were appointed delegates to the Paris Peace Conference, on which many of Sinn Féin's hopes rested. In February, shortly before the Cabinet agreed to the 'gradual and unostentatious' release of the imprisoned Sinn Féin M.P.s,[90] Michael Collins engineered de Valera's escape from Lincoln gaol, and brought him back to Dublin.[91] The Sinn Féin executive announced that his homecoming was to be 'an occasion of national rejoicing', and the Lord Mayor of Dublin planned to meet him at the gates of the city.[92] The Chief Secretary, however, had the mayoral proclamations torn down, and warned him that it would be *lèse-majesté* to meet de Valera in a way in which only the sovereign could be met.[93] After some angry exchanges the plan was abandoned, and de Valera arrived quietly. None the less, he was proclaimed president by the Dáil on 1 April, and re-acclaimed as president of Sinn Féin at the Dublin Ard-fheis a week later.

Next month he left Ireland for the U.S.A., to campaign for funds and for the recognition of the Republic. Griffith succeeded him as Acting President and Minister of Home Affairs, with a Cabinet of ten: Plunkett (Foreign Affairs), Brugha (Defence), MacNeill (Industry), Cosgrave (Local Government), Collins (Finance), Barton, later O'Connor (Agriculture), Stack (Justice), Ginnell, later Fitzgerald (Publicity), Blyth (Trade and Commerce), and Countess Markievicz (Labour). The effect of these ministries varied with the capability of their incumbents and the feasibility of their tasks. Stack, for instance, was in prison for a year, and thereafter proved a disappointing administrator, while O'Connor, with the land courts, and Collins, with the

[89] Thus the section of the Programme which, in the original draft by the Labour publicist Thomas Johnson, promised the elimination of capitalism, was deleted from the final draft. For a bitter socialist account see C. Desmond Greaves, *Liam Mellows and the Irish Revolution* (London, 1971), pp. 169–70.

[90] War Cabinet, 5, 6 February, 4 March 1919. W.C. 526, 527, 541, CAB.23 9.

[91] De Valera wished to go straight to America, but Collins and Boland persuaded him to return first to Dublin.

[92] Circular from Sinn Féin Executive, signed by Boland and O'Kelly (Hon. Secs.), C.O. 904 169/5.

[93] C.S.I. to Lord Mayor of Dublin, 31 March 1919, C.O. 904 169/5; cf. C.M.A. Orders, 26 March and 8 April 1919. C.S.O. R.P. 8257.

republican loan, did significant practical work.[94] More symbolic was the 'Commission of Inquiry into the Resources and Industries of Ireland', set up independently of Dáil Eireann so as to avoid proscription, which held a long series of public hearings and produced an 'interim' report on milk production in the summer of 1920.[95] In the circumstances it was impossible for the Dáil Government to be a regular executive body, and power was wielded by those who were capable of wielding it. The Dáil itself met only a few times.[96]

Soloheadbeg and the I.R.A.

The almost romantic façade of the Irish Republic was a revolutionary development in Irish politics, but behind it more traditional methods were also reappearing. The formidable Republican campaign which matured in 1919 combined the new ideas of civil resistance—the undermining of the British administration—with the old ideal of physical rebellion. By a notable coincidence, it was on the very day that the Dáil first met, 21 January, that Seán Treacy and eight men of the Tipperary Volunteers finally succeeded in capturing a cartload of gelignite bound for the quarry at Soloheadbeg, near Tipperary.[97] In the process they killed the two R.I.C. men who were escorting it.

Soloheadbeg shocked many moderate Sinn Féiners, and probably many nominal Volunteers as well: a new element of ruthlessness distinguished it from the attacks of the previous year. The question why it took place is fundamental to any study of the Republican movement. There can be no doubt, from the account written by Treacy's companion in arms, Dan Breen, that the attack was a conscious self-assertion by the 'physical force' wing. In the original edition of *My Fight for Irish Freedom*, he stated that the campaigning for the 1918 general election

had had a serious effect on our army. Many had ceased to be soldiers and had become politicians. There was a danger of disintegration, a danger which had been growing since the threat of conscription disappeared a few months earlier. I was convinced that some sort of action was absolutely necessary.[98]

In later editions he altered this to the statement that 'the Volunteers

---

[94] See, e.g., Dáil Eireann, *The Constructive Work of Dáil Eireann* (Dublin, 1921), ii. 9, 15; Macardle, *The Irish Republic*, pp. 263, 337; M. Forester, *Michael Collins—The Lost Leader* (London, 1971), pp. 157–8.

[95] Reports followed on 'stockbreeding farms for dairy cattle', coalfields, industrial alcohol, and sea fisheries. *Constructive Work of Dáil Eireann*, ii. Ch. II.

[96] J. L. McCracken, *Representative Government in Ireland* (London, 1958), pp. 23–4; Lyons, *Ireland Since the Famine*, p. 404.

[97] Their ambush had been prepared for five days, according to Breen. Treacy became Commandant of the Tipperary No. 3 Brigade, I.R.A., until his death in a gun fight in Talbot St., Dublin, in October 1920. Breen succeeded him. For a study see D. Ryan, *Seán Treacy and the 3rd Tipperary Brigade* (London, 1945).

[98] D. Breen, *My Fight for Irish Freedom* (Dublin, 1924), pp. 32–3.

were in great danger of becoming merely a political adjunct to the Sinn Féin organization'.[99] Both arguments are significant. If, as everyone was afterwards anxious to claim, the Irish Volunteers were from the start the legally-constituted army of the Republic, why was it a danger that they should be subordinated to Sinn Féin? The short answer seems to be that in 1919 the Republic served by the Volunteers was still a different thing from that represented by Dáil Eireann.

Since the days of James Stephens, the Fenian chief, there had been a powerful secret society which had regarded its own supreme council as the provisional government of the Irish Republic. It was this organization, the Irish Republican Brotherhood (I.R.B.), which had led the Volunteers into the streets in 1916, and declared a Republic prior to the election of a national assembly. The new Republic had begun with an elected assembly, but the I.R.B. remained. Although de Valera and Brugha disliked it, it was, as Collins's most recent biographer puts it, 'the soul of the Irish Volunteers'.[100] De Valera, the nominal president of the Volunteers, had no influence within the I.R.B., which was now dominated by Collins. Collins himself was a remarkable illustration of the divisions of power within the republican movement, being at the same time Minister for Finance responsible to the Dáil, Director of Organization (and, from June 1919, Director of Intelligence) on the Executive of the Irish Volunteers, and finally President of the Supreme Council of the I.R.B., with a notional leadership of the whole movement.

It should, in retrospect, have been easy to create a unified system of authority amidst the euphoria of 1918–19, but even then there were sharp disagreements over methods.[101] Collins, who was Brugha's colleague in the Dáil Government, was his subordinate in the Volunteer leadership, and opposed Brugha's attempts to assert Dáil control over the organization, while using his power as head of the I.R.B. to control it himself.[102] This was not because he objected in principle to governmental authority, but because he believed himself more capable of running the Volunteers than was Brugha, or even Brugha's Chief of Staff, Richard Mulcahy. His brilliant success was his immediate vindication, but in the longer term his procedure, in stunting the growth of regularized authority, sowed the seeds of division and ruin. Even in 1919, divided loyalties were reflected at the lower levels of the movement. It was thus that a local I.R.B. man and Volunteer like Breen could see subordination to the political wing of Sinn Féin as a danger.

[99] Ibid., new edn. (Tralee, 1964), p. 38.
[100] Forester, *Michael Collins*, p. 71.
[101] See, e.g., D. Figgis, *Recollections of the Irish War* (London, 1927), p. 243; R. Kee, *The Green Flag* (London, 1972), pp. 642, 647.
[102] Forester, *Michael Collins*, p. 127.

In spite of Collins's obstructiveness, the status of the Volunteers did change, albeit superficially, in 1919: the title 'Irish Republican Army' (I.R.A.) came increasingly into circulation, and the Volunteer Executive became known as G.H.Q. In August 1919 Brugha succeeded in getting the Volunteers to swear an oath of allegiance to the Dáil, though the process of administering this oath locally was slow, and the Dáil itself did not publicly take responsibility for the activities of the I.R.A. until 1921. The organizational structure of the Volunteers also began to change in 1919 to facilitate forms of warfare short of open rebellion. Hitherto the basic tactical unit had been the Company, which included Right and Left Half-Companies.[103] Now it became clear that success-ful activity would depend on a less defined group of activists within a battalion or even a brigade area. None the less, the rigid pseudo-regular hierarchy of formations remained, and could cause problems. Officers were elected by their units, and could not be replaced from above, even if they were unadventurous or inefficient.

The Captain, First Lieutenant, Second Lieutenant, Company Quartermaster, and Company Adjutant shall form a company council, which shall be presided over by the Captain. The duty of this council shall be to act in an advisory capacity on a matter submitted for its recommendation by the Captain, the Battalion and Brigade Councils, or by Headquarters staff. It shall be no auth-ority over matters of discipline, command and efficiency, for which the Captain is solely responsible.[104]

From four to seven companies formed a battalion, whose officers— Commandant, Vice-Commandant, Adjutant, Quartermaster, Lieu-tenant of Engineers, Chief of Signallers, Chief of Medical Service, and Chief of Scouting and Cycling—were elected by the company officers. On the same basis, brigades were formed with three to six battalions, though in practice they were made to conform to county areas. Large and active counties might be subdivided—thus in January 1919 the Cork Brigade was divided into three, No. 1 (East), No. 2 (North), and No. 3 (West).

An example of the operational development of these units is that of Cork No. 2, commanded by Liam Lynch, whose aide and biographer, Florence O'Donoghue, described the process as follows:

First, while his force was acquiring a mental adjustment to combat, activities were directed towards acquiring serviceable arms; secondly, these arms were used for attacks on police posts and small patrols, with the result that the small posts were driven in, leaving substantial areas clear of enemy forces; thirdly, the continuous sniping and minor attacks on enemy strongholds, creating a state of nervous uncertainty extremely destructive of enemy morale; and

[103] Irish Volunteers: General Scheme of Organization, in I.G. R.I.C. to U.S., 28 March 1918. W.O. 35 69/8.
[104] Ibid.

finally the organization of flying columns for larger operations from the best trained, fittest and keenest officers and men.[105]

Although it may be doubted whether the process was foreseen as accurately as this suggests, there is no doubt that the early grasping of opportunities was vital. Units which had failed to capture significant quantities of arms by the end of 1919 mostly failed to develop later.[106]

The growth of the rebel campaign
Violent activities remained sporadic for some time after Soloheadbeg. Seán Treacy's group wanted to press on immediately with further operations, and to issue a proclamation ordering all British forces to leave south Tipperary on pain of death.

> We sent the draft to Volunteer Headquarters for their approval; but both An Dail and General Headquarters refused to let us go ahead. We could not understand their reluctance, seeing that ours was the only logical position.[107]

Thus wrote the eager Dan Breen. The Dáil was indeed hesitant about the effect of its apparent declaration of war on 21 January, for Soloheadbeg had produced very unfavourable public reactions, even in Tipperary itself where Treacy was very popular.[108] But the initiative was taken by the Volunteer journal *An tÓglách*, which was to become the nearest thing that the I.R.A. had to a general order sheet.[109] In its 31 January number it restated the Dáil's declaration that England and Ireland were at war, adding that Volunteers were thus justified in 'treating the armed forces of the enemy—whether soldiers or policemen—exactly as a National Army would treat the members of an invading army'.[110]

The undoubted illegality of this policy left the more adventurous Volunteers isolated for some time.[111] Efforts were concentrated on the seizure of arms, and a preference for cunning rather than force was evident. Particular skill was shown in some West Cork arms raids, and in the dramatic seizure of 75 rifles, 72 bayonets, and 4,000 rounds of ammunition from Collinstown aerodrome, near Dublin, in March.[112]

---

[105] F. O'Donoghue, *No Other Law* (Dublin, 1954), p. 72.
[106] Ibid. Note the importance given to 1919 captures by the leader of the Cork No. 3. Bde flying column, Tom Barry (*Guerrilla Days in Ireland*, new edn. (Tralee, 1962), p. 17); cf. p. 62. below.
[107] Breen, *My Fight for Irish Freedom*, new edn., p. 48.
[108] Ryan, *Seán Treacy*, pp. 81–2.
[109] It was first published on 15 August 1918, edited by Piaras Béaslaí. It was issued roughly once a month until April 1921, when weekly publication commenced.
[110] P. Béaslaí, *Michael Collins and the Making of a New Ireland* (London, 1926), i. 274–5.
[111] See Breen, op. cit., original edn., p. 156, and compare the later arguments of Béaslaí (op. cit., i. 276–7) with the contemporary treatise of the theologian W. McDonald, *Some Ethical Questions of Peace and War* (London, 1919).
[112] C.S.O. Intelligence Notes, 1919. C.O. 903 19/5; *Irish Independent*, 21 March 1919; R.I.C. Reports, I.G., March 1919. C.O. 904 108.

A successful attack was made on a patrol of troops and police at Kil-
brittain, Co. Cork, on 19 June, and no casualties were caused.[113] Until
June 1919, the few deaths that occurred seemed to be accidental: for
instance, a gunfight during the attempted rescue of a Sinn Féin prisoner
in Limerick on 7 April involved the death of an R.I.C. man and of the
prisoner himself; two more R.I.C. men were killed in the famous
rescue of Seán Hogan from a train at Knocklong halt, Co. Limerick,
on 13 May. The latter incident, a bloody affray that harked more to
American gangsterism than to warfare, again involved Seán Treacy's
Soloheadbeg group, and hardly appeared part of a widening campaign.

The Knocklong incident was important for the reaction it drew
from the British authorities, as the following chapter will show. Next
month, however, an attack took place which was of far greater significance for the future. On 23 June 1919 an R.I.C. District Inspector
was assassinated in broad daylight in the centre of Thurles, Co. Tipperary; his killer or killers simply vanished, and the crowds of witnesses gave not the slightest assistance or information to the police.[114]
This was unmistakably the first blow in a methodical campaign of
terrorism. Henceforth the actions of the men whom the Government
labelled the 'gunmen' or the 'murder gang' were inseparable from
those of 'moderate' Sinn Féin; and before long they would eclipse
them almost entirely.

The response of British policy
On 10 January 1919 Lloyd George reorganized his Cabinet. Amongst
other changes, Walter Long moved from the Colonial Office to the
Admiralty, while the Chief Secretary for Ireland, Shortt, took over the
Home Office. He was replaced by the former Under Secretary at the
War Office, Ian Macpherson.[115] Among those who wrote to congratu-
late Macpherson on his risky promotion was the former Adjutant
General, now Commissioner of the London Metropolitan Police, and
soon to be Commander-in-Chief in Ireland, Sir Nevil Macready.[116]

I cannot say I envy you for I loathe the country you are going to and its people
with a depth deeper than the sea and more violent than that which I feel against
the Boche.[117]

[113] C.S.O. Intelligence Notes, 1919 (Cork W.R.). C.O. 903 19/5.
[114] R.I.C. Reports, I.G., July 1919. C.O. 904 109; *Irish Times*, 26, 27, 30 June 1919;
Tipperary Star, 28 June 1919.
[115] James Ian Macpherson, 1880–1937. Liberal M.P., 1911–31, National Liberal M.P.,
1931–5; Under Sec. of State for War, 1916; C.S.I., 1919; Minister of Pensions, 1920–2;
Baron, 1936 (Strathcarron).
[116] Cecil Frederick Nevil Macready, 1862–1946. Son of the actor; Maj. Gen., 1910;
K.C.B., 1912; G.O.C. Belfast, 1914; Adjutant General to the B.E.F., 1914, to the Forces,
1916; Commissioner of Metropolitan Police, 1918; G.O.C.-in-C. Irish Command, 1920–
1922; P.C. (Ire), 1920; Baronet, 1923.
[117] Macready to Macpherson, 11 January 1919 (Hol.). Strathcarron papers.

Macpherson's position was indeed unenviable. The Irish correspondent of the *Daily News*, Hugh Martin, a biased but penetrating commentator, wrote that

By the first month of 1919, when Mr. Ian Macpherson took over the reins as Chief Secretary from Mr. Shortt, matters had progressed so far that there was, according to my own observation,
(1) no Government policy to take up and carry through,
(2) no Government machinery in good working order, except the army,
(3) no public opinion on which to play except a mass of confused resentments.[118]

As he approached the Irish situation, Macpherson, like most of the Liberals in the Government, struggled for some firm ground on which to apply the old principle of Home Rule, away from the mire of Sinn Féin's 'impossible' demands. He was probably predisposed to a conciliatory policy, and one of his first acts was to obtain the release of the imprisoned Sinn Féin M.P.s.[119] But the growing violence in Ireland shocked and confused him. He told Lloyd George in April 1919, 'I have always been a thorough-going and consistent Home Ruler', but Ireland could not be surrendered to separatists: 'all law-abiding citizens here—whether Nationalists or Unionists—look to your support of a firm policy.'[120] He slipped easily enough into the sort of approach advocated by Long, and in his first address to the Commons on Ireland, during the supply debate on 3 April, he soon resorted to the expedient of cataloguing recent Irish crimes: in such a situation, he said, 'no steps could safely be taken by the Government to alter the present system of government'[121] (i.e. the Irish constitution). His speech produced evident disappointment, one member saying that 'We had hoped from what we knew of my right hon. Friend to have something better than he has given us', and asking the House 'very earnestly, can we leave things where they are?'[122]

Leaving constitutional things where they were did not prevent the administrative situation from worsening: if anything, the reverse was the case. Lord French was still unhappy with the machinery which was theoretically at his command. The Army, on which (as Martin saw) he depended, was being run down by demobilization and drafts to overseas units, for Ireland was still regarded as primarily a training area. On 16 January, French succeeded in getting the drafts reduced, and the War Office promised that Shaw would not be 'let down' below his minimum requirements in men and mechanical transport.[123] But

---

[118] H. Martin, *Ireland in Insurrection* (London, 1921), p. 41.
[119] See above, p. 15.
[120] C.S.I. to Prime Minister, 14 April 1919. Lloyd George papers, F/46/1/2.
[121] 114 H.C. Deb. 5s, col. 1541.
[122] Ibid., col. 1548 (speech of Maj. Hills).
[123] Telegram, Ld. Lt. to C.S.I., 16 January 1919; Gen. Harington to G.O.C.-in-C. Ireland, 16 January 1919. Strathcarron papers.

despite these good intentions a decline in strength was, in the circumstances, inevitable. French was equally worried about the police intelligence services, which he thought were dangerously weak and ineffectual,[124] and he maintained his belief that the Castle administration must be superseded by a more efficient body. In this connection he wrote to Macpherson on 23 January, 'I hope you will be able to see Haldane,[125] because his views, although decidedly impracticable at present, are interesting.'[126]

Lord Haldane had crossed to Ireland on 16 January to visit French (who had been C.I.G.S. while Haldane was Secretary for War in Asquith's government). He found him 'very worried in the midst of some 36 departments, many of them hardly on speaking terms with each other'.[127] Haldane, according to what he said later to Tom Jones,[128] 'got into touch with some of the Jesuits and Sinn Féiners', and worked out some bases for a total reform of the administration. French obviously favoured the idea, but when it was broached to Long, Haldane was told 'to "go to Hell" or words to that effect'.[129] French's subsequent illness prevented further airing of the scheme, though in any case Long's opposition presumably rendered it stillborn.

French was ill for several weeks, and did not submit a report to the Cabinet between 16 December 1918 and 15 May 1919, though on 10 April he renewed his call for an improvement in the intelligence service, telling Churchill (now Secretary of State for War and Air), 'We are suffering terribly . . . for want of a proper Criminal Investigation Department.'[130] Although his report of 15 May noted that there had been 'kaleidoscopic changes' in the situation during his illness,[131] the tenor of his régime did not alter. Special Military Areas were maintained in Clare and West Cork, where further restrictions were imposed in April after another attack on police in Eyeries. The R.I.C. reported that 70 per cent of the people were 'in sympathy with the attackers', and that 'the police have been attacked, boycotted and impeded in every possible manner'. Forty troops and police had been needed to prevent a crowd from rescuing the West Cork Volunteer leader Charlie Hurley when he received a five-year sentence for carry-

---

[124] Ld. Lt. to C.S.I., 23 January 1919. Strathcarron papers.
[125] Richard Burdon Haldane, 1856–1928. Sec. of State for War, 1905–12; Viscount, 1911; Lord Chancellor, 1912–15, 1924.
[126] Ld. Lt. to C.S.I., 23 January 1919. Strathcarron papers.
[127] Note of conversation, 10 April 1919. Thomas Jones (ed. K. Middlemas) *Whitehall Diary* (London, 1969–71), i. 83.
[128] Thomas Jones, 1870–1955. Barrington Lecturer in Ireland, 1904; confidant of Lloyd George, and Assistant Secretary to the Cabinet, 1916–30. His *Whitehall Diary* is a vital complement to the official Cabinet records for this period.
[129] Jones, *Whitehall Diary*, i. 83.
[130] French to Churchill, 10 April 1919. Churchill papers.
[131] Report of Ld. Lt. to Cabinet, 15 May 1919. G.T. 7277, CAB.24 79.

ing ammunition.[132] After the Soloheadbeg attack, French, while declaring that the mere 'commission of this crime has dealt a severe blow at the Sinn Féin organization',[133] none the less went on to declare South Tipperary a Special Military Area, with the attendant risk of focusing hostility once more upon the Government.

In so far as there was a theory behind the Special Military Areas, other than the simple necessity of supporting the police, it was that putting pressure on a whole community was the most economical way of putting pressure on the local extremists. That this had hitherto been true was, as we have seen, due to the strength of the moderates in Sinn Féin. In 1919, however, more and more Volunteers were becoming, like Treacy's group, unamenable to moderate control. Their increasing independence gave what substance there was to the Government's claim that unrest in Ireland was due to a small number of fanatics —the 'murder gang'—who terrorized the rest of the population into acquiescence. But this claim was itself a strange bedfellow for the Special Military Area theory, by which the ordinary population could be made to put a check on the extremists. As will be seen, official views diverged sharply from now on. Lord French always believed in a wide-ranging approach, aimed at the whole Volunteer organization (some 100,000 men, not just the most active members). As the conflict spread, however, this approach demanded the use of martial law, which, besides requiring a large and expensive military force, was politically unattractive to the Government. As a result, a succession of measures appeared whose common denominator was the avoidance of martial law.

The first major step, the proscription of Sinn Féin, was triggered by the Knocklong attack on 13 May. This was a shock to both French and Macpherson, for the Limerick and South Tipperary Special Military Areas had clearly had no preventive effect. Macpherson was already in a state of nerves over the arrival in Ireland of an Irish-American Commission to the Versailles Conference.[134] He looked to Lloyd George for guidance, but found none: 'we did not and do not know how to act', he wrote plaintively on 8 May.[135] This feeling of helplessness as the Commission toured Ireland amidst a welter of seditious speechmaking perhaps caused an over-reaction to the Knocklong incident: the Irish Executive now proposed to extend last year's proclamation of Sinn Féin as a dangerous association into an outright ban.

The day after Knocklong, Macpherson took his troubles to the Cabinet. He was due to speak to the Commons that afternoon,

---

[132] D.I. Castletownbere, Co. Cork W.R., to I.G. R.I.C., 13 May 1919. C.O. 904 169/3.
[133] French to Macpherson, 31 January 1919 (Hol.). Strathcarron papers.
[134] As distinct from the later American Commission on Conditions in Ireland.
[135] C.S.I. to Prime Minister, 8 May 1919. Lloyd George papers, F/46/1/3.

and said that thanks to the incident he would now most certainly be pressed to define Government policy. What was it? The answer that emerged was that there was none. Bonar Law, deputizing in Lloyd George's absence, said that Macpherson 'should have no difficulty'—'The Government's policy had been clearly defined.' Macpherson was apparently left speechless, and 'demurred by a gesture'.[136] Bonar Law then went on to say that Asquith's Government had foundered in Ireland through lack of proper information, and that the present Cabinet was no better informed. As far as he was concerned, Macpherson could 'do whatever he liked'. But when Macpherson, declaring that a rebellion was imminent and that rebel military plans had been captured,[137] proposed to proclaim Sinn Féin illegal, he met opposition from both Long and H.A.L. Fisher.[138] Fisher, the Liberal, argued that Sinn Féin was a major party containing both intellectuals and physical force groups, and that it had the moral support of the whole population. To ban it, he said, was surely wrong. By contrast Long, the Tory, objected on the ground that the Irish Executive, and especially the police, were incapable of actually enforcing such a ban, so that the Government would lose face.[139] The gulf between their arguments showed the breadth of the Coalition; and the Cabinet reached no conclusion. Macpherson had to face the Commons armed only with symbolism and rhetoric:

All I can say is that unless constitutionalism is revived, we can have no parley with Sinn Féin, which endeavours to destroy our Empire, a thing which right-minded citizens of this great kingdom will never tolerate.[140]

This outlook was to be the foundation of British policy, and to stand in the way of a practical settlement, for a long time to come.

The proscription of Sinn Féin organizations
The Irish Executive kept up its pressure for a ban. On 17 May, French declared that he would stick to this advice even if it led to open rebellion.[141] Lieutenant-General Shaw expressed his confidence in the military arrangements, though he re-emphasized the difficulty of maintaining essential garrisons in the face of constant overseas drafts.[142]

---

[136] War Cabinet, 14 May 1919. W.C. 567A, CAB.23 15.
[137] For a more sober evaluation of the captured plans see R.I.C. Reports, I.G., February 1919. C.O. 904 108.
[138] Herbert Albert Laurens Fisher, 1865–1940. Historian; Liberal M.P., 1918–26; President, Board of Education, 1916–22; active member of Cabinet Irish Situation Committee.
[139] War Cabinet, 14 May 1919. W.C. 567A, CAB.23 15.
[140] Speech by Macpherson, 14 May 1919. 115 H.C. Deb. 5s, col. 1731.
[141] Telegram, Ld. Lt. to C.S.I., 17 May 1919. Lloyd George papers, F/46/1/41.
[142] Memo by G.O.C.-in-C. Ireland, in Ld. Lt. to C.S.I., 17 May 1919. Lloyd George papers, F/46/1/5.

French was evidently thinking in terms of mass arrests of Volunteers, for he asked Macpherson to discuss the provision of extra prison accommodation with the Home Secretary.[143] The latter, however, was having serious doubts. Tom Jones reported to Lloyd George on 23 May that

Fisher, Shortt, and Addison[144] have been exchanging views and I believe all three are very concerned about the state of Ireland and disturbed at the suggestion that Sinn Fein be 'proclaimed'. They recognize that no constructive policy can be developed in the PM's absence but they don't want the pitch queered in the meantime.[145]

None the less, despite Jones's efforts, this is exactly what happened, from the point of view of the Cabinet Liberals, during Lloyd George's months at the peace conference.

In a letter to French, Long expanded on his views. He sympathized with the idea of a proclamation, but said 'my knowledge of Ireland tells me that in no country in the world is it so important . . . that strong measures should consist not merely in printed proclamations'.[146] He was convinced that the machinery for implementing them was inadequate, and that it would be necessary to replace many officers of the R.I.C. and to reform the special branches. Otherwise, 'the moment Government attempted to give effect to the proclamation, the weapon would break in their hands, and they would suffer—not the rebels'. He was particularly anxious that the Inspector General, Byrne, should be replaced by his Deputy, T. J. Smith.[147]

French was an old acquaintance of Long's and heeded his views. Especially significant for the future was another proposal, which French reported to Macpherson on 24 May:

I like Walter Long's idea to employ some discharged soldiers in the RIC. In view of the state of the country could we not get the authority to temporarily raise the establishment and spend some money on the RIC.[148]

No action was yet taken in this direction, and French stayed his hand over the proclamations for a month. The Special Military Area in Westport was lifted on 1 June, and in South Tipperary on 14 June. Still, the situation remained bad, with hostility to the police evident throughout Munster. The R.I.C. reported that military assistance was

[143] Ld. Lt. to C.S.I., 17 May 1919. Lloyd George papers, F/46/1/6.
[144] Christopher Addison, 1869–1951. Liberal M.P., 1910–22; Minister of Munitions, 1916–17; Minister of Health, 1919–21. Discredited by the excessive expense of his postwar housing programme.
[145] Jones to J. T. Davies, 23 May 1919. *Whitehall Diary*, i. 87.
[146] Long to French, 21 May 1919. (Copy to Macpherson.) Strathcarron papers.
[147] Ibid. Smith had commanded the R.I.C. in Belfast at the time of the Ulster crisis; he was I.G. R.I.C. from March to November 1920.
[148] French to Macpherson, 24 May 1919 (Hol.). Strathcarron papers.

necessary 'in nearly every case where duty of a political nature had to be performed', and that the 'absurd doctrine' that the I.R.A. was legally at war with the British Empire was becoming accepted by the fanatical youth.[149] The first recorded military operation took place on 4 June, when the roads around Dundalk in Co. Louth were picketed after warning had been received of an impending attack; but the only result was the accidental shooting of a commercial traveller.[150]

It was the shooting of D.I. Hunt in Thurles on 23 June that finally exhausted French's restraint. On 26 June he telegraphed to the Cabinet that

> The Irish Government are now forced to conclude that Sinn Féiners in this district are an organized club for murder of police and that time has come when Sinn Féin and its organization in this district of Tipperary must be proclaimed an illegal organization.[151]

Despite its moderation in referring to only one part of Tipperary, this proposal kept to the blanket proscription of Sinn Féin which had so worried the Cabinet Liberals. Oddly enough, French himself had remarked in his 15 May report that there were signs of a rift between moderate Sinn Féiners and extremists,[152] and the Cabinet had earlier shown its concern to keep such a possibility in mind.[153] But now, as the question of 'proclamation'[154] came once more under discussion, only Shortt brought up the distinction between the Irish Volunteers and the rest of Sinn Féin. In his opinion, 'no one would be more relieved than the Sinn Féiners if the Irish Volunteers were proclaimed'.[155] This was, indeed, the proper moment for any attempt to drive a wedge between them, so that the proclamation, though necessarily a cumbrous weapon, might not be absolutely blunt. But few of the Cabinet appear to have seen any force in this argument. Long even withdrew his previous objections to a proclamation, because he now 'understood' that the Irish Government had investigated and improved the Crime Section. With consent from Lloyd George and Bonar Law by telegraph from Paris, the Cabinet approved French's proposal, on the condition that the Irish Government was unanimous in its favour.[156]

Lord Haldane fumed, 'This is folly. The Sinn Féin leaders are not murderers. . . . The Government will soon be wringing its hands over

---

[149] R.I.C. Reports, I.G., June 1919. C.O. 904 109.
[150] Ibid.
[151] Telegram from Ld. Lt., War Cabinet, 26 June 1919. W.C. 585A, CAB.23 15.
[152] Report of Ld. Lt., 15 May 1919. G.T. 7277, CAB.24 79.
[153] War Cabinet, 21 November 1918. W.C. 505, CAB.23 8.
[154] The term 'proclamation' was habitually used for declaring a dangerous association to be illegal, but the correct term was 'order'. *Law Reports*, 1887, p. 54; cf. Criminal Law and Procedure (Ireland) Act: List of Proclamations and Orders in Force, 1919. W.O. 35 66.
[155] War Cabinet, 26 June 1919. W.C. 585A, CAB.23 15.
[156] Ibid.

lost opportunities.'[157] Considering the contentiousness of the issue, not the least remarkable thing about it was that the Irish Executive, which was a byword for disunity, managed to meet the Cabinet's condition of unanimity—if indeed it did. Perhaps French acted on his own. Whatever the case, the Order declaring all Sinn Féin organizations (including the Irish Volunteers, Cumann na mBan, and the Gaelic League) illegal in both north and south ridings of Tipperary was issued on 4 July.[158] Strangely, however, military restrictions were not re-imposed. According to the R.I.C., the people reacted to the Order 'with indifference, and relief that they had escaped the restrictions . . . and the pecuniary loss they would inevitably suffer had the county been declared a Special Military Area.'[159] Within four months, the Orders were to be extended to the whole of Ireland. It remained to be seen whether the improvements which Long was satisfied had been made in the police forces would make the ban effectual—and, even so, whether it could bring about a 'revival of constitutionalism'.

3. TOWARDS GUERRILLA WARFARE (August–September 1919)

Problems of the Crown forces
It was only on 7 August that dissatisfaction among the Irish police was tackled, when Macpherson introduced a Bill to improve their pay and conditions.[160] Although this was initially blocked, and did not pass until late November, a £10 gratuity was granted pending its passage, and a noticeable increase in recruitment took place during the winter. In the meantime, however, the activities of the I.R.A. developed apace. In August the number of attacks on police rose to 11, in what the Inspector General recognized as a 'deliberate campaign to break the morale of the force', amidst mounting anti-police propaganda.[161] In consequence, he reported,

In Clare and portions of Limerick and Galway it has been necessary to concentrate the police; some outlying barracks have been vacated and the remainder fortified for defence; and in a few cases the protection afforded to persons . . . has had to be withdrawn.[162]

[157] F. Gallagher, *The Anglo-Irish Treaty* (London, 1965), T. P. O'Neill's introduction, p. 18.
[158] Criminal Law and Procedure (Ireland) Act, 1887: List of Proclamations and Orders in Force, 1919. W.O. 35 66.
[159] R.I.C. Reports, I.G., July 1919. C.O. 904 109.
[160] The Constabulary and Police (Ireland) Bill was based on the recommendations of a commission of inquiry under Lord Desborough. It was introduced near the end of the session in August, and was blocked in order to obtain fuller debate in the next session. It became law on 30 November.
[161] R.I.C. Reports, I.G., August 1919. C.O. 904 109.
[162] Ibid.

Crown countermeasures were a mixture of old and new. On 7 August, fairs and markets were restricted in Clare, and the banning of Sinn Féin organizations followed on 13 August. The process of fortifying police posts (which, despite their name of 'barracks', were normally ordinary houses, neither built nor sited for defence against firearms) was extended to Cork and Kerry during the next month, military lorries being borrowed to carry gravel for sandbags.[163] Flat steel window shutters were added, though the R.I.C. were later discomfited to find that the old V-shaped iron ones which had been fitted during the Fenian troubles of 1867 were better proof against rifle ammunition.[164]

The problem of morale, though it was to go on causing the utmost nervousness in Dublin Castle, never in fact became critical. The retreat of the R.I.C. in 1919 was due to numerical weakness. In January 1919 its authorized strength seems actually to have been reduced to 10,166 excluding officers, though real strength was only some 9,300.[165] Before the retreat began, the R.I.C. was responsible for maintaining 1,332 'barracks' and 'huts', and was seriously overstretched, without reserves.[166] At the same time, although Irish Command was reinforced with five infantry battalions and four tanks in April,[167] a sharp reduction in military support for the police was impending.

It is a common Irish claim that the Republicans of 1919 took on an Empire 'fresh from victorious war'. It is true that Britain had not been essentially weakened by the war, and that in spite of war-weariness neither the people nor the Government were in a mood to give way to violence in Ireland. Sinn Féin's avowed and alleged contacts with Germany were not soon forgotten. But, as the Russian civil war and the Chanak crisis were to show, there were strict limits to any permissible British military commitment in the near future: demobilization and retrenchment were the first requirement of the times. When the Asquithian Liberal leader told the Commons on 7 August 1919 that the present cost of the military garrison in Ireland nearly equalled the net revenue of that country before the war, he touched a sensitive spot;[168] and the Cabinet was doubtless relieved next week to be told by the Secretary for War that

---

[163] C.S.O. R.P. 23835(19), 27 September 1919, R.O.
[164] See report of D.I. Egan to I.G. R.I.C., 31 May 1920 (after the attack on Kilmallock barrack). Lloyd George papers, F/19/2/11.
[165] C.S.O. R.P. 1170(19), 11 January 1919, R.O.; R.I.C. Nominal Roll, 1918–19. H.O. 184 60–1.
[166] At least 73 calls for reinforcements were made during 1919, according to the C.S.O. R.P. Index.
[167] Report of G.O.C.-in-C. Ireland, in Report of Ld. Lt., 15 May 1919. G.T. 7277, CAB.24 79.
[168] 119 H.C. Deb. 5s, col. 649. (Speech of Sir Donald Maclean, Liberal Leader while Asquith was out of Parliament, 1919–20.)

as regards Ireland, the present conditions may necessitate a garrison in excess of the normal, but within twelve months there is a reasonable probability that a normal garrison will suffice.[169]

This probability depended on the support that the Army could give to the police in restoring order. The military authorities had already made it clear that they did not want to become any more closely involved than in the emergency of 1880–2 and the strikes of 1911 and 1913–14.[170] Now, although the helplessness of the police was increasingly obvious, in the Army's view the growing threat of another open rebellion focused attention on its primary military role—as the final defence of the state against invasion or insurrection. As such its capability was at present in doubt.

Demobilization, especially the 'first in, first out' principle,[171] together with overseas commitments, caused a situation in which, after the war which had produced the greatest British army ever, the British garrisons were not only below strength but also lacking in trained men. The result in Ireland was that on 27 August 1919 the G.O.C.-in-C., Shaw, notified the R.I.C. that by Christmas, when the last of the cyclist units would have left, the Army would not be able to provide outpost detachments. It would then be concentrated for training.

In short, the Garrison of Ireland will not be in a position to carry out the police duties which have devolved upon it during the war and to respond to the constant calls made upon it to assist the police.[172]

Fifty-three detachments were to be withdrawn, and eight more altered from infantry to cavalry or artillery (much less effective for co-operation with the police).[173]

This announcement was a bombshell to the R.I.C. Byrne reacted with an urgent memorandum warning that the inevitable result would be widespread police withdrawals. These were being delayed as long as possible because of the 'apprehension and alarm' they caused to loyal citizens.[174] This argument made no impression on Shaw, however, who continued to press the logic of the Army's primary role. 'Even

---

[169] War Cabinet Discussion of the Military Estimates, 15 August 1919. W.C. 616A, CAB.23 18.

[170] For military resistance to Dublin Castle's attempt to get military patrols put at the disposal of Resident Magistrates, see Brig. Gen. Stanton to U.S., 24 January, and reply, 26 February 1918. C.S.O. File R.P. 5975(18); also the same to the same, 6 February, and reply, 9 February 1918. C.O. 904 187.

[171] Announced by Churchill in January 1919 in response to discontent in the Army. S. R. Graubard, 'Military Demobilization in Great Britain following the First World War', J. Mod. Hist., xix (1947), pp. 297–311.

[172] G.O.C.-in-C. Ireland to I.G. R.I.C., 27 August 1919. Strathcarron papers.

[173] App. to above. Of the detachments to be withdrawn, 18 were in counties Cork and Clare.

[174] I.G. R.I.C. to U.S., 9 September 1919. Strathcarron papers.

now,' he wrote to Macpherson in September, 'the military necessity for concentration and training is diametrically opposed to the Police demands for dispersion and local support'.[175] He suggested expanding the R.I.C., and proposed that, since Byrne seemed unwilling to recruit non-Irishmen, a special force of ex-soldiers might be raised. This might comprise five cyclist battalions, four for the R.I.C. and one for the D.M.P.; the ex-soldiers would retain their military arms and organization, but would be paid and commanded by the police.[176]

This proposal foreshadowed in part the 'Black and Tan' R.I.C. as well as the Auxiliary Division, but at this stage it received short shrift. Byrne argued with great clarity that such a force could not be controlled by the constabulary code of discipline,[177] and the D.M.P., while remarking that in any case it was not needed in Dublin, added that the certainty of disharmony and indiscipline meant that the proposal had 'nothing to recommend it to either police or citizens'.[178] None the less, despite their cogency and prophetic accuracy, these objections were to be overruled. Byrne's opposition was to cost him his job, and nearly to end his career.

The Fermoy attack and British reactions

Lord French's resolve to apply still wider coercive measures was reinforced in September 1919. On Sunday the 7th, when the argument over military withdrawals had hardly begun, a startling attack was carried out by the I.R.A. North Cork Brigade. The rebels fell upon a church party of 18 men of the Shropshire Light Infantry in Fermoy, the headquarter town of the 16th Brigade, and seized 13 rifles, killing one soldier and wounding four, and making a well-planned escape in cars.[179] The significance of this attack, which was as ruthless as Soloheadbeg and Knocklong but far more warlike in aim and method, was increased by its aftermath. At the inquest on the dead soldier, the coroner's jury held that the attack had been a regular act of war, and had been intended not to kill the soldiers but to seize their weapons. Therefore, although they expressed horror at 'this appalling outrage', they refused to bring a verdict of murder.[180] After this indication of the delicate balance of public opinion, the infuriated troops broke out of barracks and wrecked shops owned by members of the jury. This retaliation set a grim pattern for the future.

[175] G.O.C.-in-C. Ireland to C.S.I., 19 September 1919. Strathcarron papers.
[176] Ibid. Shaw suggested that the units might be located in Dublin city, Dublin county, Belfast, Galway city, and either Cork city or Queenstown (now Cóbh).
[177] I.G. R.I.C. to U.S., 4 October 1919. Strathcarron papers.
[178] Chief Superintendent to Chief Commissioner, D.M.P., 29 September, and Chief Commissioner D.M.P. to U.S., 30 September 1919. Strathcarron papers.
[179] C.S.O. Intelligence Notes, 1919 (Cork E.R. and City). C.O. 903 19/5; cf. O'Donoghue, No Other Law, pp. 49–50.
[180] Irish Times, 9 September 1919; Phillips, The Revolution in Ireland, p. 169.

On 10 September Sinn Féin was proclaimed in Co. Cork, and Dáil Eireann was proclaimed throughout Ireland. This sweeping step, out-lawing the elected representatives of Ireland as such, may have been connected with the Dáil's adoption of the 'Oath of Allegiance' on 20 August.[181] This was a device of Brugha's to bring the I.R.A. under the control of the Dáil rather than the I.R.B., and was hardly indicative of Republican unity. The Irish Government's reasoning, however, as Macpherson expressed it to Bonar Law on 13 September, was that 'we had to allow these members (i.e. the Dáil) to sit together *in consultation* if they wished', but that when they 'conspired by executive acts . . . to overthrow the duly constituted authority, then we could act'.[182] For the Crown forces, by contrast, the problem was whether any of the bans could actually be enforced. As a technique, Special Military Areas seemed to be at their last gasp. When restrictions were re-imposed on Tipperary on 20 September they were 'received with dismay' by the populace, but the police had to report that 'the general public is apparently prepared to suffer rather than openly condemn the criminal acts of the republican fanatics, who, as a class, have nothing to lose'.[183]

One or two successful Crown operations had in fact been carried out, notably the breaking-up of a Volunteer training camp at Glandore, Co. Cork, on 13 August.[184] But accurate intelligence was rare, and the gap between the two sides in this respect was already noticeable. On the rebel side, Collins, who had now become Director of Intelligence, was laying down an organization whose scope was to become legendary. But the police, once famed as the 'eyes and ears of Dublin Castle', were rapidly losing their local knowledge. The West Cork R.I.C. admitted at the end of 1919 that they found it 'extremely difficult to get any information' about the Volunteers. They had to rely on searches of persons and houses, which had only limited success.[185] The Galway R.I.C. reported that 'on the whole the police are receiving no support from the people'.[186] This was mainly due to the well-chosen Repub-lican course of first fomenting a 'popular' boycott of the R.I.C., who were by now widely regarded as traitors to their own race, and only then applying intimidation to cement the community against the police.

Lord French regarded the remedying of this situation as the first priority, and on 25 September he and Macpherson submitted to the Cabinet a memorandum calling for the improvement of the secret

---

181 See Macardle, *The Irish Republic*, pp. 280–1, for a pro-Brugha account of the debate; Forester, *Michael Collins.* pp. 123–7, for Collins's attitude.
182 C.S.I. to Lord Privy Seal, 13 September 1919. Bonar Law papers, 98/2/12.
183 R.I.C. Reports, I.G., September 1919. C.O. 904 110.
184 C.S.O. Intelligence Notes, 1919 (Cork W.R.). C.O. 903 19/5.
185 Ibid.
186 Ibid. (Galway W.R.).

service, the extension of the Irish Government's powers by means of D.O.R.R. 14B, and the liberal provision of prison accommodation in England. 'If these measures fail,' they concluded, 'there is no other alternative but the establishment of Martial Law wherever civil law proves ineffective.'[187] French himself asked the Cabinet to approve five additional measures: a further advance of £10 per man pending the passage of the Police Bill, to encourage the R.I.C.; an increase in the political intelligence ('G') division of the D.M.P.; an increase in the establishment of the R.I.C., 'particularly in view of the approaching reduction of the military forces in Ireland'; a scheme of economic assistance to Irish ex-servicemen (whose present plight was a poor advertisement for loyalism); and the immediate passing of the Education and Land for Soldiers Bills.[188] In Cabinet, Macpherson supported all these demands except the extension of powers—oddly, since he had put his name to the memorandum declaring this to be vital. Although he shared French's aversion to the campaign of outrage, Macpherson hesitated to combat it decisively.

This indecision was symptomatic of the Cabinet's approach. It would sanction stern measures, such as the blanket ban on Sinn Féin or, later, martial law, yet deny the means to implement them effectively. On 7 October it approved seven of French's proposals, omitting the extension of powers.[189] At the same meeting, moreover, it showed its uncertainty about the final object of its Irish policy, namely the constitutional settlement to which the restoration of order had been declared to be the necessary prelude.

[187] Joint Memo by Ld. Lt. and C.S.I., 25 September 1919. G.T. 8227, CAB.24 89.
[188] War Cabinet, 25 September 1919. W.C. 624, CAB.23 12.
[189] Ibid., 7 October 1919. W.C. 628, CAB.23 12.

II

THE BREAKDOWN OF BRITISH LAW

'The police were confronted with almost insuperable difficulties in their efforts
to obtain evidence for prosecution in cases of political crime owing to the state
of terror organized by the republican party.'

The Inspector General of the R.I.C., November 1919

4. CONSTITUTIONAL PLANS (October 1919 and after)

Principles of approach

ON 24 September, Long addressed a memorandum to the
Cabinet setting forth his views on the future of Ireland. In it
he attacked the idea of 'dominion status' as the possible basis
for a settlement;[1] Sinn Féin, he said, would use such status to move on
to complete separation. Indeed, he thought that Sinn Féin itself should
be regarded as irreconcilable, and that the Government should give up
any idea of dealing with it. Instead he proposed another constitutional
plan, federalism (or devolution),[2] as a suitable framework. This had
the advantage that when applied to Ireland it would produce several
provincial parliaments, not just one, thus drawing the teeth of the
unity/Ulster-exclusion issue. But Long insisted that nothing should
be begun until order had been restored, and the Government must
make clear to the public its 'unwavering support' of the Irish
Executive.[3] This principle had in fact been announced by Bonar Law
to the King ten days before as the basis of the Government's Irish
policy.[4]

Lord French was glad of these declarations of support, and would
doubtless have been gladder still if the Government had actually committed itself to all the measures he advocated. But his approach was
more complex than is generally recognized. It is easy to depict him as a
mere martinet, but he had a strongly liberal outlook on Home Rule.

---

[1] The Dominion Home Rule idea was to grow in strength during 1920, with the
foundation of the Irish Dominion League, and Lord Monteagle's proposal of a Dominion
of Ireland Bill in the House of Lords in June 1920. Cf. C.38(20), CAB.23 21.

[2] This principle had been pressed by Long a year before, and had been supported by
Chamberlain in a Cabinet Note of 17 June 1918. G.212, Worthington-Evans papers;
for some useful remarks on federalism see D. G. Boyce, *Englishmen and Irish Troubles*
(London, 1972), pp. 38f.

[3] Memo by Ist Lord of the Admiralty, 24 September 1919. G.T. 8215, CAB.24 89.

[4] R. Blake, *The Unknown Prime Minister* (London, 1955), p. 418.

He wrote on 25 September that

My comparatively short experience of Irish administration has convinced me that no Irish Government which is not in close touch with the representatives of the people can do the best work for Ireland.[5]

Such a sentiment was noticeably absent from the Cabinet's discussions of Home Rule, which now came into the foreground only because the 1914 Act was due to come into force as soon as the last peace treaty was ratified.[6] That Act would, in the Conservative view, 'surrender' Ulster to the Catholic majority, so that some alternative had to be rapidly found.

Although Lloyd George favoured the federal scheme, it had insufficient impetus to meet the pressing needs of the Irish situation. On 7 October, when the Cabinet approved French's proposed measures, it had to admit that 'at an early stage in the parliamentary session, some declaration of policy by the Government would be expected'.[7] But no policy existed. Some of the Cabinet felt that no settlement could be made in the present disturbed conditions; others argued that unless some form of home rule were applied—by force if necessary—there was no chance of any 'steady and sane opinion' re-emerging. Nothing was decided except to set up a committee of twelve, including Long as chairman and French and Macpherson *ex officio*, to 'examine and report on the probable effect on Ireland and on the United Kingdom and on opinion abroad of each of the possible Irish policies'.[8] On 28 October, French was made a member of the Cabinet, a revival of nineteenth-century practice which tightened the link between London and Dublin.

The Cabinet Committee, having regard, as instructed, to public and foreign (especially American and Dominion) opinion, decided on 4 November that the settling of so many European problems by the Versailles Treaties made it imperative to make 'a sincere attempt to deal with the Irish question once and for all'.[9] The committee rejected earlier ideas of excluding Ulster or of giving it special status within an all-Ireland parliament, and opted for the creation of two Home Rule parliaments, one in Dublin and one in Belfast. A Council of Ireland,

[5] Joint Memo by Ld. Lt. and C.S.I., 25 September 1919, Note by Ld. Lt. G.T. 8227, CAB.24 89.
[6] See correspondence between Acting Sec. War Cabinet and Attorney General, September 1919. G.T. 8210, CAB.24 89.
[7] War Cabinet, 7 October 1919. W.C. 628, CAB.23 12.
[8] Ibid. The other nine members were: Lord Birkenhead (Lord Chancellor), Fisher (Education), Shortt (Home Secretary), Sir Auckland Geddes (Board of Trade), Sir Robert Horne (Labour), G. Roberts (Food Control., Sir Laming Worthington-Evans (Pensions), Sir Gordon Hewart (Attorney-General), and P. Kellaway (P.S., Supply). The last four were not in the Cabinet.
[9] Cabinet Cttee. on the Irish Question, 1st Report, 4 November 1919. C.P. 56, CAB.24 92.

drawn from both, was to provide a framework for possible unification.[10] The future would prove that this compromise had little to recommend it to either unionists or nationalists. But there seemed no option but to accept it, which the Cabinet did on 11 November. The discussion was depressing. Sinn Féin was expected to control the 'southern' parliament, and 'their first action would be to declare themselves an independent republic, unless this was provided against in some way in the Bill'.[11] This was a forlorn hope. But there had to be a Bill. Dominion and American opinion demanded some constructive action. Yet how could the danger of Irish neutrality in a future war, and the consequent disruption of naval defence, be guarded against? To this the Cabinet had no answer.[12]

The exclusion of Ulster
Once the principle of the Bill was agreed, an approach had to be made to two problems which had long been in dispute—first, the size of the northern area referred to as 'Ulster', and second, the nature of the powers to be vested in the new parliaments. It is not within the scope of this study to follow the evolution of this final Government of Ireland Bill,[13] but these two points are relevant to any analysis of British policy. The main difficulty with 'Ulster' was the determination of the Unionist leaders to hold the largest area in which a permanent Unionist majority could be guaranteed. Initially the Cabinet seems not to have realized this. It accepted the Irish Committee's recommendation that all nine counties of the historic province of Ulster should be placed under the northern parliament,[14] and held to this course even when Lloyd George reported, on 19 December, that the Unionist leaders wanted a six-county area (leaving out the strongly Catholic counties of Donegal, Cavan, and Monaghan, but retaining the two counties with a marginal Catholic majority, Tyrone and Fermanagh).[15] In the Cabinet that day

It was strongly urged that if the ultimate aim of the Government's policy was a united Ireland, it would be better that the jurisdiction of the Northern Parliament should extend over the whole of Ulster, which included both Roman Catholics and Protestants, both urban and rural districts, and by its size was more suited to possess a separate Parliament.[16]

[10] Ibid.
[11] Cabinet, 11 November 1919. C.5(19), CAB.23 18.
[12] Ibid.
[13] There is copious material on the framing of the Bill and its slow passage through Parliament in the Cabinet records; a short account of the process, based on some of this, can be found in McDowell, *The Irish Convention*, pp. 195–201.
[14] Cabinet Cttee. on the Irish Question, 1st Report, discussed in Cabinet, 3 December 1919. C.10(19), CAB.23 1.8
[15] Cabinet, 19 December 1919. C.16(19), CAB.23 18.
[16] Ibid.

These arguments did credit to the Government's intentions, but they did not prevail against the Protestant demand for 'safeguards'. Although yet another committee, under Bonar Law, re-examined the question two months later, and also came down in favour of an all-Ulster assembly after 'carefully weighing the arguments on both sides',[17] Balfour asserted his authority on the other side. In a letter to Lloyd George on 19 February 1920 he dismissed the province of Ulster as a geographical term, and said that its large Catholic population would become a *Hibernia irredenta*, the cause of new troubles. But it is noteworthy that Balfour did not favour the six-county area either, for it also had a substantial Catholic population. He advocated a fair partition based on plebiscite.[18] The Cabinet took no notice of this, and when the all-Ulster proposal was finally dismissed on 24 February the six-county area held the field.[19] Of the gestures towards unity, only the projected Council of Ireland remained.[20]

The powers of the Irish parliaments

The second problem, that of powers, stemmed largely from British strategic fears about Ireland. The reason why Irish independence was so unthinkable to the Cabinet was that the loss of Ireland was seen as the first step in the break-up of the British Empire. It was generally held that without control of Irish waters, naval defence would be fatally weakened. As one M.P. put it in August 1920, 'Ireland is the Heligoland of the Atlantic'.[21] A particularly fervent believer in this threat was the Chief of the Imperial General Staff, Field-Marshal Sir Henry Wilson.[22] As late as March 1921 Wilson argued that

a hostile Ireland . . . is just as fatal to the continued existence of the British Empire as a hostile England was, is, and will be to the growth and existence of a German Empire.[23]

A more patronizing view was that of Lloyd George, who announced at Caernarvon in October 1920 that 'Irish temper is an uncertainty and

---

[17] Cabinet Cttee. on Ireland, Report by Lord Privy Seal, 17 February 1920. C.P. 664, CAB.24 98.
[18] Lord President of the Council to Prime Minister, 19 February 1920. C.P. 681, CAB.24 98.
[19] Cabinet, 24 February 1920. C.12(20), CAB.23 20.
[20] Fittingly enough it was not realized until the Bill had almost become law that it contained no provision for actually summoning this body. See Cabinet, 18 November 1920. C.62(20) App. II, CAB.23 23.
[21] 129 H.C. Deb. 5s, col. 1728. (Speech of Col. Ashley in adjournment debate for Whitsun recess.)
[22] Henry Hughes Wilson, 1864–1922. Commandant, Staff College, 1907; D.M.O., War Office, 1910–14; Chief Liaison Officer with French Army, 1915; C.I.G.S., 1918; assassinated 1922.
[23] Wilson to Lord Ventry, 30 March 1921. Callwell, *Wilson*, ii. 282.

dangerous forces like armies and navies are better under the control of the Imperial Parliament'.[24]

In order to hold Ireland in check, certain powers were to be retained by Britain: some, like defence and foreign policy, in perpetuity, and others, like postal services, transport, agriculture, and health, for a limited period. At first the list of these 'reserved services' was so long that the Irish parliaments would have been little more than glorified local councils,[25] and it was soon shortened to the judiciary, post, and income tax, these moreover being handed to the Council of Ireland as an incentive to unity.[26] So at least the Irish Committee proposed, but the Cabinet declared on 19 December 1919 that such concessions would give Ireland something like Dominion status, and that 'Dominion Home Rule had never been contemplated'.[27]

Most of the future difficulty was to be over the 'fiscal clauses', those dealing with income tax, customs, and the national debt. The Cabinet's approach was based on an analogy of Ireland not with a Dominion but with a State of the U.S.A. (at which American opinion could not cavil).[28] Indeed, as the rebellion progressed, Lloyd George took up an almost Abraham Lincoln-like stance, declaring that to concede customs and excise would be to destroy the unity of the United Kingdom. (Though he more characteristically went on to say that if customs *were* conceded to Ireland, Britain should 'get a lot in exchange', and that he was 'looking forward to using customs, excise and income tax as a means of reducing Ireland'; 'If we retain these taxes the Sinn Féiners are at our mercy.'[29]) In his open letter to the Bishop of Chelmsford in April 1921 he was to maintain that

the present struggle is not about the Home Rule Act at all. Fundamentally the issue is the same as that in the war of North and South in the United States—it is an issue between secession and union.[30]

and to refer approvingly to Lincoln's assertion that he would save the union even at the price of retaining slavery in the south. This outlook

[24] Note of speech, U.S. to Lord Chancellor, 19 October 1920. Anderson papers, C.O. 904 188,1.
[25] Cabinet Cttee. on the Irish Question, 1st Report, 4 November 1919. C.P. 56, CAB.24 92.
[26] Ibid., 4th Report, 2 December 1919. C.P. 247, CAB.24 94.
[27] Cabinet, 19 December 1919. C.16(19), CAB.23 18.
[28] Ibid.
[29] Lloyd George made another revealing remark on this occasion, possibly for the benefit of his Conservative colleagues, but consistent with his whole approach, when he complained that the concession of customs and income tax was 'not the Gladstonian Home Rule that he had grown up with'. Cabinet Conference, 13 October 1920. C.59(20) App. III, CAB.23 23.
[30] Drafts in Lloyd George papers, F/19/3/10; extensive extracts in Phillips, *The Revolution in Ireland*, pp. 197–202.

lay behind his insistence on the Oath of Allegiance in the 1921 Treaty negotiations.

The Bill and British policy

But the American analogy, and with it most of the Bill, was of little practical relevance for Ireland in 1919. The power of Sinn Féin was such that while Dominion Home Rule seemed to the Cabinet an unthinkable concession, it was now thought by many Irish nationalists to be inadequate. Conflict was inevitable, as the Government sought to scale down Sinn Féin's ambitions, so that for the first time an apparently conciliatory measure was dependent upon coercion. Many people were undoubtedly confused by this. The Cabinet's real opinion of the Bill is hard to assess. Lloyd George himself may not have thought that, in practice, it would do more than take Ulster out of the future issue, though he also gave every sign of believing that it was intrinsically 'good and generous'.[31] The Government Liberals were sincerely anxious for a settlement and were ready to go beyond the Bill and offer Dominion status; the Conservatives inevitably had a different view. Lord Birkenhead[32] took the line that the Bill afforded

an ingenious strengthening of our tactical position before the world. I am absolutely satisfied that the Sinn Feiners will refuse it. Otherwise in the present state of Ireland I could not even be a party to making the offer, for I believe that if the Sinn Feiners did accept their parliament they would only use it for the purpose of forwarding separation.[33]

The Bill might, indeed, be seen as a vulpine method of maintaining direct rule, but it was to transpire that in the end even Birkenhead could not contemplate with equanimity the prospect of an indefinitely postponed settlement.

The real grounds of the Bill and the campaign to restore order which accompanied it were two serious political misjudgements. The first may be summed up by Tom Jones's understatement that 'it was not at once that Lloyd George fully realized the fact that, in Southern Ireland, British constitutional rule was over'.[34] It will be seen that as late as May 1921 he had not finally accepted this. Nor, perhaps, had many Britons. The second misjudgement was the belief that moderate Irish opinion

---

[31] His words at Cabinet Conference, 13 October 1920. C.59(20) App. III, CAB.23 23.

[32] Frederick Edwin Smith, 1872–1930. Conservative M.P., 1906–19; Carson's 'galloper' in the Ulster crisis; Attorney General, 1915; Crown Prosecutor in Casement trial, 1916; Baron, 1919 (Birkenhead); Lord Chancellor, 1919–22; Sec. of State for India, 1924–8.

[33] Cabinet Cttee. on the Irish Question, note by Lord Birkenhead attached to note by himself and Sir Laming Worthington-Evans, 11 November 1919. C.P. 103, CAB.24 93.

[34] T. Jones, Lloyd George (London, 1951), pp. 188–9; for an attempt to penetrate Lloyd George's thinking, see D. G. Boyce, 'How to Settle the Irish Question: Lloyd George and Ireland 1916–21', in A. J. P. Taylor (ed.), Lloyd George (London, 1971), pp. 148–54.

could be made to return to 'constitutionalism' if Republican terrorism were crushed. As a proposition this was doubtless true, but as a practical guideline it was dangerously misleading. As all such forms of warfare had shown, the governing power could not hope to strike at guerrilla forces without involving the ordinary population also. By September 1919 the Republicans were clearly determined on, and capable of, waging a guerrilla struggle which would be difficult and unpleasant to deal with. The critical question was whether they had sufficient moral support from the population for British repression to turn their struggle into a war of national liberation. The 'murder gang' theory suggested that they did not, and therefore led to coercion rather than negotiation. But at the same time it stressed the necessity of reconciling moderate opinion, and thereby weakened the exercise of coercion.

In thinking that it could apply selective repression against the Republican extremists, the Government overestimated the capability of the Crown Forces. As we have seen, only Long had recognized this as a vital factor, and even he did not press his investigations. Yet without an efficient intelligence service it is hard to see how the rebels could have been rooted out cleanly. Lord French's policy of crushing the Sinn Féin movement in its entirety had at least the merit of depending on force, which could be made quickly available, rather than on skills which would take a long time to acquire. But French's ideas ran into political opposition. On 20 October he failed to get approval for the limited application of martial law,[35] and on 14 November the senior officers of the Crown Forces reported to the Cabinet that martial law would do little good. They said, or the Cabinet thought they said,[36] that it would provide few powers that were not already available under D.O.R.A. They also suggested that the effect of one or two capital convictions on murderers would be far greater than the deportation of suspected murderers—in other words that the moral effect of exemplary punishment would be greater than the physical effect of removing troublemakers.[37] This belief, another serious underestimation of the scale of opposition in Ireland, fatally undermined Lord French's approach, and was to colour British policy for many months to come.

[35] French to Macpherson, 20 October 1919. Strathcarron papers.
[36] It is not clear from the Cabinet minute whether the officers concerned—Shaw (G.O.C.-in-C.), Byrne and Smith (R.I.C.), and Johnstone (D.M.P.)—gave this view directly to the Cabinet, or whether it was drawn by the Cabinet from their reports. Nor is it clear whether French's arguments in favour of martial law and deportation were also put to the Cabinet.
[37] Cabinet Conference, 14 November 1919. C.8(19) App. IV, CAB.23 18.

5. THE MILITARIZATION OF THE POLICE
(October–December 1919)

The decision on 'police war'

In June 1921 Lloyd George was to tell the Cabinet that 'the Irish job . . . was a policeman's job', and that if it became 'a military job only' it would fail.[38] But though the use of military force in Ireland had by then been under discussion for eighteen months, it is a striking fact that no record exists of any other statement of this vital priority. The Government never defined the conflict, and the issue was obscured by attempts to distinguish between war and insurrection, summed up in Lloyd George's phrase, 'You do not declare war against rebels.'[39] The Government was unwilling even to admit that a rebellion existed which had to be countered by military methods. The roles of the Army and the Police were never to be properly understood.

In his autobiography, H. A. L. Fisher, who in late 1919 was at the height of his political influence,[40] stated that he had been a party to 'the decision which led to the police war', though he put no date to this.[41] He added that

The Irish troubles raised no military problem. Sinn Féin was not challenging the British Army, for that would have been insanity; it was assailing the police. Only by making this too dangerous a game to be pursued with any chance of success was it possible to maintain the British administration in Ireland, and it was only when they found that their efforts were frustrated by the Black and Tans that a powerful section of the gunmen were ready to treat.[42]

This simple analysis owed a good deal to hindsight, and nothing like it can be found in the contemporary documents—such as Fisher's own diary. The evidence rather suggests that there was no specific decision, but an acquiescence in the drift of events. The British Government did not start the 'police war'; the rebels did so by concentrating their attacks on the R.I.C. And though there was no strategic military problem, there were a host of tactical problems which were unquestionably military. The R.I.C., in fact, had to become military in order to survive. The question of a political decision would only have arisen if the Cabinet had deemed it better to disarm or withdraw the R.I.C. The process of rearming and reinforcing it arose naturally out of events.

[38] Cabinet, 2 June 1921. Jones, *Whitehall Diary*, iii. 73. See below, p. 184.

[39] Cabinet Conversation, 30 April 1920. CAB.23 20.

[40] Lloyd George described him to C. P. Scott as 'another Morley', and Scott saw him as Lloyd George's 'chief support on the Liberal side'. T. Wilson (ed.), *The Political Diaries of C. P. Scott 1911–1928* (London, 1970), p. 379 (30 November–1 December 1919).

[41] His assent, he said, was 'not without cruel misgivings'. H. A. L. Fisher, *An Unfinished Autobiography* (London, 1940), p. 129. The decision may possibly have been over the recruitment of non-Irishmen into the R.I.C., though no record exists of this.

[42] Ibid.; see the banality of Fisher's diary for, e.g., the important Cabinet of 14 November 1919. Fisher papers.

From a political rather than an executive standpoint, there was much to be said for trying to keep the R.I.C. in the forefront of the campaign against Sinn Féin. It suited the Cabinet to suggest that, while disorder in Ireland made an immediate constitutional settlement impossible, it did not amount to a national rebellion. In the context of postwar retrenchment, also, it was easier to obtain funds for the police than for the Army.[43] What the Cabinet failed, or refused, to recognize was that, as Maxwell had pointed out in 1916 and Byrne in September 1919, the nature and discipline of the R.I.C. were unsuited to the control of armed men in a combat situation. It was a frail skin into which to pour the new wine of reinforcements.

The retreat of the R.I.C.
The framework of the old R.I.C. was gradually weakening. The social and economic boycott had alienated it from the community, destroying the normal basis for police investigation of crime. Republican intimidation was now bringing the judicial machine to a halt. By November 1919, according to the Inspector General,

> The police were confronted with almost insuperable difficulties in their efforts to obtain evidence for prosecution in cases of political crime owing to the state of terror organized by the republican party.[44]

This situation crippled the service of political intelligence, which was perhaps the R.I.C.'s most vital function.[45] In the R.I.C., intelligence information was supplied by a member of each station, and the whole force was in a sense a special branch. This was partly the reason for the I.R.A.'s ruthlessness in attacking it. The Dublin Metropolitan Police,[46] by contrast, who were mostly unarmed and less widely employed on 'political' duties, were left alone by the I.R.A., who made only the special intelligence section, G Division, a major target. On 14 November the Chief Commissioner of the D.M.P. told the Cabinet that

[43] Cf. the remarks of Maj. Gen. Tudor plausibly recalled in F. P. Crozier, *Impressions and Recollections* (London, 1930), p. 251.

[44] R.I.C. Reports, I.G., November 1919. C.O. 904 110.

[45] G.H.Q. Ireland, *Record of the Rebellion in Ireland in 1920–21*, vol. ii (Intelligence), May 1922, pp. 4–5. Jeudwine papers. (See Bibliography.)

[46] Henceforth references to the police will usually refer to the R.I.C. Not only was the D.M.P. much smaller, and confined to the capital, but it also took little part in counter-insurgency operations. Its unarmed constables came to a tacit understanding with the I.R.A. that they could perform ordinary (i.e. non-political) duties without fear of attack. (Cf. Chief Commissioner D.M.P. to H.Q. D.D., 11 January 1921. D.D. H.Q. File, W.O. 35 71.) The fine physique and limited brainpower of these constables was brilliantly portrayed by Mrs Woodcock, *An Officer's Wife in Ireland* (Edinburgh, 1921), pp. 14–15, and more bitterly by Shaw Desmond, *The Drama of Sinn Féin* (London, 1923), p. 207. Macready described them as 'mere ornaments standing about at street corners', but they did some useful work, searching for arms and mounting road blocks—on one occasion arresting Seán MacBride and Countess Markievicz for driving a car without a tail light (D.D. H.Q. File, 27 September 1920, W.O. 35 70; Markievicz, *Prison Letters* (London, 1934), p. 251).

With regard to the moral effect of [I.R.A.] outrages on the D.M.P., . . . on the whole force this was negligible, but . . . in regard to the Political Section . . . which consisted of ten men only, it was having an effect which was not surprising in view of the fact that out of this small number, two men had been killed, one dangerously wounded, and two had had attacks made upon them.[47]

The last really capable head of D.M.P. intelligence, Inspector Redmond, was assassinated on 21 January 1920, a few days after he had been appointed Assistant Commissioner. After this, in the Army's opinion, G Division 'ceased to affect the situation'.[48]

During the winter of 1919–20 organized attacks on the R.I.C. multiplied, and were 'delivered with greater determination and skill than heretofore'.[49] Many of the smaller barracks and huts became untenable: in Meath, for instance, out of 31 R.I.C. stations, 11 were closed during the winter 'as a temporary measure', and one permanently.[50] Although barrack garrisons of a dozen or so remained common, the R.I.C. aimed at concentration in 20s or 30s, and later in 30s and 40s.[51] As a result substantial rural areas were abandoned, a process which noticeably lowered the morale of the R.I.C. and raised that of the rebels.[52] But the psychological effect of actual rebel attacks may not have been destructive. More resignations from the R.I.C. seem to have been due to intimidation of relatives than to personal fear, and, once the force became clearly embattled, recruitment increased dramatically. Leaving aside the addition of non-Irish recruits, the intake of native Irishmen went up 100 per cent between September and December 1919, and another 95 per cent in January 1920.[53]

Nevertheless the R.I.C. remained grievously ineffective if its task was to police the whole country and to resist the I.R.A. Although it was armed, it was neither disciplined by military law nor given military training. Its weapons were not rifles but Martini-Metford carbines,[54] and the standard of musketry was not rigorous.[55] The last generation of constables had found little use for firearms in their job, and they were regarded as mere encumbrances, a psychological barrier between the R.I.C. and the community. It has been well said that 'In practice and experience' the R.I.C. 'was a civil force'.[56] Thus even the simple steps

[47] Cabinet Conference, 14 November 1919. C.8(19) App. IV, CAB.23 18.
[48] G.H.Q. Ireland, *Record*, ii. 5.
[49] R.I.C. Reports, I.G., December 1919. C.O. 904 110.
[50] C.S.O. Intelligence Notes, 1919 (Co. Meath). C.O. 903 19/5.
[51] Cf. Note by I.G.; Resolution of Representative Body, R.I.C., 11 May 1920. Bonar Law papers, 102/5/19.
[52] General Staff 5th Division, *History of the 5th Division in Ireland 1919–1922* (?1922), p. 19. Jeudwine papers. (See Bibliography.) Henceforth cited as Hist. 5th Div.
[53] The figures were: September—26, October—36, November—55, December—50, January 1920—95. R.I.C. Register, H.O. 184 36.
[54] Hist. 5th Div., p. 33.
[55] See the excellent study by Hawkins, 'Dublin Castle and the R.I.C.', p. 174.
[56] Ibid.

taken in 1919 to increase its military capability, though apparently just a matter of survival, were fundamentally alien. In September and November 1919 large quantities of revolvers and Colt automatics were ordered; hand grenades were issued; and there was even a request for supplies of body armour.[57] Most types of military stores could be provided by the Army, but motor transport posed a severe problem. Lord French himself declared that motor vehicles were 'absolutely necessary for the efficient working of the already weakened Police forces',[58] but even he could not obtain priority on surplus stocks—to his disgust the Disposals Board decided that the Irish Government must bid for them in the open market like anyone else. An R.I.C. officer thus had to be sent over in late December to purchase 45 motor vans and 5 lorries.[59]

The move to non-Irish recruitment

The necessity of these steps was emphasized by the still declining condition of the Army. Towards the end of 1919, demobilization and drafts began to strip away the experienced N.C.O.s and men; the new recruits were unimpressive, and although officer demobilization had gone at a slower rate,[60] one Irish divisional staff later wrote that 'it may be frankly stated that the standard of efficiency of the officers was not a high one'.[61] In November 1919, Irish Command's minimum requirement in bayonets (effective infantry) was laid down as 25,000, with a total of all arms of some 40,000. At that moment there were 37,259 troops in Ireland, but the proportion of bayonets was below the minimum and still decreasing.[62] Battalions were often hard put to muster 300 officers and men, and owing to drafts a battalion might 'for short periods . . . consist of its headquarters and the band'.[63] At least 36 infantry battalions would have been needed to meet the November requirement, but even in January 1920, when military involvement had vastly increased, only 34 were available, and 6 of them were due for disbandment. Strength would then fall to 19,000 bayonets.[64] The garrison of Britain itself, totalling over 200,000 in November 1919, was to fall to 38,000 bayonets by February 1920, and to 25,000 by March—5,000

[57] Summary of Ordnance Services in Dublin District and 5th Divisional Areas, 1919–21. W.O. 35 182(1)/1. (Henceforth Ordnance Summary); C.S.O. R.P. 8419(19), 9480(19), 27726(19).
[58] French to Macpherson, 11 December 1919. Strathcarron papers.
[59] C.S.O. R.P. 31819(19), 32003(19), 21 December 1919. R.O.
[60] 55·5 per cent of officers as against 78·3 per cent of men by the summer. Graubard, 'Military Demobilization in Great Britain', p. 309.
[61] Hist. 5th Div., p. 8.
[62] Brig. Gen. Brind (G.S.O. 1, G.H.Q. Ireland) to Saunderson (P.S. to Ld. Lt.), 8 November 1919. Strathcarron papers.
[63] Hist. 5th Div., p. 9.
[64] Strength of the Army and its Capacity to Aid the Civil Power: Memo by C.I.G.S., 3 January 1920. C.P. 472, CAB.24 96.

below the minimum requirement.[65] Industrial strife was daily expected, and the Army's weakness so alarmed Sir Henry Wilson that he flew to Paris to communicate his fears to Lloyd George.[66] They were doubt-less exaggerated, but certainly neither the British nor the Irish garrison was well placed to give effective aid to the civil power in anything more than local crises.

In Ireland, the military structure of command remained unwieldy until November 1919, when the three old military districts were replaced by seven brigades in two regular divisions. The 5th Division, with headquarters at the Curragh, had four brigades, including Dublin and Belfast, and was commanded by Major-General Sir Hugh Jeudwine.[68] The other three brigades formed the 6th Division, at Cork, under Major-General Sir Peter Strickland.[69] This reorganization allowed much greater local control, such as would be necessary for work in support of the civil power; but it was some time before any of the new headquarters were fully functional.[67]

The weakness of the Army made it clear by October 1919 that if the R.I.C. were to be kept 'in the field', it would have to be strengthened, not only in armament and equipment but also in sheer numbers. As we have seen, the G.O.C.-in-C. had already tacitly criticized the R.I.C. Inspector General, Byrne, for being unwilling to recruit British ex-soldiers into the R.I.C., and had suggested an alternative scheme for employing them. Byrne rebutted this criticism (though his general attitude did not), and reported on 4 October that 'thousands' of recruiting leaflets had already been distributed among servicemen due for demobilization. The response, however, had been 'practically nil'.[70] This result was almost certainly to Byrne's own taste. He had made clear his belief that such recruits would not fit into the R.I.C. Now he soft-pedalled. But Lord French wanted to expand the police, and when he found that he could not push Byrne along, he swept him aside. As far back as May, Long had told French of his firm belief that 'the head of the police had lost his nerve',[71] and since then the dispute over the withdrawal of military detachments had caused friction between Byrne and Shaw. By November, French was ignoring Byrne and treating his

---

[65] Ibid.; cf. Strength of the Army: Memo by Sec. of State for War, 15 November 1919, showing the extent of overseas commitments. C.P. 282, CAB.24 94.

[66] S. W. Roskill, *Hankey: Man of Secrets*, ii (London, 1972), p. 144. Hankey was 'unimpressed' by Wilson's warning that even some of the Guards battalions were not reliable; he thought that the C.I.G.S. 'fairly had the "wind up"'.

[67] Hugh Sandham Jeudwine, 1862–1942. Commanded 55th (W. Lancs.) Div., 1916–1919; K.C.B., 1918; C.G.S., British Army of the Rhine, 1919; G.O.C. 5th Div., 1919–22; Acting G.O.C.-in-C. Ireland, Dec. 1920.

[68] Edward Peter Strickland, 1869–1951. Maj. Gen., 1916; K.C.B., 1918; G.O.C. 6th Div., 1919–22, 2nd Div., 1923–6; G.O.C. British Troops, Egypt, 1927–31; General, 1931.

[69] Hist. 5th Div., p. 5.

[70] I.G. R.I.C. to U.S., 4 October 1919. Strathcarron papers.

[71] Long to French, 21 May 1919. Strathcarron papers.

deputy, T. J. Smith, as *de facto* Inspector General. He wrote to Macpherson,

I find that Byrne is still showing great weakness and giving considerable umbrage to the Commander-in-Chief. I consider it most prejudicial to the accomplishment of what we have to do that he should remain in his present position.[72]

It is undoubtedly significant that the authority under which non-Irishmen were eventually recruited into the R.I.C. was an order issued from the Inspector General's office on 11 November,[73] and it seems reasonable to assume that it was Smith, not Byrne, who put his hand to this measure. Finally, in December, after more prompting by Long,[74] French sent Byrne on a month's leave.[75]

Byrne's departure was noticed by the press in January 1920, and the Government's refusal to make a statement caused some unfavourable comment.[76] Thereafter Byrne's 'dismissal' remained something of a mystery, even in well-informed circles.[77] In fact he proved hard to get rid of. He had shrewdly insisted on becoming a permanent civil servant when he took up the post, and difficulties in finding him another job meant that French and Macpherson could not remove him until 11 March 1920.[78] But his influence in Ireland ended in December 1919, and heralded the second stage in the passing of the old R.I.C. itself. Already it was alienated from the community; now it was to be made truly alien by an influx of foreign recruits.

Lloyd George, with a mixture of perception and shortsightedness, wrote to Bonar Law on 30 December that

It may of course very well be that the task in Ireland is a hopeless one and that Byrne has simply the intelligence to recognize it. However, until we are through with Home Rule a man of less intelligence and more stolidity would be a more useful instrument to administer the interregnum.[79]

[72] French to Macpherson, 4 November 1919. Strathcarron papers.
[73] Acceptance of a recruit into the R.I.C. depended on a reference from the D.I. in his home area. The name of this D.I. was entered in the R.I.C. Register alongside that of the recruit. In the case of non-Irish recruits in January 1920 and after, reference was to 'I.G.'s Order, 11 November 1919'. No copy of this order itself has yet been located. R.I.C. General Register, H.O. 184 36.
[74] Cabinet Memo by 1st Ld. of the Admiralty, 4 December 1919. Lloyd George papers, Encl. in F/31/1/17.
[75] French to Macpherson, 10 December 1919. Strathcarron papers.
[76] *Cork Examiner*, 9 January; *The Times*, 10 January 1920.
[77] Gen. Sir C. F. N. Macready, *Annals of an Active Life* (London, 1924), ii. 438. (Henceforth cited as Macready, *Annals*.)
[78] Ld. Lt. to Prime Minister, 29 December 1919. Lloyd George papers, Encl. in F/31/1/17; C.S.I. to Prime Minister, 21 February 1920. Ibid., F/46/1/20; Note by C.S.I., 11 March 1920. Ibid., F/46/1/22. Byrne later enjoyed a comfortable round of colonial governorships.
[79] Lloyd George to Bonar Law, 30 December 1919. Lloyd George papers, F/31/1/16.

This concept of an 'interregnum' indicates that Lloyd George had accepted that the old Irish administration was over. Yet his pragmatism was bound by his nineteenth-century Liberal roots; 'Home Rule' remained the utmost horizon of his outlook on Irish affairs. The reform of the police force was aimed at restoring an orderly situation in which Home Rule could flourish, and Lloyd George was not particular about the methods that the police chose to use. It was enough that they stayed in the field, showing that although a policy of force was being applied in Ireland, it was being applied within a civil and not a military context. In a short time, however, any such idea became meaningless. Byrne's successors did not share his determination to preserve the civil character of the R.I.C. Their 'stolidity' was to be a dedication to keeping the R.I.C. in the fight, no matter how much its character changed in the process.

The man who was subsequently to be most closely identified with this attitude, and with the growth of violence on the part of the police, was Major-General H. H. Tudor,[80] who became overall police commander during the reforms of May 1920; and it has been common for historians to date the creation of the 'Black and Tans' from this period.[81] It is now clear that the recruitment policy originated at least six months earlier. Recruiting offices were set up in Britain before the end of 1919, and a special recruiting officer began to travel the country.[82] The first British ex-serviceman to join the R.I.C.—Henry Batters of Nottingham, described as a 'musician and ex-soldier'—was appointed on 2 January 1920,[83] and another 110 followed that month.[84] Although recruitment remained fairly static for five months afterwards, with non-Irishmen forming about one-third of the total intake, the foundations were laid for the massive expansion which took place during the summer of 1920. Grasping at an expedient, Lord French had taken— and Lloyd George was soon to deepen—a step whose imprint would be seen on the whole future of Ireland.

[80] Henry Hugh Tudor, 1871–1965. Commanded 9th Div. Artillery, 1916–18, 9th Div., 1918; Maj. Gen. 1919; Police Adviser, Ireland, 1920 (Chief of Police, Nov. 1920–2); G.O.C. and Director of Public Safety, Palestine, 1922; K.C.B., 1923.

[81] Recent instances are R. Rhodes James, *Churchill: A Study in Failure 1900–1939* (London, 1970), p. 126; K. Middlemas, Jones, *Whitehall Diary*, iii. 22; Boyce, *Englishmen and Irish Troubles*, pp. 49–50.

[82] Recruiting Offices were opened first in London, Glasgow, and Birmingham; they later existed in over 20 towns. The special recruiting officer, Major Fleming, held the rank of C.I., R.I.C. See R.I.C. General Register, H.O. 184 36.

[83] Ibid.

[84] Ibid. Full statistics of intake and proportion of non-Irish recruits are given in Appendix I below, p. 209.

6. THE COMMITMENT OF THE ARMY (December 1917–March 1920)

The question of martial law
There was one curious aberration from the general hesitancy of Irish policy in this period. Walter Long, in his capacity as 'liaison officer' between the Cabinet and the Irish Government,[85] took the Admiralty yacht to Dublin early in December, and there drew up a memorandum which stated that henceforth 'the Irish Government will be at liberty to impose martial law when and where they please without reference to the Cabinet'. 'I have satisfied myself', Long went on, 'that the policy to be adopted ... will be carefully thought out, and adopted with every regard for ultimate success.'[86] By this he meant simply that it would only be imposed if it could be effectively enforced. In view of the Cabinet's previous, and subsequent, attitude to martial law, this was a remarkable undertaking. But the Cabinet did not disavow it; on the contrary, Lloyd George wrote to French on 30 December that 'Mr Walter Long's memorandum fairly represents our attitude', and he promised formal repressive legislation next parliamentary session if French still wanted it.[87] It is none the less hard to believe that the Cabinet was really ready for martial law, and it may be that Lloyd George had not fully digested the memorandum. In any case, Lord French was unable to seize the opportunity it presented, for, as we have seen, the Irish Government was far from unanimously in favour of martial law.

Macpherson, as he had shown on 25 September, did not share French's belief in the need for radical measures. Nor did French's own Viceregal Council, which French had set up in an attempt to resolve some of the confusion at the Castle—an attempt in which, to his disappointment, neither Shortt nor Macpherson gave him any assistance.[88] Macpherson, indeed, was now making the confusion worse by virtually boycotting the Under Secretary, the Catholic and nationalist James MacMahon,[89] and working instead through the Assistant Under Secretary, Taylor.[90] Macpherson's Protestant religious prejudices

[85] French's phrase, to Lloyd George, 14 January 1919. Lloyd George papers, F/48/6/24. Long had been designated as having chief responsibility in the Cabinet for Irish affairs on 10 May 1918 (W.C. 408), but it is not clear how this placed him *vis-à-vis* the Chief Secretary.
[86] Memo by 1st Ld. of the Admiralty, 4 December 1919. Strathcarron papers.
[87] Lloyd George to French, 30 December 1919. Lloyd George papers, Encl. in F/31/1/17.
[88] See French to Bonar Law, 18 April 1920. Bonar Law papers, 103/2/11.
[89] James MacMahon, 1865–1954. Secretary, Post Office, Ireland, 1916; U.S., Ireland, 1918–22; P.C. (Ire), 1920.
[90] On the evidence it seems to have been Macpherson who encouraged Taylor's over-centralizing tendencies. G. C. Duggan's opinion ('The Last Days of Dublin Castle', *Blackwood's Magazine*, mcclxxxii (1922) pp. 139–41) that French was under Taylor's influence seems quite wrong, especially in view of the events of April 1920. But the tangle of evidence is tantalizingly hard to penetrate.

appear to have been exercising an increasing influence over his policy and behaviour,[91] though not sufficiently to drive him into decisive action. The Irish Lord Chancellor had earlier in the year been 'at loggerheads' with the G.O.C.-in-C.,[92] but when he now took up a more militant stance and proposed the issue of a D.O.R. Regulation making it a capital offence triable by court martial to 'compass the death or injury of any member of the police or Army', Macpherson told him to wait: 'we will be in a much better position to secure the assent of the Cabinet when we have proved that the existing law has failed'.[93] Dramatic proof to this effect was soon to be forthcoming. Meanwhile, the Castle, in the shape of Taylor and the Chief Crown Solicitor, Wynne, put its faith in a new Criminal Injuries Bill.[94]

The Ashtown ambush

The deliberations of the British authorities usually ignored one vital factor, the continual increase in the tempo of the rebel campaign. The hope that Sinn Féin had 'shot its bolt' frequently arose, only to be dashed by a new rebel stroke. The I.R.A., apart from a minority who actually thought that they could physically eject the British, showed a natural grasp of the political and psychological bearing of guerrilla warfare applied in conjunction with modern publicity techniques. It has been well said that Collins 'knew the gun to be but a propaganda weapon, its power of destruction a headline, its detonation a slogan'.[95] By December 1919 the first phase in the I.R.A.'s development, that of securing arms, was sufficiently advanced to permit operations aimed primarily at public opinion. The most dramatic of these was the ambush at Ashtown, near the Viceregal Lodge, on 19 December.

The ambush was an attempt to kill Lord French himself. Dan Breen, who took part in it, stressed that there was no personal spite against the old soldier, but 'His name was known throughout the civilized world,' and 'we knew that his death would arouse all peoples to take notice of our fight for freedom'.[96] In fact, owing to confusion over the number of cars in French's convoy, the attack narrowly failed of its physical object,[97] and at first its moral effect was also in doubt. Lloyd George, as Macpherson bitterly recorded, reacted only with the

[91] They were sufficiently well known for Macready to suggest them as the reason for the dismissal of Byrne. *Annals*, ii. 438.

[92] Sir John Ross to Long, 19 February 1919. Copy in Long to Lloyd George, 21 February 1919. Lloyd George papers, F/33/2/15.

[93] Lord Chancellor of Ireland to C.S.I., 2 November; and reply, 5 November 1919. Strathcarron papers.

[94] Duggan, 'The Last Days of Dublin Castle', p. 141.

[95] J. Gleeson, *Bloody Sunday* (London, 1962), p. 36; an Irish account unusually frank in its treatment of propaganda and terrorism.

[96] Breen, *My Fight for Irish Freedom*, new edn., p. 86.

[97] See official inquiry, C.O. 904 188; The Kerryman, *With the I.R.A. in the Fight for Freedom* (Tralee, 1955), pp. 43-5.

remark, 'they are bad shots'.[98] British public opinion was similarly un-moved.[99] But on French and Macpherson the effect was undoubtedly traumatic. Macpherson forgot his disagreements with French in a wave of sentiment. Eloquent testimony to his distress can be found in a rambling, plaintive memorandum, unaddressed and uncompleted, which he wrote on 20 December. He bewailed the influence of Shortt, 'the worst of all Chief Secretaries', over Lloyd George, and gave rein to a string of prejudices:

I never had a word of sympathy from the P.M. He preferred to have the views of a man who was notoriously a Jesuit. . . . The same views were accepted by the Minister of Education, who had the P.M.'s ear. He was essentially a theorist, guided by that stupid egotist Sir Horace Plunkett, who ruined the Convention.[100]

It is, at least, descriptive of Irish policy at this time that while Macpherson felt that he was being undermined by Fisher's influence, C. P. Scott was despairing of making Fisher understand the need for 'putting a bridle on the Irish Executive'.[101]

Macpherson's shock, together with the Cabinet's momentary approval of strong measures, permitted a dramatic response to the Ashtown ambush. French had accepted defeat over the reform of the Irish Government. He told Lord Riddell in November, 'It is as bad as can be. I don't mean that the system is corrupt, but it is bad. There is no proper control.' But he added, 'It is impossible to make a satisfactory alteration under existing conditions.'[102] Now, in January 1920, the Army was introduced into this system as virtually a supplementary department of the administration, with powers which fell far short of martial law, but pushed the Defence of the Realm Act to its limits. Irish Command later recorded that

Briefly, the policy was to transfer to the Competent Military Authority[103] the powers, previously vested in the police authorities and magistrates, of instituting and organizing action against the perpetrators of outrage and the organizers of lawlessness, and to deport and intern under DRR 14B such persons on a warrant signed by the Chief Secretary for Ireland. Secondly, the Competent Military Authority was to be empowered to search individuals and buildings for arms, explosives, and seditious literature.[104]

[98] Note by Macpherson, 20 December 1919. Strathcarron papers.

[99] Boyce, *Englishmen and Irish Troubles*, pp. 45–6.

[100] Note by Macpherson, 20 December 1919. Strathcarron papers. Plunkett was the founder of the Irish agricultural co-operative movement of the early 1900s, and had presided over the Irish Convention in 1917–18.

[101] Wilson, *Political Diaries of C. P. Scott*, p. 379 (1 December).

[102] Lord Riddell, *Intimate Diary of the Peace Conference and After* (London, 1933), pp. 146–7 (26 November 1919).

[103] The usual Competent Military Authorities were brigade commanders, though in certain important matters authority was confined to divisional commanders.

[104] G.H.Q. Ireland, *Record*, i (March 1922), p. 5.

The Army decided on the mass arrest of all known I.R.A. leaders, and the deportation of those who could not be legally convicted. Orders to this effect were issued on 7 January 1920, and destroyers were placed on standby at Kingstown, Arklow, Greenore, and Waterford to take deportees to Britain. Military commanders were to prepare lists of wanted men, and arrest substitutes for those who could not be found; they were given the 'widest latitude' in carrying out searches at any time of the day or night; and they were also instructed to carry out random street searches.[105]

The problem of intelligence

It was soon to become evident that this scheme was over-ambitious, as regards both the Army's powers and the Cabinet's determination. The historian of 5th Division was subsequently to analyse the military and political options thus:

> When a country is drifting into armed rebellion through the action of a small extremist section, it is open to argument whether the majority, as a deterrent, should suffer for the sins of the few, or whether the organizers and party leaders ... should be removed ... until reasonable political grievances are redressed. But, if the second course is chosen, it is necessary
>
> (a) to know the names of the leaders
> (b) to be able to arrest them
> (c) to make certain they do not get back to their country until the trouble is over.[106]

These three requirements may be otherwise described as (a) effective intelligence, (b) effective operational capability, and (c) political determination to keep suspects imprisoned. In January 1920 the Army was hampered in all three respects.

The weakness of the intelligence services was of the first importance. Until 1919, intelligence in Ireland had been almost entirely the work of the police, there being only three military intelligence officers in the country. The police intelligence services, even the highly efficient G Division of the D.M.P., worked on 'touch'—experience and intuition—without formal systems of written records, so that when experienced men were killed in the attacks of 1919, their knowledge went with them. Moreover, the police were reluctant to convey their knowledge to the military: Irish Command wrote in 1922 that

> even to the very last, it was exceedingly difficult to obtain information from almost any R.I.C. man unless he were seen and examined personally by some officer whom he knew and trusted.[107]

[105] G.H.Q. Ireland General Instructions, 2/15115G, 7 January 1920. D.D. H.Q. File, W.O. 35 70.
[106] Hist. 5th Div., p. 23.
[107] G.H.Q. Ireland, *Record*, ii. 23.

Although R.I.C. officers and Head Constables were instructed on 13 January 1920 to supply Competent Military Authorities with all necessary information,[108] 'it took a lot of talking before you got very much out of them', as one military intelligence officer remarked.[109] And when it came to compiling, at that time, the lists of I.R.A. leaders to be arrested, it dawned on the Army 'how completely the R.I.C. service of information was paralysed':

It was then found that the local R.I.C. could give little reliable information about such persons beyond a statement that so and so was 'a bad boy' or 'a bad article'. The police lists were out of date and to them every Sinn Fein club was a battalion.[110]

Irish Command still felt that 'officers who were able to establish friendly relations with the R.I.C. got, as a rule, more than those who worked independently',[111] but by and large the Army soon found that it had to construct a system of its own from scratch.

In this it faced not only the daunting problem of a population whose mouths were already closed against the authorities, but also a severe shortage of personnel. Until 1919 there were no trained intelligence officers in Ireland, and only in the middle of that year was a small 'I.' staff created at G.H.Q., with one G.S.O. 2, one G.S.O. 3, and one clerk.[112] Divisional and brigade intelligence did not appear until some time after the creation of these units in November 1919, while at battalion level, the most vital of all, the appointment of I.O.s was 'encouraged rather than ordered', and depended entirely on whether battalion commanders appreciated the necessity of intelligence work.[113] Even where they did, I.O.s were ordinary regimental officers without specialized training, and perhaps without aptitude for the work. And where, as was all too common, they did not, I.O.s would have to fit their intelligence work in with their regimental duties. The Army as a whole tended to leave intelligence work to the 'secret service', and was slow to realize that no amount of 'secret service' work could replace the gathering of comprehensive 'front-line' information by every officer and man.[114]

Military strength and methods
It was at battalion level that the Army faced its second handicap, physical weakness. Without sufficient men, units were too thinly

[108] Hist. 5th Div., p. 20.
[109] Major (later General) A. E. Percival, 'Two lectures on Guerrilla Warfare' (?1925), No. 2, p. 6. Percival papers. (Henceforth cited as Percival, Lectures 1 and 2.) Percival was I.O. of the 1st Essex Regt., in southern Cork from January 1920.
[110] G.H.Q. Ireland, *Record*, ii. 8.
[111] Ibid., ii. 21.
[112] G.H.Q. Ireland, *Record*, ii. 5–6.
[113] Ibid., ii. 7. [114] Ibid., ii. 8, 29, 33.
3

distributed to permit them either to gather detailed intelligence information or to translate information into action—to arrest the rebel leaders.
At the beginning of 1920, for instance, the 1st Essex Regiment,
stationed at Kinsale in southern Cork, had at most 600 men available
for all purposes. Its area, which consisted of hilly terrain with a network of small fields enclosed by high stone walls affording superb cover
for guerrilla operations, was no less than 100 miles from east to west
and 20 from north to south.[115] The need for closer control was obvious.
With only 29 weak battalions for the whole of Ireland, however, no
improvement could be expected, and the only advance that was made
in this period was the further multiplication of headquarters. The nine
counties of Ulster were placed under a new division, the 1st, at Belfast,
and another divisional command was created for Dublin District.[116]
The latter was an important step, bringing the capital city under close
military supervision, which became more effective there than elsewhere
because of the absence of the R.I.C. The commander of Dublin District
was a youngish Major-General, G. F. Boyd.[117] His two provisional
brigade H.Q.s were short-staffed, and lacked even typewriters until
late April (though so, amazingly, did Lord French himself).[118] The
structure of Irish Command at this time is shown in Table 1.

   Of equal importance to the Army's numerical weakness was its
generally poor state of training. It contained a high proportion of raw
recruits, and even its veterans had little experience of anything but
trench warfare and frontal assaults. In Ireland it was fieldcraft and
marksmanship which were at a premium, and duty was both physically
and psychologically arduous. Shortage of numbers, coupled with the
need for as many local detachments as possible, meant that

The young infantry soldier was soon reduced to a monotonous succession of
one night in bed, one night on guard, and one night on inlying picquet or out
on raiding duties.[119]

Within a short time, no infantryman in Ireland could hope for more
than three consecutive nights in bed. This pressure of duty made it

[115] Percival, Lecture 1, pp. 3–4, 11. The terrain of much of southern Ireland at this time
bore a remarkable resemblance to that of Brittany, whose guerrilla potential was
graphically described by Balzac in *Les Chouans*.
[116] General Routine Orders, Lt. Gen. Sir F. Shaw, 7 January 1920. W.O. 35 173/1.
Dublin had previously been a brigade command of 5th Division, and this brigade (13th)
was transferred to the west. Its commander, Col. T. S. Lambert, was later killed in an
ambush. Hist. 5th Div., p. 107.
[117] Gerald Farrell Boyd, 1877–1930. Commissioned from the ranks: commanded 46th
(N. Midland) Div. in France, and Dublin District, 1920–3; K.C.B., 1923; Mil. Sec. to
Sec. of State for War, 1927.
[118] D.D. War Diary 'A', 24 February 1920. W.O. 35 90/1; Ibid., 21 April 1920; cf.
H. A. L. Fisher's diary, 28 May 1920. Fisher papers.
[119] Hist. 5th Div., p. 25.

TABLE I

Irish Command: Distribution, Spring 1920[a]

Division	Brigade	Battalions	Location
5th (Curragh)	13th (Galway)	3	Westmeath, Longford, Mayo, Galway, Roscommon, S. Leitrim
	14th (Curragh)	3	Carlow, Kildare, King's, Queen's, part of Wicklow
	15th (Belfast)	4	Antrim, Londonderry, Armagh, Down, Tyrone, Fermanagh, Cavan, Monaghan, Louth, Sligo, N. Leitrim
6th (Cork)	16th (Fermoy)	4	Waterford, Wexford, Kilkenny, S. Tipperary
	17th (Cork)	4	Cork, Kerry
	18th (Limerick)	4	Limerick, Clare, N. Tipperary
Dublin District	24th(P) (Royal Bks.)	4	Meath, N. Co. Dublin, Dublin City north of River Liffey
	25th(P) (Kilmainham)	3	Dublin City south of River Liffey, S. Co. Dublin, part of Wicklow

[a] Source: G.H.Q. Ireland, *Record*, i. 5.

difficult to give even basic training to the new recruits, and the Imperial General Staff stated in June 1920 that of the 23,000 'effectives' available in Ireland, 3,000 had not fired a musketry course.[120]

The work into which these inexperienced troops were precipitated was of probably the most difficult type for any Army, especially that of a democratic society with a traditional aversion to any sign of military presence. Simple military logic, which in essence is the application of superior force, is, in operations in aid of the civil power, complicated by many political and social factors. Power has to be tempered with restraint, and exercised according to criteria which were not, until the mid-twentieth century, habitual among soldiers. Individual self-control and judgement are as vital as corporate discipline; indeed, the best qualities of soldiers and of policemen need to be fused for successful internal security work, and it is not surprising that Sir Henry Wilson feared that the Army was unreliable in this respect. In the event, the discipline and temper of the Army proved equal to the strain of Irish conditions, but the general lack of skill and initiative was a constant drag on military flexibility.

To begin with, raids and searches of private houses and other buildings formed the bulk of offensive military operations. Their objective was the arrest of wanted men and the seizure of arms and equipment or 'seditious literature'—the latter including any material of interest from an intelligence point of view (diaries, letters, lists of names, and so on),

[120] Imperial General Staff, Note on the Garrison in Ireland, 15 June 1920. C.P. 1467, CAB.24 107.

as well as proscribed publications—*An tÓglách* and the *Irish Bulletin*—and any other papers connected with Sinn Féin organizations, such as the Bonds issued by Michael Collins's Republican Loan.[121] Even photographs of de Valera were removed, though they were not illegal.[122] Raiding parties usually consisted of an officer and twelve men, and operated at night, so as to increase the possibility of locating wanted men. Raids were ordered on the basis of information from the police or the public, or on 'hot' information from other raids or prisoners. A high percentage of searches drew a blank, and it became necessary to take elaborate security precautions to prevent advance knowledge of raids from falling into the hands of the very active rebel intelligence organization.[123] Raiding parties learnt that instead of driving their lorries up to the house which was to be raided, and thus, in the still of the night, giving advance warning to its occupants, it was better to halt some way off and surround the building on foot.[124] They also had to take precautions to counter allegations of theft, which were a staple ingredient of Republican propaganda.

A typical example of raid conduct can be seen in the following report, commended by Major-General Boyd as 'a useful illustration of good method'.

On the night of the 27th/28th (February 1920) I was in charge of a raid on Dr. Lynn's house No. 9 Belgrave Road. So that there should be no chance of any trouble from the soldiers going where they should not or taking anything, the following arrangements were made. Immediately on entering the house, one soldier and one constable proceeded to the top landing to prevent any escape that way, one soldier was put over the telephone and three soldiers were under the charge of a police Sergeant to assist him in the search in any way required. No other soldiers entered the house at all. Miss Ffrench Mullen was inclined to be troublesome so I told her she must wait in the study till the search was over. As far as I know no soldier entered a room except with a Police Sergeant or Constable.[125]

Even in this case a claim for the theft of several articles was made by Miss Lynn (who stated that the police could not have taken them because they had had 'the fear of God put into them').[126] In future it became necessary for raid officers to search their troops and sign a declaration that nothing had been removed.[127]

[121] Notes and Raid Proformas A and B issued by H.Q. Dublin District, in 25th(P) Brigade Reports, W.O. 35 72.
[122] Macready to Anderson, 5 January 1921. Anderson papers, C.O. 904 188/2.
[123] For a graphic impression of these precautions see Woodcock, *Experiences of an Officer's Wife in Ireland*, p. 60.
[124] Cf. C Coy. 1st Cheshire Regt. Orders, 2 November 1920. W.O. 35 72; Dublin District Orders for 26th(P) Bde, W.O. 35 71.
[125] Bt. Lt. Col. Charlton, 1st Prince of Wales Volunteers, to H.Q. D.D., 29 February 1920, and note by G.O.C. D.D. W.O. 35 70.
[126] Miss Lynn to G.O.C. D.D., 29 February 1920. Ibid.
[127] H.Q. D.D. Orders, 25 March, 6 April, 8 September 1920. Ibid.

The Army and the police

The problem of co-operating with the police was never to be fully solved, and in some ways was rather to grow more serious. The Army had resisted the idea that military patrols should be put under the control of the police or magistrates,[128] but the situation in January 1920, with the Army acting as a sort of supplementary police force, was highly unsatisfactory. The warrants for the arrest of I.R.A. leaders were issued by the civil government, and it was arranged that wherever possible actual arrests should be made by policemen.[129] Raiding parties therefore contained a police contingent, though its presence was not fully explained. For instance, on 8 March one Dublin District unit formally asked the reason for constables accompanying the troops, adding that if they were supposed to be guides, they were incompetent. Dublin District replied only that the constables went along 'as an authority'.[130] Even the basic principle that in any joint operation the command must rest with the senior military officer present, and that troops must not take orders from police, was not commonly grasped, though it was frequently reiterated.[131]

In January 1920 the Army not only took over much police work in seeking out political criminals, but it also had to protect the police themselves from these criminals. During that month there were ten rebel attacks on police posts, a new phase of guerrilla activity; and though none were successful, only four police being wounded, the Inspector General felt that 'all the attacks showed careful preparation and good discipline'.[132] The police had been unable to identify the attackers, and had no success in searching for them.[133] Nine more attacks occurred in February, while indictable offences totalled 659. Of these 557 were regarded by the R.I.C. as part of what was now called 'the guerilla warfare' of Sinn Féin.[134] Military detachments in rural areas were extensively employed in going to the assistance of threatened police posts, and Dublin District ordered its units to instruct the R.I.C. in musketry and tactics, and to inspect their arrangements for barrack defence.[135]

The militarization of the R.I.C. continued. The first of the British

---

[128] Military Forces in Aid of the Civil Power: C.S.O. File R.P. 5975(18).
[129] G.H.Q. Ireland, *Record*, i. 7.
[130] Capt. Clifton, Sherwood Foresters, to H.Q. D.D., 8 March 1920, and reply. D.D. H.Q. File, W.O. 35 70.
[131] Initially by the police themselves—R.I.C. and D.M.P. Circulars, 9 January 1920; cf. C.-in-C.'s Conference, G.H.Q. Ireland, 4 July 1920. W.O. 35 90; H.Q. D.D. note, 29 March 1921 (Robinstown 'incident'). D.D. H.Q. File, W.O. 35 71.
[132] R.I.C. Reports, I.G., January 1920. C.O. 904 111.
[133] Ibid.
[134] R.I.C. Reports, I.G., February 1920. C.O. 904 111.
[135] Percival, Lecture 1, pp. 14–15; D.D. Orders, 20 February 1920. D.D. War Diary 'D', W.O. 35 90/1.

ex-soldier recruits arrived in Ireland to begin police training on
25 March and a small number of ex-officers were also taken on to
supervise the defence of barracks.[136] At the same time the R.I.C.'s
old organization of four Divisions, Ulster, Leinster, Munster, and
Connaught, each under a Divisional Commissioner, was re-established,
and an extra Divisional H.Q. was set up in Dublin.[137] This reorganization has often been credited to Major-General Tudor,[138] but
it took place well before his arrival, apparently at the instigation of
Sir John Taylor.[139] The function that seems to have been envisaged
for the D.C.s was the laudable one of improving co-operation between
the R.I.C. and the Army, but neither they nor the Army showed much
understanding of how this could be done. Their sphere of responsibility
within the R.I.C., and their position *vis-à-vis* the military authorities,
remained vague for a long time.[140] Some of them eventually gave up
the attempt to combine alien methods, and, having established tactical
control of the R.I.C., became virtually independent warlords, scarcely
connected with either their military counterparts or with the police
authorities in Dublin.

Some improvement was clearly necessary. On 27 March the Irish
Unionist peer Lord Desart[141] wrote to Lord Midleton,[142] leader of the
Irish Unionists in the House of Lords (who had been offered the Lord
Lieutenancy in 1918 before Lord French), that according to his own
observation 'the military authorities do not assist effectively or really
collaborate with the police'.[143] Desart criticized Lieutenant-General
Shaw as 'neither energetic nor specially capable', and argued that,
although no one expected the Army to perform technical police duties,
'as to patrolling and working with the police, if they will not do that,
they do not serve the most immediate purposes for which they are
wanted'.[144] He had been told in confidence by his local County Inspector that there was no defined system of co-operation between the
police and the military:

[136] R. Bennett, *The Black and Tans*, new edn. (London, 1970), p. 28; the number of the
cumbrously-named 'Defence of Barracks Sergeants' remained a handful until May; for
recruitment statistics see Appendix I below, p. 209.
[137] Hist. 5th Div., pp. 31–2. It appears from subsequent evidence that the Dublin H.Q.
was moved or amalgamated with the Leinster H.Q. at Dundalk.
[138] See Brig. O. de L'E. Winter, *Winter's Tale* (London, 1955), p. 315.
[139] Duggan, 'The Last Days of Dublin Castle', p. 143.
[140] Hist. 5th Div., pp. 31–2. Eventually, in March 1921, they were accorded the status
of colonels for military liaison purposes.
[141] Hamilton John Agmondesham Cuffe, 5th Earl of Desart, 1848–1934. British
plenipotentiary at London Naval Conference, 1908; British member of Hague
International Court.
[142] St. John Brodrick, 1st Earl of Midleton, 1856–1942. Conservative M.P., 1880–1906;
Sec. of State for War, 1900–3; for India, 1903–5; succeeded to Viscounty, 1907; Earl,
1920.
[143] Desart to Midleton, 27 March 1920. Midleton papers, P.R.O. 30 67/42.
[144] Desart to Midleton, ibid.

they sometimes act together for particular purposes and in special emergencies, but there seems to be little or no use of soldiers to prevent danger and disturbances.

When this Inspector had made arrangements with the 15th Hussars for joint night patrolling, Major-General Strickland (commander of 6th Division) had quashed them, saying that he would not have his men 'joy-riding' around the country.[145]

Transport and communications

The final military handicap was shortage of material, especially for communication and transport. In December 1919, the signals commander of 6th Division had reported that full communications could not be maintained in an emergency, owing to shortage of personnel,[146] and the efforts made during the following year to remedy the situation were risible. (A handful of signals personnel were sent to Ireland in May 1920, but most of them were found unfit for service; one was an ex-batman with no signals experience, another was unable to climb poles because of malaria, and two had been waiting for medical discharge when they were drafted to Ireland.)[147] The scarcity of wireless meant that much reliance was still placed on pigeons, but these also required trained operators, and good loftmen were hard to find; besides which the pigeons had to be transported by road or rail to their starting positions, thus throwing an extra burden on the communication system.[148]

As far as motor transport was concerned, the Army was no better off than the R.I.C. The military administrative system had rapidly reverted to peacetime standards of triplicate bureaucracy and 'red tape', and the flow of vehicles was sluggish. Sir Henry Wilson had drawn attention to this situation in a Cabinet memorandum of 3 January,[149] but it was several months before significant steps were taken to meet the real requirements of the units in Ireland.[150] Concerning the transport which was available in early 1920, 5th Division wryly observed that

[145] Ibid. The reference to the 15th Hussars appears to be an error, as this unit was part of Dublin District, not of 6th Division; the reference is probably to the 19th Hussars, stationed at Ennis, Co. Clare, (18th Brigade).
[146] O.C. Signals 6th Div. to G.H.Q.(I.), 30 December 1919. W.O. 35 172/1.
[147] O.C. Special Signal Coy. (I) to Chief Signal Officer, G.H.Q.(I), 11 May 1920. W.O. 35 172/1.
[148] See G.O.C. 6th Div. to G.H.Q.(I), 17 July 1920; G.O.C. 5th Div. to G.H.Q.(I), 23 November 1920. W.O. 35 172/1.
[149] Memo by C.I.G.S. (Strength of the Army: Capacity to Aid the Civil Power), 3 January 1920. C.P. 472, CAB.24 96.
[150] G.H.Q. Ireland, *Record*, i. 17. Cf. below, p. 84.

The Disposals Board appeared to have sold all the best vehicles and to have retained those which were nearly worn out, or which were deficient in the necessary spare parts.[151]

Breakdowns were frequent, and, to begin with, neither workshops nor trained personnel were available to deal with them. (Even a year later, 20 to 35 per cent of transport vehicles were off the road under repair at any time.)[152] Numbers inexorably declined through cannibalization of mechanical parts,[153] and the heavy demands on lorries for supply purposes restricted their availability for tactical use. In March 1920, the R.A.S.C. was even forced to resort to commercial hiring—and still its supply work remained in arrears.[154]

Military policy and political uncertainty

Altogether, therefore, there were considerable handicaps to the successful identification and arrest of Republican leaders at the beginning of 1920. The policy of arresting these leaders was none the less persisted in for three months, and appears to have improved the morale of the Crown Forces, especially the police, by giving them a sense of direction and purpose. As to its effect, Lieutenant-General Shaw declared in March that

> The first real result of this policy has been the capture of most valuable documents from which the organization of the Irish Volunteer Army has been deduced. . . . They have a very powerful organization, which can only be crippled through its leaders.[155]

This was an admission that the attempt to arrest the leaders in January had been premature, and that an effective intelligence service was the first necessity. But Shaw still claimed that the organization 'can and will be broken' by such arrests, and that 'No other course is possible.'[156] Later events were to suggest that this was a false analysis of the dependence of the Republican movement on its leaders, and that the new movement had more internal drive and resilience than former Irish political organizations. For the time being, however, it was not weakness of intelligence or falseness of analysis that wrecked the military policy, so much as oscillation in the Government's approach.

[151] Hist. 5th Div., p. 28. This document provides (pp. 27–8) a good analysis of available transport, including horse and bicycle, and of the necessity for motor vehicles for ease of operation and bulk carrying capacity.

[152] Hist. 5th Div., p. 89. The heavy (3-ton) lorries suffered a higher percentage of breakdowns than the lighter (15- and 30-cwt.) types.

[153] This was very noticeably so with obsolescent types like the Austin and Jeffrey Quad armoured cars. Cf. G.O.C.-in-C.'s Weekly Situation Report, 4 December 1920. S.I.C. 61, CAB.27 108.

[154] R.A.S.C. to H.Q. D.D., 16 March 1920. D.D. War Diary 'D', W.O. 36 90/1. In Dublin district only 50 per cent of 3-ton lorries were allotted for tactical use.

[155] The Military Situation: Memo by G.O.C.-in-C. Ireland, 25 March 1920. C.P. 1131, CAB.24 104.

[156] Ibid.

To begin with, the military instructions of 7 January concerning the arrests were changed even before they were put into effect. Originally each division was given a quota of internment warrants—80 to 5th Division, 120 to Dublin District, and 200 to 6th Division—and left to work out its own list of wanted men.[157] On 21 January these warrants were withdrawn, and a scheme was substituted whereby each case was to be reviewed by the Dublin Castle legal department after the men had been arrested, so that deportations were neither certain nor immediate. This was the first sign of a dichotomy which was to become more serious, between the Castle's scrupulous regard for justice—or at least for legal form—and the Army's belief in the necessity of firmness and dispatch. In this case the Army was annoyed by the delay in deporting suspects, and by the release of many of them after their cases had been reviewed, which led to many allegations of false arrest.[158] But in spite of this confusion, the mass arrests went ahead on the night of 30 January, when 57 out of 74 wanted men were taken, and by 14 April the number had risen to 317, of whom 27 were brigade commandants or staff.[159] Lieutenant-General Shaw, as we have seen, was optimistic about the eventual effect of this policy. But at this point the Government's determination to keep the suspects imprisoned gave way in the face of a renewed adoption of the hunger-strike by Sinn Féin prisoners. A sudden reversion to 'conciliation' was to nullify any positive achievement—though not the adverse public effect—of the first three months of 1920.

7. THE REPUBLICAN GUERRILLA CAMPAIGN (January–July 1920)

The Republic and its Army

British authority in Ireland was opposed by a campaign of subversion and confrontation which was now growing dramatically. In its fusion of the distinctive approaches of Sinn Féin, the Irish Volunteers, and the Irish labour movement, this campaign was a classic prototype of guerrilla action across the whole face of society. Its most striking aspect was its psychological focus: purely physical objectives played little part in it. It was the publicity given to the acts of a comparatively small Republican group which led to their mastery over a population of three million, and gave them a voice which carried beyond the shores of Ireland.

At the heart of the campaign was the ideal of a free and Gaelic

[157] G.H.Q. Ireland, Record, i. 6.
[158] G.H.Q.(I) to Dublin District, 21 January 1920. D.D. H.Q. File, W.O. 35 70; G.H.Q. Ireland, Record, i. 6–8.
[159] G.H.Q. Ireland, Record, i. 7, 9; Macready, Annals, ii. 440.

Republic, an ideal which has remained the most potent of modern Irish political concepts. Its great strength as a nationalist rallying-cry after 1916 was its romantic vagueness, which detached it sufficiently from practical detail to allow it to secure the adherence of many groups whose real aims and approaches were significantly different. It may be that, as some have suggested, the Republic was originally seen as a bargaining-counter, not a practical demand. From January 1919 onwards, however, it began to take on a life of its own[160]—or, to use an expression later attributed to de Valera, to become a political and moral straitjacket.

The group which took the Republic most seriously, and which did most to make it a reality, was the Irish Volunteers, whose campaign of killing and terrorism was based on the legality of the Declaration of Independence and the declaration of war against Britain—as, indeed, was the title 'Irish Republican Army' which it had widely adopted by 1920. The activity, efficiency, and fighting potential of this group were now increasing rapidly. Although its system of organization retained the somewhat artificial hierarchy of pseudo-regular formations, such as battalions and brigades, which involved a certain security risk, and which were of limited use from a guerrilla point of view, these did not unduly interfere with its essentially territorial nature.[161] It is worth quoting at length the account of Ernest O'Malley,[162] an organizing officer sent out to the provinces by I.R.A. H.Q.:

The organization scheme had to be elastic. A company contained 120 men, four sections and eight squads; in practice the number varied from full strength in some city companies to an average of thirty or thirty-five, but the parade strength would be twenty or twenty-five. Officers were elected by the company on parade; captain, lieutenant and second lieutenant; the voting was by ballot. Section and squad leaders were appointed by the captain at a company council of his lieutenants. When there were enough companies, five to eight, according to regulations,[163] to form a battalion, officers met to elect a commandant, vice-commandant, adjutant and quarter-master. The lieutenants of the Special Service were appointed by the commandant. In like manner the battalions elected a brigade staff. The average parade strength of a brigade in the spring of 1920 was close on nine hundred men.[164]

[160] Cf. W. K. Hancock, *Problems of Nationality 1918–1936* (London, 1937), pp. 103–5, 110.

[161] It is worth noting that when, in 1921, an attempt was made to overcome the arbitrariness of county boundaries for brigades, it was by creating an even bigger and more impractical formation, the division. See below, pp. 177–8.

[162] Later (1921) Commandant General of 2nd Southern Division; anti-Treaty Republican; author (1936) of perhaps the most expressive account of the guerrilla conflict.

[163] According to earlier (1917) regulations the number of companies required had been 4–7. I.G. R.I.C. to U.S., 23 March 1918. W.O. 35 69/8. See above, p. 18.

[164] E. O'Malley, *On Another Man's Wound* (London, 1936), p. 118. This account is remarkable not only for its literary quality but also for its view of relations between the I.R.A. and the people.

The 'Special Service' included engineers (mainly concerned with explosives), scouting, signals, transport, and musketry, one to three specialists of each sort being theoretically allotted to each section.[165] Training was circumscribed by the general shortage of equipment and the need for secrecy. Great attention was paid to formal drill—apparently irrelevant, but reflecting the emphasis on discipline throughout the Republican movement. Weapon training had to be confined to a handful of live rounds, and the general standard of marksmanship left much to be desired, even among the comparatively few men who were armed with service rifles. Irishmen, however, turned out to be natural adepts at fire and movement, the vital fusion of discipline and initiative which governed every guerrilla combat.

Operational planning remained largely a local affair. There is not much evidence of liaison at or above brigade level concerning specific operations.[166] (This is another reason why these over-large formations seem to have been unnecessary.) I.R.A. G.H.Q. in Dublin, though served by a fairly effective communications network, could hardly hope to exercise much local control, and could only encourage, and supply weapons to, units which showed most activity. General operational directives were issued from time to time, and regular exhortation and advice was supplied in the columns of *An tÓglách*, but even the broad strategic developments of the campaign depended less on decisions made at top level than on the ideas and abilities of local units. It is a question, especially in view of events after the Treaty in 1922, whether the I.R.A. succeeded in striking the correct balance between initiative and obedience. During the conflict with Britain, however, remarkably few of the actions taken by the multitude of independent rebel groups proved to be politically counterproductive.

Operations themselves were closely linked with the problem of weapons, especially ammunition supply. During 1919 the securing of arms had been the main object of operations. By 1920 the more determined units were sufficiently well endowed to embark on operations with objectives which were more psychological than logistical. Raids for arms were no longer a 'front-line' activity, though they continued, and indeed increased, reaching a startling peak in September 1920. According to police figures, some 900 such raids had occurred up to the end of August 1920, 240 of them in August itself. By the end of September this total had risen to some 2,800.[167] In his remarkable book *The Administration of Ireland 1920* Major C. J. C. Street, supervisor of

[165] I.G. R.I.C. to U.S., 23 March 1918, loc. cit.
[166] One of the few examples appears to have been the famous attack on Kilmallock R.I.C. barrack in May 1920, carried out by some 60 rebels assembled from Limerick, Cork, Tipperary, and Clare, J. M. MacCarthy (ed.), *Limerick's Fighting Story*, new edn. (Tralee, n.d.), p. 80.
[167] C.S.I. Weekly Surveys. CAB.27 108 (S.I.C. 33, 35, 37, 39, 40).

the publicity section of the Irish Office,[168] attributed this to the fact that only in September were I.R.A. arms raids finally carried out to a general plan rather than on local initiative.[169] We no longer have access to the material on which Street based his investigation, but it appears from other sources that the spate of activity was rather due to a military order in September to impound all guns left in private possession (a belated enough measure), which led, according to 5th Division, to 'a great race between the I.R.A. and the troops' to see who could seize most, in which honours were about even.[170] To give an idea of the quantities involved, 352 shot guns were taken by one brigade of 5th Division in the first fortnight of September. It is noticeable that in October the number of rebel arms raids entered on a sharp and sustained decline.[171]

The supply of effective weapons was never much more than a trickle. The prime need of rebel units outside the towns was for service rifles. and these were harder to come by than shot guns or revolvers (the latter being relatively easy to smuggle into the country). Table 2 shows the endowment of a battalion in the famous and very active West Cork Brigade in June 1920, which had 25 service rifles. For the sources of such weapons there is testimony concerning the 6th Battalion of the same brigade: this had 29 rifles, of which 21 had been seized from Eyeries coastguard station, 4 from Eyeries R.I.C. barrack, 2 in an ambush on a supply escort rearguard, and 2 stolen from the military camp on Bere Island.[172] Virtually the whole of this battalion's armament was acquired in 1919; subsequent supplies, for instance from G.H.Q. in Dublin, appear to have been minimal.

Besides weapons, the other major precondition of guerrilla operations was an effective intelligence service. Liddell Hart has observed that it is vital for all guerrillas that their enemies be kept in the dark while they themselves 'operate in the light of superior local knowledge combined with reliable news about the enemy's dispositions and moves'.[173] For the I.R.A. this was less a military principle than a fact of life, and it is often hard to see where the intelligence service stopped and the ordinary population began. It is, however, apparent that the

---

[168] Street wrote his first book, published in 1921, under the pseudonym of 'I.O.'; his second, *Ireland in 1921*, appeared under his own name the following year. Both are full of quotations from original police and other documents and can to this extent be seen as primary sources. For Street's position in the publicity organization see the lists of personnel in C.O. 904 168/2/G.H.Q. (Organization).

[169] Street, *The Administration of Ireland 1920*, p. 198.

[170] Hist. 5th Div., p. 59.

[171] cf. Appendix V.p-214

[172] Liam O'Dwyer to Padraig Ó Maidin, 2 December 1969. Cork County Library. This battalion was later asked to supply arms to another unit.

[173] B. H. Liddell Hart, 'Lessons from Resistance Movements—Guerrilla and Non-Violent', in A. Roberts (ed.), *Civilian Resistance as a National Defence* (London, 1969), p. 235.

TABLE 2

Arms Roll, 1st (Bandon) Battalion, Cork No. 3 Brigade I.R.A.,
4 June 1920[a]

				Companies							
	A	B	C	D	E	F	G	H	I	K	L
Rifles											
service	6	8	1	2	6			1	1		
smallbore	1	1					1		1		
Shot guns											
double bl.	15	32	15	20	10	2	13	15	6	8	10
Revolvers											
·32+	7	10		4	1	4	3	6	3		4
·22	1									1	
Rifle ammunition											
service	340	400			900	150		360	70		
smallbore											
Revolver ammunition											
·32+	140	103	38			10		126	24		
·22					20			500			
Gelignite											
sticks	15	4			½			1			½

[a] Source: document captured by R.I.C., cited in G.H.Q. Ireland pamphlet, 'Sinn Féin and the Irish Volunteers', issued to officers October 1920. W.O. 32 4308.

I.R.A. was able at first to rely on the information network provided by the public, and that it was no quicker than the British military to create intelligence specialists at battalion level as an integral part of its own organization. Under its original organizational scheme, quartermasters doubled as intelligence officers, and the practice of appointing specialists did not become universal until December 1920.[174] Whether this development reflected a growing unreliability on the part of the public, caused perhaps by pressure from the Crown Forces, or whether it merely answered the need for a more flexible and professional service after the creation of flying columns, cannot at present be decided.

I.R.A. methods

At all events it is clear that throughout the conflict the I.R.A. enjoyed a decisive advantage both in obtaining information and in denying it to the British. This 'intelligence gap' resulted from its overwhelming psychological domination of the community. The rebels of 1920 were

[174] See especially the concise account in P. Béaslaí, 'How It Was Done—I.R.A. Intelligence', in *Dublin's Fighting Story 1916–21* (Tralee, 1949), pp. 198–200. Cf. also G.H.Q. Ireland, 'Sinn Féin', confidential pamphlet, May 1919. W.O. 32 4308; G.H.Q. Ireland, *Record*, ii. 41.

the heirs not only to the exalted legacies of the United Irishmen and the Fenians, but also to a deeper and darker tradition of agrarian secret society terrorism. This is what Lord French had meant when he spoke of the Volunteers in December 1918 as a 'secret society in the worst and most dangerous sense', though even he did not comprehend the breadth of their power. In the hard currency of fear, in which the British were to seek to deal by means of the Black and Tans, the rebels had bottomless reserves. Most Irishmen were very ready to believe in the omniscience of the I.R.A., and the certainty of vengeance upon informers, summed up in the words 'remember Carey'.[175] And although the 'execution' of 'spies and informers' did not become common until late in 1920, the earlier part of the year saw a noticeable upsurge in less violent intimidation.[176]

Also, the I.R.A. was using terrorism to cement and buttress the loyalty of a population whose fundamental sympathies were already, except in the north-east, anti-British. This is not to say that the bulk of Irish nationalists were yet Republicans, much less that they approved of the physical force methods adopted by the I.R.A.[177] But to betray Irish patriots to the Government was very different from disapproving of their methods. This fact was not grasped by the British, who continually condemned the lack of 'moral courage' of the Irish moderates who refused to stand up against terrorism. Irish terrorism was unpleasant, but it had many justifications, not the least of which was that 'informing' had previously been habitual in the Irish way of life. To gain some understanding of the relationship between the I.R.A. and the community one can probably do no better than to turn once again to the words of Ernest O'Malley.

I was on the outside. I felt it in many ways by a diffidence, by an extra courtesy, by a silence. Some were hostile in their minds; others in speech; often the mother would think I was leading her son astray or the father would not approve of what the boys were doing. . . . Yet there was a tradition of armed resistance, deeply felt; it would flare up when we carried out some small successful raid or made a capture. Around the fire it would be discussed; it would heighten the imagination of those who were hostile. In their minds a simple thing became heroic and epical. Perhaps the sense of glory in the people was stirred, and the legend that had been created about myself, whom they did not know, helped them to accept me as part of it.[178]

[175] Cf. Winter, *Winter's Tale*, p. 296. Carey had informed against the 'Invincibles' of 1882; for his far from inevitable death, see T. Corfe, *The Phoenix Park Murders* (London, 1968), p. 258.

[176] Summary of Outrages against the Police, etc., 1920–1. C.O. 904 150. Cases of intimidation reported to the R.I.C. rose from 25 in February to 100 in May, and these can only be a fraction of the real total.

[177] No satisfactory study of the development of Irish opinion in this period has been found, but it is clear that distrust of Britain was growing markedly from the 1918 Conscription crisis onwards. See Kee, *The Green Flag*, pp. 618–50.

[178] O'Malley, *On Another Man's Wound*, p. 128.

It is in considering these fireside discussions that one realizes how immense a weight of British action and publicity would have been necessary to deflect their inexorable course. The 'hearts and minds' of the Irish people were at last finding a true allegiance to replace their uneasy subjection to the British Crown.

The operations undertaken by the I.R.A. depended very largely upon the co-operation of the public, which, whether through loyalty, respect, or fear, ensured protection from pursuit by the Forces of the Crown. Daylight assassinations, notably those of Assistant Commissioner Redmond of the D.M.P. on 21 January and Resident Magistrate Bell (who was investigating the Republic's secret bank accounts) on 26 March, became an important part of the campaign. Much more ambitious were attacks on R.I.C. barracks which began in January 1920. Thirteen were mounted that month in counties Cork, Limerick, Galway, Longford, Waterford, and Wicklow; the first actual capture of a barrack was at Ballytrain, Co. Monaghan, on 14 February.[179] Such attacks were a definite risk for the guerrillas, as they required the assembly of substantial forces for a protracted period; and they usually took place at night, both to cause the maximum disruption to the inmates, and because most I.R.A. men still carried on their normal occupations during the day. On 28 May the barrack at Kilmallock, Co. Limerick, was destroyed by fire despite the heroic stand of its ten-man garrison in an all-night battle.[180] Altogether, 16 occupied barracks were destroyed and 29 damaged in the first six months of 1920; another 424 abandoned ones were also destroyed (298 of them in a well-co-ordinated *feu de joie* to mark Easter Week), together with 47 courthouses.[181] Here the psychological element was well to the fore. These evacuated buildings were no longer of use to the Government, but as scorched shells they became a chilling advertisement of its retreat.

The authorities condemned the I.R.A.'s methods as 'those of common assassins, careful never to act until they are in overwhelming numbers and have covered their line of retreat'.[182] But outraged feelings (perhaps exacerbated by the degree of rebel success) seem here to have blinded the British to the fact that this must be the aim of all sound strategy. Where the I.R.A. really differed in principle from regular armies was in its adherence to the 'fundamental principle', later to be laid down by a guerrilla leader of another continent, that 'no battle, combat, or skirmish is to be fought unless it will be

---

[179] Irish Office, 'Monthly Commentary', 4 August 1920. C.O. 906 19; C.S.O. R.P. 295, 296, 299, 362, 434, 462, 1050, 1854, 2273, 2274, 2288, 2653, 3634, 5621 (all 1930). R.O.
[180] D.I. Egan to I.G. R.I.C., 31 May 1920. Lloyd George papers, F/19/2/11.
[181] C.S.I., Weekly Survey of the State of Ireland, 4 August 1920. S.I.C. 25, CAB.27 108. (Cabinet Irish Situation Committee, vol. ii (Memoranda); henceforth C.S.I. Weekly Surveys.)
[182] Street, *The Administration of Ireland 1920*, p. 215.

won'.[183] Unlike regular armies, guerrillas do not have to stand their ground in defence of strategic points or lines; they can, and must, operate only at the time and the place that suit them. For the I.R.A., with a few thousand poorly-armed men, any idea of fighting 'by the rules' was absurd. The conventions of war, which now seemed akin to civilized morality to the well-matched European states, meant certain destruction to Irish rebels, whose prime concern was not to act with honour but to survive. Tom Barry records that when the West Cork I.R.A. started to form a flying column, they accepted that its 'paramount objective . . . in the circumstances then prevailing, should be, not to fight, but to continue to exist'.[184]

This new realism, so significant a contrast with the 'blood-sacrifice' of Easter 1916, does not seem to have entirely replaced the older way of thinking, at least in early 1920.[185] An I.R.A. document captured by the D.M.P. in February contained an interesting appreciation of rebel military options.[186] Its writer dismissed the idea of an outright offensive as 'suicide', and advocated an 'offensive defensive', by which simultaneous blows at R.I.C. barracks and post offices would initially cause three-quarters of the country to fall into rebel hands. After this the main aim would be to hamper any British counter-offensive, and possibly even to concentrate 'larger bodies of Volunteers on the Garrison towns with a view to at least holding the military in these towns'.[187] Great stress was laid on the disruption of communications, and this was indeed effectively carried out during 1920 through ambushes, raids on the mails, and the republican sympathies or forced co-operation of most Post Office workers. The thesis that large rural areas could be liberated was also borne out. But the further stage of open confrontation around the 'Garrison towns' was unduly ambitious, and it is worth noting that the overall thesis was in fact pessimistic.

All our training, lectures, etc., drive us to one conclusion, namely that no matter what strategy we may adopt we will evidently be beaten, in a military sense.[188]

This document was therefore still strongly influenced by conventional ideas, whereas the I.R.A. of 1920 was to find that by matching its

---

[183] Che Guevara, *Guerrilla Warfare* (London, 1969), p. 18.

[184] Barry, *Guerrilla Days in Ireland*, new edn., p. 26; cf., again, Guevara's dictum 'At the outset, the essential task of the guerrilla fighter is to keep himself from being destroyed'.

[185] Nor even in 1921: see p. 180 below.

[186] 'The Strategy that the Volunteer Force as at present armed and trained is likely to use in case it takes to the field voluntarily': R.I.C. Reports, I.G., February 1920. C.O. 904 111.

[187] Ibid. (Circulated to Cabinet as 'Military Aims of the Irish Volunteers' by C.S.I., 8 March 1920. C.P. 821, CAB.24 100.)

[188] 'Military Aims of the Irish Volunteers', C.P. 821, CAB.24 100.

operations to its means it could ensure its survival for long enough to achieve psychological victory out of military stalemate.

Republican government and publicity

The importance of propaganda in the Republican campaign was indicated by the cabinet status of Dáil Eireann's Department of Publicity. The activities of this department were largely concentrated on producing the *Irish Bulletin*, a cyclostyled news-sheet which first appeared on 11 November 1919, and which was later issued every few days.[189] Printed in secret, and widely circulated to political and public figures, the press, and so on, it excelled in portraying an exchange of shots as a battle, the sniping of a police barrack as an assault, or the breaking of windows by Crown Forces as the sacking of a town. It did so in a matter-of-fact style which encouraged credence, and it proved to be a strong influence on the Irish press, especially the two biggest daily papers, the *Irish Independent* and the *Freeman's Journal* (the former organ of the Nationalist party), which were anti-British in tone by 1920.[190]

The line taken by Republican publicity was that Ireland was an independent state *de jure*, and not only this, but also that the operations of the I.R.A. represented its defence of the state against a foreign invader. It was not in the least deterred by the manifest fact that the invaders, who had been in apparently legitimate possession for several centuries, were defending themselves against rebel attacks, and it seized on every raid or arrest carried out by the Government as examples of 'aggression'. The singleminded determination of Republican propaganda was backed by a strong effort to turn Dáil Eireann into the *de facto* governing power. The method adopted, well characterized by O'Hegarty as 'butting in on everything',[191] was what had been preached by Arthur Griffith before Sinn Féinism became synonymous with physical force republicanism.

One major line of development was the takeover of local government. In the municipal elections of January 1920, Sinn Féin won 550 out of 1,806 seats, gaining control of 72 out of 127 town councils.[192] The Dublin Corporation resolved on 3 May to acknowledge 'the authority of Dáil Eireann as the duly elected government of the Irish people', and asked the Dáil Minister for Foreign Affairs to communicate this resolution to the United States Congress.[193] Sinn Féin

[189] The complete series is in the National Library of Ireland; a number of the fakes later circulated by Dublin Castle intelligence can be seen in the Bodleian Library, Oxford.

[190] The *Independent* was to declare on 30 October 1920 that 'Nobody in Ireland accepts as truthful any statement made by the British Government.'

[191] P. S. O'Hegarty, *The Victory of Sinn Féin* (Dublin, 1924), p. 34.

[192] Irish Office, 'Monthly Commentary', 4 August 1920. C.O. 906 19.

[193] *Irish Times*, 4 May 1920.

control of local government increased in the rural elections of May, when Republican majorities were gained on 28 out of 33 county councils and 182 out of 206 rural councils.[194] By 21 June, 85 public bodies had pledged formal allegiance to the Dáil, and an effective Republican local government policy was being implemented.[195]

These developments vastly increased Sinn Féin's credibility. Of still greater relevance to the campaign itself was the effort to supersede the British legal system and break down the power of British law. Dáil Eireann decreed the establishment of 'National Arbitration Courts' as early as June 1919, but in spite of a few local initiatives it was not until 17 May 1920, when the first Dáil land court sat in public at Ballinrobe, Co. Mayo, that they really began to function.[196] By early June such courts were working in 21 counties.[197] They served a vital function, for land disputes were still undoubtedly the major issue in ordinary Irish life, and Sinn Féin saw the need to 'keep the national demand for freedom clear from class issues': as Darrell Figgis wrote, 'Dublin Castle would have been well content to see the larger pretensions of the Republican Government crumble into the general disorder of an agrarian war.'[198] This endemic source of conflict, which traditionally reached its peak of violence during the summer, and which obviously threatened to be far worse in the disturbed conditions of 1920, was effectively defused by the Dáil land courts. Claims were arbitrated with a fairness 'bordering on Quixotism', as one British newspaper reported,[199] and even loyalist landlords were ready to accept their judgements.[200]

While they confined themselves to arbitrating claims, these courts were within the British law. On 29 June, however, the Dáil revised their constitutions, giving them the power to compel attendance and enforce judgements in the name of the Republic.[201] Local Volunteers took on additional duty as Republican police, carrying out court sentences and controlling the distillation and sale of liquor (over which the Republic was more severe than the British authorities): groups of men sporting 'I.V.' armbands were often to be seen at fairs and races. Indeed, policing became so popular with the I.R.A. that *An tÓglách*

---

[194] Macardle, *The Irish Republic*, Appendix 33, p. 910.

[195] *Irish Times*, 16 June 1920; *Saturday Herald*, 21 June 1920.

[196] Dáil Eireann, *The Constructive Work of Dáil Eireann* (Dublin, 1921), No. 1, p. 6; No. 2, p. 9; *Irish Times*, 19 May 1920.

[197] *Freeman's Journal*, 3 June 1920.

[198] D. Figgis, *Recollections of the Irish War* (London, 1927), p. 293.

[199] *Daily Graphic*, 1 May 1920.

[200] Phillips, *The Revolution in Ireland*, p. 181, admits that they 'occasionally weakened' when they found that the Sinn Féin courts imposed a higher price for land compulsorily purchased than that allowed by the Land Commission.

[201] Dáil Eireann, Decree No. 5, Session 1, 1920. *The Constructive Work of Dáil Eireann*, No. 1, p. 22.

was forced to issue a reminder in August that 'there is a war on' and that their main duty was to fight.[202]

By June 1920, one of Walter Long's friends in Co. Limerick told him that 'everybody is going over to Sinn Féin, not because they believe in it, but because it is the only authority in the county'.[203] The reports of Resident Magistrates showed that British law had broken down across 13 southern counties. At New Ross, the Sinn Féin appeal court was presided over by an ex-Indian Army officer; in some places, Sinn Féin local councils were even levying a 6d. rate to pay the Republican police.[204] The summer assizes next month became a laughing-stock: at Sligo, 35 out of the 40 civil bill appeals listed had been transferred to Republican courts;[205] at Cork, Galway and Waterford the assizes fell through completely for lack of jurors—the 'Competent Military Authority, I.R.A.' having notified them that to attend would be regarded as an act of treason.[206]

The Republic held the initiative at many levels across most of Ireland, and the King's writ had ceased to run. It is hardly an exaggeration to say that British authority, as distinct from mere power, was broken, and that any future British policy in Ireland could only be implemented by coercion. In the last fortnight of July 1920 'Sinn Féin outrages' reached record totals, four times those of late April: their pattern can be observed in the graph on p. 123. *An tÓglách* was able to draw an impressive 'War Map' of rebel operations (Map 2, p. 70). This was not all, for in May 1920 began one of the most remarkable contributions to the Republican cause, and one which has been virtually ignored by historians[207]—the dock and railway strike.

The transport embargo

On 20 May the quayside workers in Dublin met and issued a declaration that they would not handle 'certain war material' now being imported into Ireland; shortly afterwards they were joined by the Irish Transport and General Workers' Union.[208] The first ship affected was the freighter *Polberg*, at Kingstown, which had to be unloaded by

---

[202] *An tÓglách*, vol. ii, No. 17, 15 August 1920.

[203] Cabinet Irish Situation Cttee., note of conversation by W. Long, 30 June 1920. S.I.C. 3, CAB.27 108.

[204] Reports Received from Resident Magistrates, June 1920; extracts circulated to Cabinet Irish Situation Cttee. by Sec. of State for War. S.I.C. 24, CAB.27 108.

[205] Mr Blood, K.C., to Long, 7 July 1920. S.I.C. 12, CAB.27 108.

[206] Gregg to Wylie, 3 August 1920, and reply. Irish Office telegrams, C.O. 904 150; *Freeman's Journal*, 7 July 1920.

[207] Even the committed socialist (and extremely inaccurate) account by C. D. Greaves hardly mentions it except to take a swipe at J. H. Thomas. *Liam Mellows and the Irish Revolution* (London, 1971), p. 190.

[208] Home Office, Report on Revolutionary Organizations in the U.K. No. 56, 27 May 1920. CAB.24 100. (Henceforth Rev. Org.)

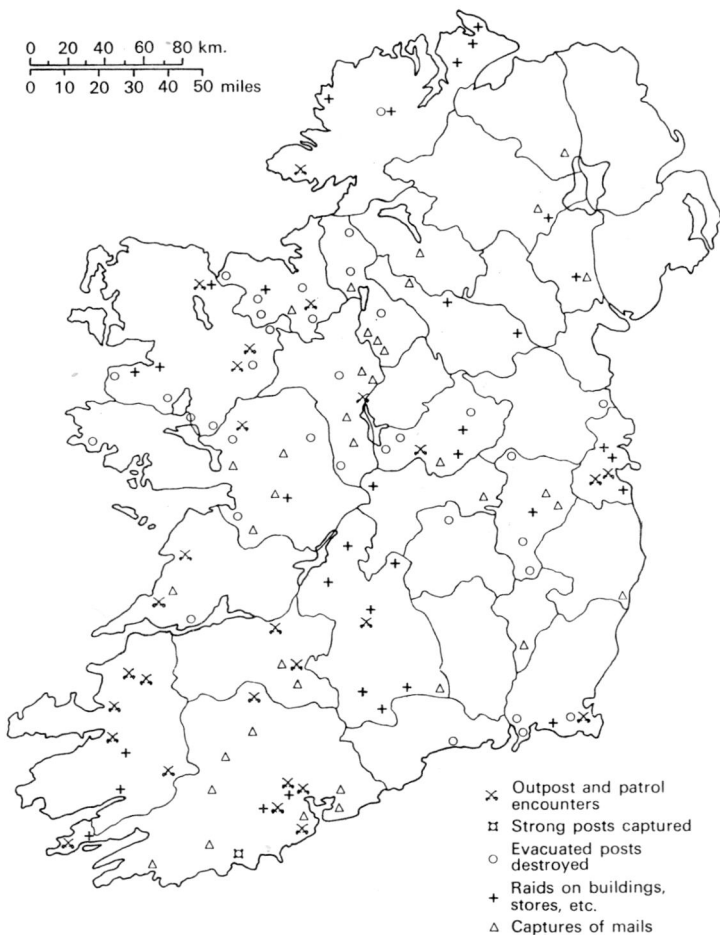

0   20 40 60 80 km.
0 10 20 30 40 50 miles

× Outpost and patrol
   encounters
⊓ Strong posts captured
○ Evacuated posts
   destroyed
+ Raids on buildings,
   stores, etc.
△ Captures of mails

Map 2: I.R.A. Operations, July 1920
(derived from the 'War Map' for the second half of July 1920, in *An tÓglách*,
vol. ii, no. 17 (15 August 1920))

troops. The railwaymen then refused to take the cargo on from the docks, and appealed for solidarity from the National Union of Railwaymen in Britain, comparing their action to that of the British workers who had refused to handle munitions for Poland.[209] In fact this cargo turned out to be pressed beef, not munitions, but within a week the cargo of a real arms ship, the *Czaritza*, was immobilized at Queenstown, the port of Cork.[210] In June the embargo spread across Ireland and embraced armed troops and police as well as munitions, though certain other military stores, such as food and building material, were excluded from the ban.[211]

On 3 June the Executive of the Irish Labour Party and Trades Union Congress made a public appeal for funds to support the embargo, which, it declared, was not a strike in the railwaymen's own interests 'but on behalf of the whole Nation'.[212] By 10 June only £100 had been received, while railwaymen at North Wall alone had lost over £5,000 in wages.[213] The railway companies were retaliating by dismissing or suspending men who refused to work trains carrying munitions, and though they could not actually get the trains moving, they were confident that they would soon break the embargo.[214] Disappointingly little help came to the railwaymen from Britain. The *Westminster Gazette* warned that 'the trade union leaders are up against a very difficult test case of the use of the strike for political purposes'.[215] J. H. Thomas, the N.U.R. General Secretary, was no extremist, and it became clear by late June that hopes (or fears) of co-operation between Irish and British labour were unfounded.[216] The Labour Party conference at Scarborough contented itself with passing a resolution calling for the 'withdrawal of the British Army of occupation' from Ireland, a step which was of some importance in the development of British public opinion, but of no assistance in the struggle of the Irish railwaymen.[217]

Despite this, they were to press on for another six months. By 11 August over 900 of them were out of work, and there were signs that the whole railway system was inexorably running down.[218] The Cabinet's only response was to put pressure on the companies, and to discuss whether their subsidies could be withdrawn on the grounds

---

[209] *Irish Times*, 24 May 1920.
[210] Ibid., 31 May 1920.
[211] Hist. 5th Div., p. 50.
[212] *Irish Independent*, 3 June 1920.
[213] 'Munitions of War Fund', advertisement in *Freeman's Journal*, 10 June 1920.
[214] *Irish Times*, 28 May 1920.
[215] *Westminster Gazette*, 29 May 1920.
[216] Home Office, Rev. Org. No. 60, 24 June 1920. CAB.24 108.
[217] Greaves, *Liam Mellows*, p. 190, regards it as 'an enormous accretion of political strength . . . to the Irish cause'.
[218] Cabinet, 11 August 1920. C.47(20), CAB.23 22.

that they were failing in their obligation to act as common carriers.[219] In fact the Governments both in London and in Dublin took, throughout, a cavalier attitude to the embargo, an attitude evident in C. J. C. Street's account.

The strike hit every section of the community in Ireland except the Government, who were able to use their own vessels, their own labour, and their own motor transport to convey such material as they chose to any part of Ireland.[220]

But the Army, which actually had to provide that labour and that transport from its already strained resources, did not share this view. At the very least, as we shall see, the embargo was a severe military inconvenience, and it certainly absorbed time and effort which would otherwise have been spent in pursuit of the I.R.A. On another level, it broadened the Republican campaign and heightened the atmosphere of alienation from British authority; it was a true example of civil resistance. By the summer of 1920 it seemed that what a percipient French observer called Sinn Féin's 'clear and deliberate determination to ignore what is, and to take account, nay to admit the very existence, only of what ought to be',[221] had successfully turned its plans, as one Sinn Féin leader put it, 'from alleged dreams into practical realities'.[222]

---

[219] Memo by C.S.I., 20 July 1920. C.P. 1657, CAB.24 109; Cabinet, 26 July 1920. C.41(20), CAB.23 22.
[220] Street, *The Administration of Ireland 1920*, p. 90.
[221] S. Briollay, *Ireland in Rebellion* (London, 1922), p. 18.
[222] Speech by Chairman of Mayo County Council, *Irish Times*, 2 August 1920.

III

LOW PROFILE GOVERNMENT

'I have impressed on my Generals the importance of taking no measures that
may cause irritation. . . .'

Sir Nevil Macready, April 1920

8. THE REFORM OF THE ADMINISTRATION (April–May 1920)

Sir Nevil Macready, the Army, and the police

IT IS not easy to assess British public feeling about Ireland at this
time, but it seems certain that as the Government turned from
European peacemaking to yet another Irish crisis, it was under
definite pressure to find a solution. Up until now, Irish problems had
been shelved, or at best cursorily treated. Lloyd George had evidently
not yet turned his full attention to them, and apart from producing the
Government of Ireland Bill, which few people regarded as a potential
solution, the Cabinet had hardly been involved in the making of Irish
policy: this had effectively been left to the Viceroy and his rivals in
Dublin.

In April 1920, however, the Cabinet made a sudden intervention. Its
apparent aim was a radical reform of the Irish Executive, but its actions,
as so often, had mixed results. In a sense, this reform granted Lord
French's oft-expressed wish for a new system. Yet, in the process,
French's own power was to vanish, while some of the old confusions
became worse confounded. It is clear that, because of its uncertainty
over Ireland, the Cabinet wanted an executive which would respond
more swiftly and effectively to initiatives from London. This it failed to
achieve. Instead of a single strong, flexible body, another piecemeal
system was created, in which the ambiguity of the Cabinet's policy
produced an uneasy division of powers, each operating on different
principles towards different ends. The failure to unite the civil administration, the police, and the military, was to be a constant source
of weakness and confusion.

It began with the failure of an attempt to unite the military and
police commands in the hands of the successor to General Shaw.[1]
Although the Secretary of State for War, Churchill, had emphatically

---

[1] Shaw's appointment was temporary, though French asked that it be confirmed for
four years. Churchill refused on grounds that Shaw had not sufficient seniority, and that
'when and if the Army of the Rhine is broken up the Royal Hospital is the only place I
have for Robertson'. Churchill to French, 17 April 1919. Churchill papers.

and repeatedly advised that Shaw should be succeeded by Field-Marshal Robertson (who not only had seniority, but seems actually to have wanted the job),[2] a soldier of a very different stamp was finally chosen. General Sir Nevil Macready, son of the famous actor, had made his mark as Adjutant General in the last two years of the war, and as Commissioner of the London Metropolitan Police, where he had dealt with the police strike of 1919. His career had embraced the command of troops in aid of the civil power in South Wales at the time of Tonypandy, as well as in Belfast during the crisis of 1914. Lloyd George told the Commons on 29 March 1920 that Macready 'combines' both military and police experience and remarkable powers of organization with exceptional judgement and tact'.[3] The following month, Bonar Law indicated that public criticism of the poor co-operation between police and military had been instrumental in the decision on Shaw's replacement:

the Viceroy and the Government thought it was essential they should have somebody at the head of the forces in Ireland who understood the police system, and who could in some way co-ordinate the military and police.[4]

Macready's qualifications, together with Lloyd George's personal liking for him,[5] secured him the job.

Not that he was keen to take it up. His Belfast experiences had given him a distaste for Irish affairs which we have already observed,[6] and he later wrote that only the persuasion of his old chief, French (who had been C.I.G.S. when Macready was Director of Personal Services at the War Office), made him accept

a task which I instinctively felt would be affected by every variation of the political weathercock, and in which it was doubtful if any satisfactory result could be attained.[7]

As a matter of fact, his attitude when he first arrived in Ireland was not so anti-political as this might suggest. His Liberal sympathies, which had led him to detest the unconstitutional behaviour of the Unionists in 1914, and which made him a consistent advocate of Home Rule throughout the conflict of 1920–1, coupled with his frank admiration

[2] Sec. of State for War to Prime Minister, 11 October, 11 November, 29 November 1919; 29 February, 6 March 1920. Lloyd George papers, F/9/1/36, 44, 47; F/9/2/10, 12.
[3] 127 H.C. Deb. 5s, col. 870.
[4] Speech during Lord Robert Cecil's adjournment motion, 26 April 1920. 128 H.C. 5s, col. 989. (Cecil had been the leading critic of military-police co-ordination.)
[5] Macready had been a member of the dinner party on the anniversary of Lloyd George's appointment as Prime Minister in 1919 (Riddell, *Diary of the Peace Conference*, pp. 150–1) and had other personal links with him.
[6] See above, p. 20. Macready demanded £5,000 disturbance allowance for leaving his job with the Metropolitan Police.
[7] Macready, *Annals*, ii. 425.

for Lloyd George, then dominated his view.[8] It was only with the rise of the Black and Tans that his disgust with the Government's policy led to a cooling of his relations with Lloyd George, an exaggerated contempt for politicians and all their works, and an aloofness which came in for criticism from his civilian colleagues in Dublin.

He showed from the start a lack of enthusiasm for perfecting the machinery of coercion in Ireland. His most important action, in its future consequences, was his refusal to take up the joint command of the Army and the police. That he should have been offered it at all was, in view of later developments, remarkable. His refusal, on the grounds that to make the Irish police efficient would be in itself a full-time job,[9] was short-sighted. He could not have guessed how deep a rift was to open up between the two forces, and he thought at first that it would be sufficient to bring in a competent overall commander for the police. Shortly after arriving in Ireland he carried out a somewhat cursory investigation of the R.I.C. and D.M.P., and concluded that

In my opinion they are disorganized, and I am prepared to say, without perhaps having any proof, that even before the present troubles arose, they were hopelessly out of date.[10]

Several 'little instances' confirmed him in this opinion, and he made sweeping criticisms of the abilities of police officers in general, and in particular of the Chief Commissioner of the D.M.P. (who did not have 'a grip on police work'), and T. J. Smith, the favourite of French and Long, who lacked breadth of outlook and freedom from political leanings.[11] Unfortunately, the man whom Macready wanted to take over the police, Lieutenant-General Bulfin,[12] refused the post, and though Macready described this as 'a misfortune I never ceased to regret',[13] he made no further suggestion for filling the new position. The officer who was eventually to be appointed was unknown to him.

The civil government
Before this final complication, striking changes took place in the civil

---

[8] Austen Chamberlain thought that he had 'a good civilian mind' (Jones, *Whitehall Diary*, iii. 67). Macready's political capacity has recently been sadly misjudged (Kee, *The Green Flag*, p. 674), presumably owing to the anti-political tone of his memoirs.

[9] Macready, *Annals*, ii. 425.

[10] Macready to Long, 23 April 1920. Lloyd George papers, F/34/1/19.

[11] Macready to French (Report on the Irish Police Forces), 23 April 1920. Bonar Law papers, 103/2/16. When Long protested against this judgement, Macready said that Smith was 'worn out', and was in any case not 'a big enough man'. Macready to Long, 1 May 1920. Ibid., 102/5/10. Smith was, of course, a Protestant Unionist, which was why Long had favoured him.

[12] Sir Edward Stanislaus Bulfin, 1862–1939. Irish by birth; commanded XXI Corps in Palestine, 1917–19.

[13] Macready, *Annals*, ii. 453; cf. Cabinet Conference, 11 May 1920. C.29(20) App. II(g), CAB.23 21.

administration. Early in April the unhappy Macpherson resigned the
Chief Secretaryship, and was replaced by Sir Hamar Greenwood,[14]
a Canadian Liberal with an Imperial style of oratory and Conservative
political tendencies,[15] whose bluff courage and sanguine outlook
seemed well suited to his discouraging task. Not so well suited, however, was the fact that this outlook stemmed from mental inflexibility.
Greenwood was 'a man of one idea at a time',[16] and his optimism was
often based on failure to take account of facts which were, it sometimes
seemed, obvious to everyone but himself. Moreover his success as a
head of department was limited by a domineering approach which
marked him as not being of the 'old school', and which was especially
damaging when applied to his most talented subordinates. His wife, by
contrast, had charm and political intelligence. 'The Lady' was much
admired by Greenwood's senior civil servants, but, whether through
loyalty or weakness, she never materially altered his ideas.

Greenwood took up his appointment with the determination, like
many former Chief Secretaries, to make a gesture of conciliation. He
met a tense situation, with many of the Republican leaders who had
been arrested since January on hunger-strike in Mountjoy prison in
Dublin, demanding 'political' treatment. Some of them were convicted
under D.O.R.A., some were untried. Huge demonstrations were taking
place in their support, and on 12 April the streets around Mountjoy
were thronged with crowds estimated by the Army at 5,000 and by the
police at 10,000; the air was filled with prayers and the lamentation of
women.[17] Next day the demonstrations were reinforced by a one-day
strike throughout the city. On 14 April the prisoners were suddenly
released, apparently at Lord French's instigation, in the hope of
generating a wave of popular support.[18] The Assistant Under Secretary,
Taylor, was so shocked by this surrender that he took a month's leave.
Macready simply saw it as a necessity, writing later that if any of the
hunger-strikers had died the Government would have released the rest
in any case, and 'a situation created worse than anything that might
happen from their release at the moment'.[19] None the less, it was a
severe blow to police morale, and may be held partly responsible for

[14] Hamar Greenwood, 1870–1948. Barrister; Liberal M.P., 1906–22; Conservative
M.P., 1924–9; Baronet, 1815; D.A.A.G., War Office, 1916; Sec. Overseas Trade Dept.
1919; C.S.I., 1920, Baron, 1929; Treasurer, Conservative Party, 1933–8; Viscount, 1937.
[15] He was accepted as a 'natural Conservative' by the die-hard 'Woman of no importance' (?Mrs A. C. Stuart Menzies) in her book of portraits, As Others See Us (London,
1924).
[16] Duggan, 'The Last Days of Dublin Castle', p. 156.
[17] For the overpowering emotional pressure generated, see Sir James O'Connor,
History of Ireland (London, 1925), ii. 321; for the difficulties of the troops (an infantry
company and 2 tanks) guarding the prison, see 1st Lancs. Fusiliers to H.Q. D.D.,
13 April 1920. D.D. War Diary 'D', W.O. 35 90/1.
[18] Duggan, 'The Last Days of Dublin Castle', p. 146.
[19] Macready, Annals, ii. 447.

the excessive pampering of the R.I.C. that became an established custom from the early summer onwards. Equally startlingly, the special powers which had been given to the military authorities in January were cancelled on 3 May,[20] so that the whole policy of the first quarter of 1920 was more or less reversed.

Macready and Greenwood were for the time being in complete harmony. Within a fortnight of his arrival, Macready was horrifying Walter Long by advocating amendment of the Government of Ireland Bill in the direction of greater concessions.[21] He wrote to Lloyd George on 1 May that the people he had talked to in Ireland felt that,

knowing the Irish temperament, the moment has come, and may slip away, when a dramatic turn in policy, may have an instantaneous, and possibly lasting effect.[22]

The only alternative, he insisted, was a drift towards martial law, an extremity which, even if it could be enforced without alienating British public opinion, could never induce the Irish to make a sincere settlement.[23] This assessment of the limits and difficulties of military rule Macready did not alter throughout the conflict (though he did come to regard martial law as less of an evil than 'police warfare'). On 8 May, Greenwood wrote to Bonar Law that 'if we now act quickly as [Macready] suggests, we can save this country from the bitterness of war.'[24] Four days later he was still more enthusiastic, saying 'I am in accord with Macready, and will not enlarge on his views. They are mine.'[25] Greenwood's own formula, as he described it to Bonar Law on 16 May, was to 'focus every mind on murder, arson and other outrage, and to leave no grievance unremedied that can be remedied'; he hoped that 'this focussing may rally the moderates'.[26] To the same end he curtailed deportations drastically, reviewing all cases himself, and releasing many suspects, whose 'daily press and "martyrdom"', he said, 'does the Govt. more harm than their freedom can'.[27] Greenwood was by nature a propagandist—though, as time was to show, an insensitive one—and he felt that these concessions would have a major public impact. Bonar Law, however, worried about the legal implications

[20] G.H.Q. Ireland, *Record*, i. 11.
[21] Macready to Long, 23 April 1920. Lloyd George papers, F/34/1/19; Long to Bonar Law, 27 April 1920. Bonar Law papers, 103/5/3.
[22] Macready to Prime Minister, 1 May 1920. Lloyd George papers, F/36/2/13.
[23] Ibid.
[24] C.S.I. to Ld. Privy Seal (Bonar Law), 8 May 1920. Bonar Law papers, 103/3/1. All Greenwood's early correspondence as C.S.I. was addressed to Bonar Law in Lloyd George's absence.
[25] C.S.I. to Ld. Privy Seal, 12 May 1920. Ibid., 103/3/9.
[26] C.S.I. to Ld. Privy Seal, 16 May 1920. Ibid., 103/3/13.
[27] C.S.I. to Ld. Privy Seal, 18 May 1920. Ibid., 103/3/18.

of the releases, and feared that the Irish Executive 'may get into a mess through not carefully thinking out what they are doing'.[28]

The arrival of Macready and Greenwood put Lord French's star into eclipse. Although he retained his membership of the Cabinet until April 1921, he soon became out of touch with the making of policy, and by July 1920, H. A. L. Fisher found him 'a shadow of his former self and quite useless'.[29] He did, however, make a significant contribution to the reforms of April and May 1920. After the Assistant Under Secretary at the Castle went on a month's leave in pique at the release of the hunger-strikers, French wrote to Bonar Law to emphasize once again the appalling confusion of the Castle administration and the need for a re-shaping,[30] and this time he met with success. Bonar Law accepted the idea of an investigating committee, under the head of the Civil Service, Sir Warren Fisher.[31] This committee completed its work by 12 May, and its conclusions were as bald and uncompromising as French could have wished. Fisher wrote that

The Castle administration does not administer. On the mechanical side it can never have been good and is now quite obsolete; in the infinitely more important sphere (a) of informing and advising the Irish Government in relation to policy and (b) of practical capacity in the application of policy it simply has no existence.[32]

He could not find where real responsibility rested. The Chief Secretary was 'skied on Olympus', while even his top officials were down 'hewing wood in the remotest valley'.[33] Although the civil authority was 'at present (theoretically) in the saddle', it preferred to lean on the military and to avoid responsibility: the relationship of government, police and military was nowhere adequately defined.[34]

There is a hint in this report that Fisher would have liked to see the appointment of an overall civil–military supremo, for he wrote, referring to Macready, that

During the past few weeks the unsoundness of the prevailing Irish system has been somewhat disguised in consequence of the appointment to command the military forces of a man who would be admirably equipped to play the dual role of Under Secretary and G.O.C.[35]

[28] Bonar Law to Prime Minister, 22 May 1920. Ibid., 103/3/18.

[29] H. A. L. Fisher's diary, 22 July 1920. Fisher papers.

[30] Ld. Lt. to Ld. Privy Seal, 18 April 1920. Bonar Law papers, 103/2/11.

[31] Norman Fenwick Warren Fisher, 1879–1948. Chairman, Board of Inland Revenue, 1918–19; Permanent Sec. of the Treasury and Head of the Civil Service 1919–39.

[32] Report of Sir Warren Fisher, 12 May 1920. Encl. in Bonar Law to Prime Minister, 13 May 1920. Lloyd George papers, F/31/1/32.

[33] Ibid.

[34] Ibid.

[35] Ibid. Sturgis later remarked that Macready was 'extraordinarily enlightened for a general' and that 'Nathaniel (Warren Fisher) adores him'. Sturgis's diary, 15 July 1920. P.R.O. 30 59/1.

'But', he added, 'this is incidental': he evidently recognized that the idea was politically unattractive. Unified control was to remain a distant, and indeed a receding, prospect. Turning back to his brief, Fisher recommended instead the appointment of a 'powerful civil servant' to work out a *modus operandi* for the administration, and he insisted that a cardinal principle of any arrangement must be that 'the Civil Authority controls the police and is responsible not only for policy but also for its proper application.'[36] For, set out in a further report prepared by Fisher's assistants, were the ghastly facts about the confusion of the police forces and intelligence services. The investigators found that the Inspector General of the R.I.C., Smith, had no idea on what basis the police and military were supposed to co-operate; he thought that, 'contrary to the expressed view of the Military, the latter were not assisting the police, but the reverse was the case.'[37] Raids were carried out by the Army as reprisals for outrages, and policemen were only taken along to identify men whom the Army wanted to arrest. Smith himself was obviously worn out, admitting frankly that he wanted only to go back to Belfast or take his pension.[38]

Fisher's choice of 'powerful civil servant' was the Chairman of the Board of Inland Revenue, Sir John Anderson,[39] whom Whitehall regarded as 'the greatest administrator of his time, perhaps of any time in the country's history',[40] and whose ability and ambition were afterwards to bring him into still greater prominence. Fisher wrote to Bonar Law on 15 May that 'with wise strong men like Macready and Anderson working as one, the future wd be far from hopeless', though he lamented the effects of the Government's blanket proscription of Sinn Féin, as a result of which even intelligent, influential people did not distinguish between moderate Sinn Féin and violent Republicanism: this was 'as if retired warriors and dowager ladies who denounce socialism in England were to secure the banning of the Labour Party'.[41] Fisher denounced the use of military force as a magnification of this original blunder. The military policy of raids and arrests he characterized as 'merely blind hitting out', and he thought that even now Macready was almost alone in opposing the indiscriminate use of violence.[42]

[36] Report of Cope and Harwood, App. to Fisher's report.
[37] Ibid.
[38] Ibid.
[39] John Anderson, 1882–1958. Chairman, Board of Inland Revenue, 1919–22; K.C.B., 1919; Joint U.S., Ireland, 1920–2; Permanent U.S., Home Office, 1922–32; Governor of Bengal, 1932–7; Independent M.P., 1938–50; Home Secretary, 1939–40; Chancellor of the Exchequer, 1943–5; Viscount, 1952 (Waverley, of Westdean).
[40] Lord Salter, in *Dictionary of National Biography*.
[41] Sir Warren Fisher to Bonar Law, and memo to Prime Minister, Ld. Privy Seal, and Chancellor of the Exchequer, 15 May 1920. Lloyd George papers, F/31/1/33.
[42] Ibid.

Anderson arrived in Dublin on 22 May, and must have borne in mind Fisher's opposition to coercion. He was not, however, a man who was easily led. His stern, proud Scots temperament proved somewhat unsympathetic to Irish problems,[43] and though he had a striking impact on Dublin Castle (where he was technically Joint Under Secretary with Macmahon, but rapidly became unquestioned chief), he confined himself to administrative matters. The task of keeping open channels of negotiation with Sinn Féin, he left to his remarkable deputy, Alfred ('Andy') Cope,[44] an ex-customs detective, highly-strung and with something of Taylor's greed for work, but with more ability and greater personal magnetism. Duggan described Cope as

the maid-of-all-work, to be flung into the breach whenever the opportunity offered, and in the waiting-time he would be employed in toning up Irish departments, most of which certainly needed it.[45]

Working to secret instructions from Lloyd George, who often, in Cabinet, disowned his moves, Cope tirelessly struggled to establish common ground for negotiations. But his dedication in this sphere limited his success in other directions, especially the vital one of liaison with the Army. G.H.Q. looked on him as a virtual Sinn Féiner, and he in turn was brusque when speaking to soldiers; Macready saw staff officers 'fairly dancing with suppressed rage' while on the telephone to him.[46]

Fortunately another of the civil servants who accompanied Anderson, in what might be described as a transfusion of talent from Whitehall to Dublin,[47] was tailor-made for smoothing contacts between the civil, military, and even, though with less success, the police authorities. Mark Sturgis,[48] who became in effect Joint Assistant Under Secretary with Cope (though he was not so gazetted for two years, apparently for fear of wounding Cope's sensibilities), was an amiable man and a dashing huntsman, who brought a rare quality of gaiety to the dismal surroundings of the Castle. He also kept a diary which, though selfconscious in style, provides a unique picture of the day-to-day working of the new administration.[49] The English group set up

[43] J. W. Wheeler-Bennett, *John Anderson, Viscount Waverley* (London, 1962), p. 59. (Henceforth *Anderson*.)

[44] Alfred William Cope, 1877–1954. In detective branch, Customs and Excise, 1896–1919; Asst. U.S., Ireland, 1920–2; K.C.B., 1922; Gen. Sec., National Liberal Organization, 1922–4.

[45] Duggan, 'The Last Days of Dublin Castle', p. 149.

[46] Macready, *Annals*, ii. 493

[47] Some dozen officials altogether, including G. G. Whiskard and L. N. Blake Odgers of the Home Office, M. T. Loughnane of the Ministry of Pensions, and three Treasury men who formed a miniature Treasury in Dublin. See Wheeler-Bennett, *Anderson*, p. 56.

[48] Mark Beresford Russell (Grant-) Sturgis, 1884–1939. P.S. to Asquith, 1906; Chairman, Treasury Selection Baord, 1919; Joint Asst. U.S., Ireland, 1920–2; K.C.B., 1923.

[49] The typescript of this diary, with holograph corrections, is in P.R.O. 30 59/1–4 (Diary of Sir Mark Sturgis); it is referred to here as Sturgis diary.

their offices in the Castle, but resided like a rather precarious colony in the Royal Marine Hotel, Kingstown.[50]

The command of the police and intelligence
The fundamental principle enunciated by Fisher, that the civil authority must control the police and direct policy, was not imposed by the new administration. The reason was not that the police fell increasingly under the control of the Army, but that they became increasingly independent and unamenable to any control. The nature of the new chief of police had much to do with this. After Lieutenant-General Bulfin had turned down the job proposed by Macready, the joint command of both R.I.C. and D.M.P., Macready was asked to interview two other generals selected by the Secretary for War, Churchill. He knew neither of them,[51] but one of them was Major-General Hugh Tudor, an intrepid artillery officer who had treated Churchill to a hair-raising gunnery display on the western front.[52] On 15 May 1920, Tudor was appointed Police Adviser to the Irish Government.

In this post he showed two important failings. First, he was an ordinary military officer with nothing like Macready's grasp of police or political matters. One of his bitter critics said not altogether unjustly that the Police Adviser, 'being without previous police experience, was not in a position to advise'.[53] More importantly, no one seemed to know whom he was supposed to advise. This was hardly his fault; but his second failing was more personal. As even one of his most dedicated admirers admitted,

If he had a fault it was that he was too prone to excuse others and shoulder blame himself, and I sometimes doubt his having been a sufficiently strict disciplinarian.[54]

The imposition of military standards of discipline upon the armed police was undoubtedly one of Macready's basic intentions in placing a military officer in overall command. For various reasons, Tudor was not to carry this out, and Macready, and even Anderson, found it extremely difficult to force him to do so. Tudor's position in the executive hierarchy was only vaguely defined, and he soon made it into one of considerable independence. From the start he took direct

[50] Sturgis diary, 15 July 1920. P.R.O. 30 59/1.
[51] Macready, *Annals*, ii. 459.
[52] For the incident see M. Gilbert, *Winston S. Churchill* (London, 1971), iii. 663–4; Churchill regaled his Cabinet colleagues with the story on 1 January 1921. Riddell, *Diary of the Peace Conference*, p. 262.
[53] Brig. Gen. F. P. Crozier, *A Word to Gandhi: The Lesson of Ireland* (London, 1931), p. 19. For Crozier's quarrel with Tudor, see below, pp. 163–4.
[54] Quoted in 'A Woman of No Importance' (? Mrs. A. C. Stuart Menzies), *As Others See Us*, p. 100. This work includes a number of studies of lesser figures such as Brigadier Wood and Brigadier Prescott Decie.

command of the police, and his title of 'Adviser' was a curiosity (he took the more explicit title 'Chief of Police' when Smith retired as Inspector-General in November 1920). His friendship with Churchill strengthened his position, and as the pattern of 'unauthorized' police reprisals grew up during the summer of 1920, it suited Greenwood, and more importantly Lloyd George, to back Tudor against the demands of the civil and military authorities in Dublin for a tightening of discipline and control.[55] This process of allowing rifts to develop between the police and the other authorities, symptomatic of the Government's fundamental inability to choose between a 'civil' and a 'military' approach, was to be a continuing obstacle to effective command in Ireland.

The final appointment made during the May reforms was theoretically very promising. The Army had realized that the key to anything more than accidental success against the rebels was an effective intelligence service, and it was clear that the Crown Forces could only hope to overcome the advantage already secured by the I.R.A. in its domination of the general public if they built up a superior organization based on expertise. On 11 May the Cabinet approved Macready's suggestion that Crown intelligence should be placed under a single officer,[56] but yet again the appointment was a strange one. The officer chosen, Colonel Ormonde Winter,[57] had no specific experience of intelligence work. Though seconded by the War Office, his position as Director of Intelligence for the Crown Forces was a police, not a military post, and Winter was technically Tudor's deputy.[58] Notwithstanding the impression conveyed by his autobiography,[59] he was only a qualified success as an intelligence chief. Under the *nom de guerre* of 'O' he excelled in the secret service operations that went on in Dublin, but the Army was at first unimpressed, and at last exasperated by his slowness in building up a more general organization, his inability to impose a single system, and his lack of an overall perspective.[60] To G.H.Q. he personified the mistaken tendency of equating 'intelligence' with 'secret service'.

As soon as it was created, therefore, the new Irish administration began to generate frictions as harmful as those of the old. The reforms had been superficial, not structural. Although the new machine had greater potential capacity than any earlier one, it could not realize this

---

[55] See below, pp. 100, 163.

[56] Military Requirements in Ireland, IV; App. to C.29(20) App. II (Cabinet Conference, 11 May 1920), CAB.23 21.

[57] Ormonde de l'Epée Winter, 1875–1962. Brig. Gen., Royal Artillery, 1917; Dep. Chief of Police and Director of Intelligence, Ireland, 1920; Director of Resettlement, Irish Office, 1922; K.B.E., 1922.

[58] His title was Deputy Chief of Police. Note in Winter papers, C.O. 904 177.

[59] O. de l'E. Winter, *Winter's Tale* (London, 1955); especially pp. 288–347.

[60] G.H.Q. Ireland, *Record*, ii. 10, 20; cf. pp. 125–8 below.

potential unless a clear line of policy was laid down and enforced from London. In the event it was to work in different, often conflicting, directions.

9. MILITARY AND POLICE MEASURES (April–July 1920)

The policy of General Macready

Macready explained his military policy to Long on 23 April as being to try 'to get breathing space to enable Hamar Greenwood to start on the Bill[61] and to get an undisturbed hearing'.[62]

> I have impressed on my Generals (he wrote) the importance of taking no measures that may cause irritation, except in retaliation; that is to say, a murder or outrage is committed, and we at once retaliate by a raid for arms or persons in the immediate vicinity.[63]

As far as 'reinstating' the R.I.C. in districts which had been abandoned was concerned, he said that he had conferred with Strickland on the subject, but had considerable doubts—'not so much on account of their morale, as in [sic] that crass stupidity which is so often found among police officers who have not been carefully selected'.[64] This low opinion of the R.I.C., and faith in the value of military 'retaliation' (a word which did not yet possess the odour it later acquired) was not entirely shared by the Cabinet. On 30 April, Bonar Law reported that Lord Carson was highly critical of the decision to withdraw the police from outlying areas, saying that 'in the past it had been impossible to control disturbances from the centre'.[65] Greenwood, however, was satisfied that mobility was the panacea for dealing with the rebel campaign, and said that if the Army were supplied with sufficient motor transport and armoured cars 'it could be moved out quickly to the centres of attack'.[66] This showed little conception of the methods used by the I.R.A. Hankey, indeed, described Greenwood on this occasion as talking 'the most awful tosh', though he reflected that 'he has not been to Ireland yet, and will no doubt be sobered by responsibility'.[67] Unfortunately, Greenwood's ideas were not simply those of an inexperienced politician: they were those of the Irish military authorities themselves. The Army was withdrawn, by the orders of 3 May, from its close involvement in the judicial process, and the policy of raids and

---

[61] i.e. to try to gain public suport for the Government of Ireland Bill.
[62] Macready to Long, 23 April 1920. Lloyd George papers, F/34/1/19.
[63] Ibid.
[64] Ibid.
[65] Note of Cabinet Conversation, 30 April 1920. CAB.23 20.
[66] Ibid.
[67] Hankey's diary, 8 May 1920. Roskill, Hankey, ii. 153.

4

arrests was drastically curtailed.[68] Macready made it clear that henceforth the Army would depend on mobility, and he called for a doubling
of the available motor transport.[69] This demand was agreed to by the
Cabinet on 11 May, when it pledged itself to meet 'all the requirements' of the Irish Executive.[70] It also agreed to reinforce Irish Command by 8 battalions and (according to Hankey) to bring all units in
Ireland up to war strength.[71]

Macready offered the Cabinet remarkably little in the way of a
concrete plan, beyond a proposal to make the troops 'so mobile that
by moving about the country they may from time to time surprise the
Sinn Fein bands'.[72] This was extremely vague, and Wilson aptly
described it to Hankey as 'useless'. In his diary, Wilson was still more
hostile, writing that

A vain ass like Macready goes over to Ireland and in a week thinks he can solve
the Irish problem. I told Winston that before I would agree to send over 8
Batts. (which would completely break up the Army—Z Divs. we are struggling
to form) I must have knowledge what it was all for.[73]

Whether or not Macready explained his plan to Wilson's satisfaction,
the reinforcements eventually went. Macready's ideas sprang largely
from his own character. He was, as one critic said, an 'office soldier' and
not a 'fighting general':[74] during the fifteen months in which he
commanded active operations in Ireland, the available records show
only three occasions when he visited units outside Dublin—all three
being confined to Cork city.[75] His attitude was well expressed at the
Gairloch conference, after the Truce in 1921, when he deprecated
Lloyd George's idea that 'actual operations could be commanded by
senior officers flying about the country'.[76] In a sense he was right to do
so; but the problem was not simply one of operational command. By
not moving around, encouraging units and getting the feel of the
guerrilla challenge, Macready perhaps did his troops and himself a
disservice. He always retained an idea that by purely military display—
which he called 'showing the flag'—the moderate majority could be
won over.[77] It would be tempting to suggest that he failed to see the
depth of Irish alienation from Britain, were it not for his consistent

---

[68] G.H.Q. Ireland, *Record*, i. 11; cf. 'Notes for Guidance of Troops when Acting in
Aid of the Civil Police in Ireland', 3 May 1920. D.D. War Diary 'D', W.O. 35 90/1.
[69] For details see Appendix VI below, p. 215.
[70] Cabinet, 11 May 1920. C.29(20) App. II. CAB.23 21.
[71] Hankey's diary, 23 May 1920. Roskill, *Hankey*, ii. 153.
[72] Ibid. I am indebted to Captain Roskill for supplying the full text of this quotation.
[73] Wilson's diary, 10 May 1920. Wilson papers.
[74] Crozier, *Impressions and Recollections*, p. 254.
[75] 'G' (Operations) War Diary, G.H.Q. Ireland. W.O. 35 93(1)/1.
[76] Macready, *Annals*, ii. 598.
[77] See below, p. 182.

championing of Home Rule and his belief that military measures could not bring about a political solution. It is probably truer to say that he saw the complexity of the issues too clearly to be able to dedicate himself simply to coercion. His attitude was best summed up in his remark, 'Whatever we do we are sure to be wrong.'[78]

Little evidence remains on which to evaluate the use of military mobility in 1920. Orders were issued on 3 May for the preparation of flying columns, equipped for 7 days' continuous operations, bivouacking by the roadside,[79] but only a few scattered press reports show any resulting activity.[80] In his memoirs, Macready skirted the topic, restricting his description of operations in the summer of 1920 to the successful use of military pounds to discourage cattle-driving.[81] His reports to the Cabinet mentioned only one mobile operation, and this was very much a sledgehammer against a nut. A column of 100 lorry-borne infantry, 50 cavalry, and 2 armoured cars was sent to confront a group of Republican 'police' at Bellewstown Races (some 6 miles from Drogheda) on 9 July. Forty 'I.V.' armbands, thirty Volunteer uniform caps, two flags, a bugle, and some documents were confiscated by the troops, and

The Volunteer Commander, Mr. Mullaney, was made to explain to some 40 of his men ... that the Military Authorities would not recognize any such body, wearing any article which tended to make them into a force.[82]

No arrests were made, though the Volunteers were not only advertising their membership of an illegal organization, but also usurping the functions of the law itself. Macready perhaps approved of the use of mockery rather than brute force, but this subtlety was lost on the Irish press, whose reports made the military action seem merely ineffectual,[83] while the tacit recognition of the Volunteer Commander's status was evident in both the press reports and Macready's own report.

The general military posture was defensive. Dublin District was told on 3 June that under the new policy little retaliation would be possible—'We were to hope for catching offenders in the act of committing some outrage.'[84] (The idea that Wilson had described as

---

[78] G.O.C.-in-C. to C.S.I., 27 April 1921. Lloyd George papers, F/19/3/10. Cf. Sturgis's question, regarding martial law in June 1921, 'if Macready is the man or if we want a Prussian?' (diary, 4 June, P.R.O. 30 59/4).

[79] D.D. H.Q. Conference, 3 May 1920. D.D. War Diary 'C', W.O. 35 90/1.

[80] e.g. *Irish Independent*, 22, 27 May, 9–10 July 1920.

[81] Macready, *Annals*, ii. 467.

[82] Weekly Situation Report by G.O.C.-in-C. Ireland, 13 July 1920. S.I.C. 15, CAB.27 108. These reports were made to the Cabinet Irish Situation Committee from June to December 1920, and thereafter circulated to the Cabinet in the C.P. series. (Henceforth cited as G.O.C.-in-C. W.S.R.)

[83] e.g. the *Dublin Evening Mail*, 10 July 1920, reported that 'the Volunteer officer was told ...' (not 'made to explain ...'); see also the *Daily Express and Mail*, 10 July.

[84] D.D. H.Q. Conference, 3 June 1920. D.D. War Diary 'C', W.O. 35 90/1.

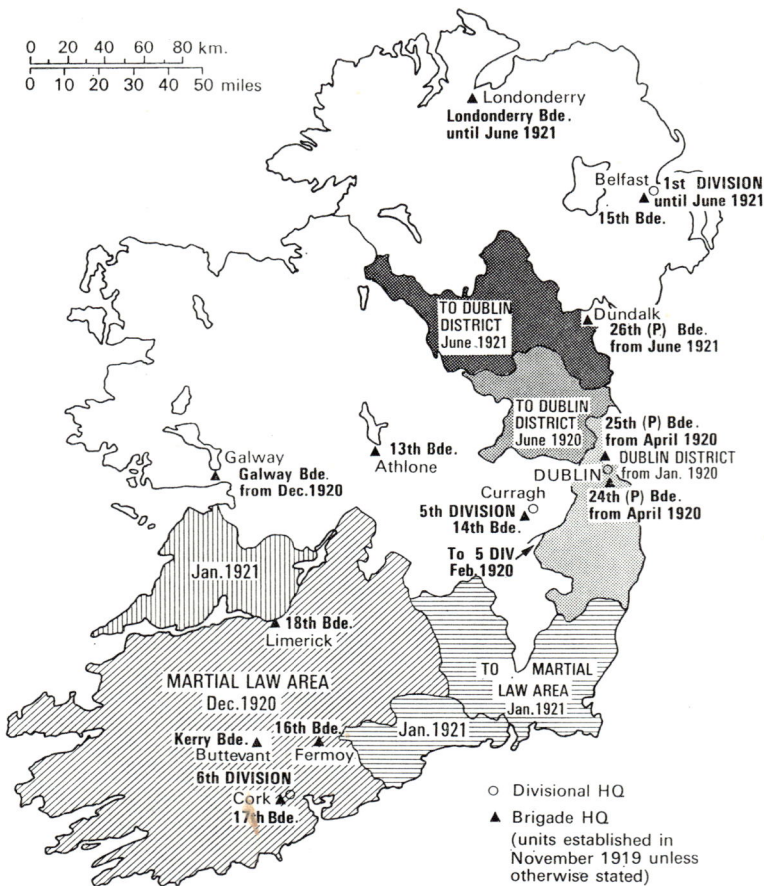

Map 3: British Military Areas in Ireland

'useless'.) Military detachments were multiplied, to provide more protection for R.I.C. barracks, and patrols were increased as far as strength permitted.[85] Irish Command was reinforced by 4 battalions in May, 3 in June, and another 3 in July;[86] but on 15 June Wilson asked the Cabinet,

Is it realized that at the present moment we have absolutely no reserves whatever (in formations) with which to reinforce our garrisons in any part of the world where an emergency may at any moment develop without warning.[87]

There were 40 infantry battalions and 8 cavalry regiments in Ireland by the end of July.[88] Effective strength is hard to gauge, because of the weakness of nearly all units.[89] Out of Dublin District's total of 7,726 men, only 4,270 were available for operations, and an idea of the strength and distribution of this division and of 6th Division in the south can be gained from a study of Appendices VII and VIII.[90]

Turning back to military measures, the curfew, which had been imposed on Dublin in February, was maintained, and was extended to Cork in July.[91] Curfew patrols were very active and made many arrests, but they could not hope to stop all nocturnal activity, nor could they work effectively over a wide area. Outside the cities the rebels for their part often blocked roads which were used by day patrols, and the Army experimented successfully with Stokes Mortar bombs to blow obstacles away.[92] In late May the provision of cyclist escorts for patrols and the makeshift armouring of lorries with planks became necessary, though on the whole the military authorities in the Dublin area thought that patrolling had been successful in 'supporting the police and protecting loyal people'.[93]

The disadvantage of the defensive posture was that any grip which had been secured on the rebel organization between January and April was now lost. Macready admitted to the Cabinet on 31 May, when he was asked whether 'a better type of evidence' was yet being obtained, that the reverse was true, as the curtailment of raids had shut off the main source of information.[94] But he and Greenwood held to the principle of mobility, and pointed out that vehicle supplies were not

[85] G.H.Q. Ireland, *Record*, ii. 9; Macready, *Annals*, ii. 486.
[86] G.H.Q. Ireland, *Record*, i. 17.
[87] British Military Liabilities: Minute by C.I.G.S., 15 June 1920. C.P. 1467, CAB.24 107.
[88] Ibid., Note on the Garrison in Ireland by the Imperial General Staff.
[89] The 32 battalions available in late May could muster altogether only 23,000 effectives. Ibid.
[90] Below, pp. 216–19.
[91] G.H.Q. Ireland, *Record*, i. 8, 15.
[92] H.Q. D.D. to 24th and 25th (P) Bdes., 17 May 1920. D.D. War Diary 'D', W.O. 35 90/1.
[93] Ibid., and D.D. H.Q. Conference, 22 May 1920. D.D. War Diary 'C', W.O. 35 90/1.
[94] Cabinet Conference, 31 May 1920. Jones, *Whitehall Diary*, iii. 22.

yet sufficient to make it work. At this 31 May Cabinet there was an evident contrast between Greenwood's (and by implication Macready's) belief that serious outrages were due to a few 'Thugs' by whom the majority of the population were terrorized, and Lord French's view that the whole Volunteer organization was involved, and that mass arrests were still the only answer.[95] Macready did, however, raise the subject of martial law, also long advocated by French. This caused predictable alarm, and the Cabinet preferred to consider something like the resuscitation of the old Special Military Areas in order to permit extensive searches for arms. Something had to be done in this direction, for, as the Irish Attorney-General[96] pointed out, 'We made 10,000 raids in 6 months. We did not get hold of the revolvers.'[97] But despite the urgency of the problem, the Cabinet could not bring itself to reach a decision.

The Army itself was still scarcely well-adapted to the guerrilla campaign. On 26 June the North Cork I.R.A. took a remarkable trick by capturing the G.O.C. 16th Brigade (not, as has recently been said, the 'Commander of the forces in the South'[98]), Brigadier Lucas, and two staff colonels, while they were on a fishing trip.[99] That night, soldiers at Brigade H.Q. in Fermoy left their barracks and ran amok in the town (where there had been an earlier reprisal after Liam Lynch's attack in September 1919), doing £18,000 worth of damage. Churchill angrily ordered a full-scale 'drive' to find Lucas, and when Macready postponed the operation on 29 June, because he felt it might endanger Lucas himself, Churchill tersely informed him that the Cabinet took 'a serious view' of the brigadier's carelessness in allowing himself to be captured, and that the drive was to go ahead.[100] A big operation was duly mounted throughout the 6th Division area, in which 38 arrests were made: Lucas, however, was not found.[101] (He escaped after about a month.) Following this fiasco, Churchill instructed that officers would henceforth forgo recreation rather than endanger themselves, and warned that 'officers and men who allow themselves to be deprived of their weapons or kidnapped . . . are liable to severe disciplinary action.'[102] But, contrary to Macready's assertion in his memoirs, the Army was not yet placed on an active service footing.[103] The military

---

[95] Ibid., iii. 17–18.
[96] Denis Stanislaus Henry, 1864–1925. Barrister; Unionist M.P., 1916–21; Attorney-General, Ireland, 1919–21; Lord Chief Justice, Northern Ireland, 1921; Baronet, 1922.
[97] Jones, *Whitehall Diary*, iii. 21.
[98] Kee, *The Green Flag*, p. 676.
[99] G.O.C.-in-C. W.S.R., 29 June 1920. S.I.C. 2, CAB.27 108.
[100] G.O.C.-in-C. Ireland to C.S.I., 29 June; Sec. of State for War to G.O.C.-in-C. Ireland, 30 June 1920. 79/Irish/658, W.O. 32 4309.
[101] G.O.C.-in-C. W.S.R., 6 July 1920. S.I.C. 10, CAB.27 108.
[102] Memo by Sec. of State for War, 2 July 1920. 79/Irish/658, W.O. 32 4309.
[103] Cf. Macready, *Annals*, ii. 469.

lawyers made this far too hot a political issue: the Judge Advocate General, Cassel,[104] wrote on 5 July that the Government 'have no power of declaring that troops serving in the United Kingdom are on active service'. Such a declaration could only be made by the courts, and 'would almost involve as a necessary corollary a Proclamation of Martial Law'.[105]

The general outlook was depressing. A military and police conference at G.H.Q. on 4 July produced few ideas. It was decided to make an announcement that if I.R.A. raids on mails continued, postal services would be curtailed (a suggestion of the old system of communal punishments), and a long-overdue decision to review and restrict arms permits was also taken.[106] Searches and raids were to continue, but on the initiative of local commanders rather than a general plan. Close study was to be given to seditious reports in the press. And regarding the railway embargo, no 'provocative' action would be taken, but parties of Crown Forces would stay on board, and thus immobilize, trains which would not move them. Co-operation between the Army and police in 5th and 6th Divisional areas was to be improved by the appointment of a D.C. to each brigade.[107] Macready wrote to Greenwood on 17 July that

while we cannot during the last four months show any definite gain for the number of troops and transport that have been sent over, matters would have been a great deal worse if we had not been so reinforced.[108]

Though court-martial convictions for carrying arms and so on had increased, he said, the numbers were merely 'a drop in the ocean'.[109] More overt criticism came at this time from Lord Midleton, who told Churchill on 15 July that since April, when Midleton and Desart had complained of the lack of co-operation between the Army and the police,

patrols had been established, and some posts had been occupied by troops, but soldiers had apparently not been successful in a single instance and in one or two notable cases . . . culpable laxity had been apparent.[110]

The same theme was taken up in a Cabinet committee on 22 July by Balfour, who 'expressed his surprise that the military had on all

---

[104] Felix Cassel, 1869–1953. Barrister; Conservative Candidate, W. Hackney, 1910; Judge Advocate General, 1916–34; Baronet, 1920.

[105] Note by J.A.G., 5 July 1920. 79/Irish/658, W.O. 32 4309. For an opinion of Cassel's grasp of martial law and its procedures, see below, pp. 104–5.

[106] Conference, Royal Hospital, Dublin, 4 July 1920. D.D. War Diary 'C', W.O. 35 90/1.

[107] Ibid.

[108] G.O.C.-in-C. Ireland to C.S.I., 17 July 1920. Lloyd George papers, F/19/2/12.

[109] Ibid.

[110] Note of a meeting at the House of Commons, 15 July 1920. Midleton papers, P.R.O. 30 67/43.

occasions been defeated and that they shot nobody'. Churchill, far from denying this, only replied that the position of the troops was very bad, owing to their youth and the strain put on them by poor accommodation and the constant threat of attack, not to mention the fact that (thanks to his new instruction) they were punished if they were taken prisoner.[111]

At this time also Macready received an important appreciation of military developments since April, from the G.O.C. 5th Division. Jeudwine ('Judy' to Macready) stated frankly that

Owing to the increase in detachments, and the absence of railway communications, we are little if at all more mobile, a large amount of transport being absorbed by administrative requirements which are constantly increasing. The long lines of road communication would be impossible to guard thoroughly in the event of railways failing altogether, and convoys would have to be strongly guarded as they would certainly be attacked.[112]

All in all the situation had 'altered considerably for the worse'. Jeudwine felt that senior officers were 'dissatisfied by a consciousness of the utter inefficacy of any measures hitherto adopted', and believed that 'we are drifting without any settled course or goal.' The Government, said the general, should choose either peace or war; if the latter, 'the more drastic, complete and immediate the measures taken the less will be the cost, and the quicker the end will be reached.' But without some definite decision, the present policy could, from a military point of view, 'only end in disaster'.[113]

Intelligence
In this report, Jeudwine singled out two main handicaps, the problems of communication and of intelligence. Wireless was still so scarce that only brigade H.Q.s could use it; aircraft were confined to a handful of landing-grounds.[114] These were due to weakness in material and personnel—as Churchill pointed out on 31 May, the Army of the Rhine was having to employ Germans as wireless operators.[115] The intelligence problem was of a different order, inherent in the Irish situation, and could only be overcome by a special type of expertise. There were signs, in the first three months of 1920, that the foundations of such expertise were being laid. The flow of intelligence material captured in raids was so great that a Documents Branch was formed at

---

[111] Cabinet Irish Situation Cttee., 22 July 1920. Note, ibid. (Not in official minute, C.P. 1672, CAB.24 109.)
[112] G.O.C. 5th Div. to G.O.C.-in-C. Ireland, 23 July 1920. Jeudwine papers, I.W.M. 72/82/2.
[113] Ibid.
[114] Ibid. For the role of aircraft in Ireland, see below, pp. 170–1.
[115] Jones, *Whitehall Diary*, iii. 18.

G.H.Q. to collate it, and the compilation of an Irish Republican Army list began.[116] The curtailment of raids in April–May virtually cut off this source, and the only consolation for intelligence was that the reinforcements of May–July made it possible to reduce the size of local intelligence areas. Divisional intelligence staffs were also expanded, and overdue recognition was given to the importance of brigade I.O.s by grading them as G.S.O.s.[117] But one of the many imbalances which marred the Crown intelligence system appeared when Dublin District was given an intelligence chief who outranked the intelligence officer at G.H.Q., so that the latter was reduced to providing only 'a small bureau for the Commander-in-Chief rather than the directing and controlling force for military intelligence throughout Ireland'.[118]

The curtailment of raids inevitably increased reliance on 'secret service' methods, where the problem was much less one of lack of expertise than one of unassailable obstacles. Only in Dublin District, where a Special Branch had been built up unofficially in mid-1919,[119] was there any consistent success in penetrating Republican organizations. The G.S.O. 1 who took over Dublin intelligence in May 1920, Lieutenant-Colonel Wilson, proved a brilliant secret service chief.[120] Even so, D.D. Special Branch suffered daunting casualties, and other intelligence groups suffered still more and achieved less. Typically, it was decided in 1919 to place Irish secret service, 'with the exception of any agents already employed by the Intelligence Branch at G.H.Q.', under the control of the head of C.I.D. in London, Sir Basil Thomson.[121] For various reasons, including one which might perhaps have been obvious from the start—the difficulty of co-ordination—the contribution of the London-based organization was minimal.[122] Walter Long admitted to Lord Midleton on 15 July 1920 that

every species of operation by Secret Service had been tried by American and other detectives, with the result that 6 of the detectives sent over from here had been shot. The Secret Service was almost impossible to establish under present conditions.[123]

In Ireland the projected fusion of the Crown intelligence services under Colonel Winter got under way only slowly. Local co-ordination between the Army and the police depended on the Divisional Commissioners, whose position and powers remained uncertain; in Leinster,

[116] G.H.Q. letter C/3532/i, 23 March 1920. D.D. H.Q. File, W.O. 35 70.
[117] G.H.Q. Ireland, *Record*, ii. 9.
[118] Ibid.
[119] Ibid., ii. 6.
[120] Winter, *Winter's Tale*, p. 294.
[121] Basil Home Thomson, 1861–1939. Barrister; Sec. to the Prison Commission, 1908; Asst. Commissioner, Metropolitan Police, 1913; Director, Home Office Intelligence, 1919.
[122] G.H.Q. Ireland, *Record*, ii. 7.
[123] Note of a meeting at the House of Commons, 15 July 1920. Midleton papers, P.R.O. 30 67/43.

moreover, the D.C.'s office was in Dundalk, well away from any military headquarters.[124] In general the R.I.C. was no nearer to effective co-operation with the Army than before, and its strengthening in itself had rather served to strengthen its independence.

Tudor and the new R.I.C.

In the spring of 1920 the R.I.C. was in a state of flux and, it appeared to many people, disintegration. According to Sir John Anderson, the situation when he took up his post on 22 May was that

> The police forces were in a critical condition. The morning I arrived in Dublin the Inspector General of the Royal Irish Constabulary stated in my presence that he was in daily fear of one of two things, either of wholesale resignations 'from the force or of his men running amok. Either he said would mean the end of the RIC.[125]

This was the pass to which the 'stolid' T. J. Smith had come. He had already informed the Chief Secretary that the number of men asking for transfer from the south-west to the north was a sure sign of demoralization, while on 11 May the Representative Body of the R.I.C. had passed a resolution calling for the complete withdrawal of the police from the most lawless counties and their replacement by military rule.[126] There was still unrest in both the R.I.C. and the D.M.P. over delays in implementing the 1919 Police Act.[127] Greenwood told the Cabinet on 31 May that resignations from the R.I.C. were running at 200 a month, as against 25 before the war (he made the figures even more startling by mistakenly referring to them as weekly, not monthly totals).[128] During May, June, and July there were 566 resignations, and recruitment exceeded this number by only 250.[129] The men left, it seems, not so much through personal fear as through the intimidation of their families,[130] but in June the Inspector General warned that 'the boycott of the police is growing and it is questionable how much longer the Force will stand the strain without largely increased support.'[131]

The task that faced Tudor as Police Adviser was therefore a daunting one, to which his determination and energy were initially well suited. Macready wrote to Lloyd George on 25 May (via Miss Stevenson) that Tudor 'is going, I am sure, to be a great success, and I fancy will later

---

[124] G.H.Q. Ireland, *Record*, ii. 18.
[125] U.S. to C.S.I., 20 July 1920. Anderson papers, C.O. 904 188/1.
[126] Enclosures in C.S.I. to Ld. Privy Seal, 12 May 1920. Bonar Law papers, 102/5/19.
[127] C.S.O. R.P. 11681 (20), 30 April 1920. R.O.
[128] Jones, *Whitehall Diary*, iii. 17. The error does not appear to have been questioned by the Cabinet.
[129] Oral Answer, C.S.I., 9 August 1920. 133 H.C. Deb. 5s, col. 24.
[130] Jones, loc. cit.; cf. entries in R.I.C. General Register, 1920–1. H.O. 184 36–40.
[131] R.I.C. Reports, I.G., June 1920. C.O. 904 11

lay bare a good deal of rottenness in the Police Force here'.[132] To Anderson, Macready gave it as his opinion that the R.I.C. needed

a thorough reorganization from top to bottom, and there is no doubt that if they were turned into an ordinary unarmed police force they would fulfil their functions in time of peace a good deal better than at present.[133]

He admitted, though, that 'to take away their arms while the inhabitants enjoy the privilege of being armed and shooting at anyone they like is impossible.'[134] None the less, it soon became clear that over the question of reinforcing and expanding the R.I.C. he did not see eye to eye with Tudor.

On 11 May the Cabinet had considered the idea of creating a special 'gendarmerie' as a supplement to the R.I.C., and appointed a military committee to report on the proposal. This committee, chaired by Macready himself, came out unequivocally against the alien concept of a 'gendarmerie'. It declared that

Police discipline is too weak in the circumstances now prevailing in Ireland, the more so as the men we may expect to recruit are largely men of the New Army, willing to join up again for a short period, who will need the strictest discipline.[135]

Macready's committee believed, justly enough, that armed forces should be under military law, and recommended instead that eight special garrison battalions (not employable outside the U.K.) should be enlisted by the War Office, with a high establishment of officers and N.C.O.s.[136] The Cabinet seemed to accept this recommendation, though at the 21 May meeting fears were expressed that 'it would evoke a good deal of protest and would be represented as the beginning of a reconquest of Ireland.'[137] These fears were in the end to permit the creation of a force which evoked far greater protest than can then have been imagined. Once again the Government's antipathy to overt 'military' measures—as distinct from coercion—seems to have been decisive. No further discussion or decision on this matter can be found in the Cabinet records, but on 27 June Tudor was writing to Churchill that

The formation of ex-soldier battalions would probably militate against recruiting for the RIC. It is far better to very largely increase the RIC in my opinion.[138]

[132] Macready to Frances Stevenson, 25 May 1920. Lloyd George papers, F/36/2/14.
[133] G.O.C.-in-C. to U.S., 28 May 1920. Anderson papers, C.O. 904 188/2.
[134] Ibid.
[135] Report of Committee under Gen. Sir C. F. N. Macready, 19 May 1920. C.P. 1317, CAB.24 106.
[136] Ibid.
[137] Cabinet, 21 May 1920. C.30 (20), CAB.23 21.
[138] Police Adviser to Sec. of State for War, 27 June 1920. S.I.C. 4, CAB.27 108.

and in late July he began, as we shall see, apparently on his own initiative, to recruit exactly the type of force that Macready had rejected.

In the meantime he fostered the recruitment of ex-servicemen into the regular R.I.C. The first of these had arrived in Ireland in late March, and though their numbers were at first fairly small it was found necessary to dress them in khaki 'pending the arrival of R.I.C. uniform'.[139] After a cursory training in the civil law, which was to become still more cursory as time went by,[140] they were sent out to stations, where they immediately sensed the weakness of discipline. On 28 April a group of them went on a spree in Limerick, breaking windows and assaulting civilians, where they earned the immortal soubriquet 'Black and Tans', after a local pack of hounds. This name was originally a graphic description of their mixture of khaki and dark-green R.I.C. uniform, but it was quite specifically applied to British recruits into the R.I.C., and later the Auxiliary Division, and not to any Irish recruits who may have suffered from the same uniform shortage.[141] The name survived on the tongues not only of the Irish but also of the 'Tans' themselves.

The number of Black and Tans recruited by the time of Tudor's appointment was about 500, and the monthly intake rose to 333 in July and 667 in August.[142] The overall strength of the regular R.I.C. was fluctuating, rising to 10,129 in mid-July, falling to 9,903 in mid-August, and not exceeding 10,000 again until late September.[143] Tudor worked hard to increase the capability of the force, and his executive methods excited general admiration. He was frequently on the move by road or air, inspecting and encouraging units. He brought a new efficiency to the R.I.C. Office at the Castle by importing female clerical staff—'Tudor's typists'—who were a sensation in their dull surroundings.[144] He created from scratch a Transport Division, with 1,500 trained personnel by the end of the conflict, and replaced the Ford vans which had been bought in 1919 with more suitable vehicles like Lancia 'cage cars' and Crossley 'tenders',[145] while he rearmed the R.I.C. at large with rifles and Lewis guns.[146] He 'pushed' recruitment

[139] C.S.O. R.P. 9393(20), 10 April 1920. R.O.

[140] The situation by early 1921 is tellingly described in D.V. Duff, *Sword for Hire* (London, 1934), pp. 58–61.

[141] Cabinet Conference, 29 December 1920. C.79A(20), CAB.23 23; Capt. Poynting to A.A.G., 29 December 1920, encl. in G.O.C.-in-C. to U.S., 5 January 1921; cf. Anderson to Deputation, House of Lords, 15 April 1921. C.P. 2883, CAB.24 122.

[142] Including Auxiliary Division. For statistics, including recruitment of Irishmen, see Appendix I below, p. 209.

[143] See Appendix III below, p. 211.

[144] Duggan, 'The Last Days of Dublin Castle', p. 169.

[145] Light (15 and 30 cwt.) lorries originally developed for R.A.F. use. For the drawbacks of the vans see War Office *Manual of Military Vehicles*, 1930, p. 7.

[146] Strength of the Police Forces in Ireland, 1 July 1921. Hemming papers; Winter, *Winter's Tale*, p. 293.

'in every way', as he wrote to Churchill on 27 June 1920,[147] and pressed on with the process of evacuating such barrack buildings as could not be made fully defensible.

> The policy decided on is to concentrate sufficiently to ensure proper defence of barracks whilst leaving a mobile force. As soon as the transport difficulty is got over we hope that constant patrolling of the country will help to re-establish the ordinary law.[148]

As far as morale was concerned, Tudor stressed the bad effect of releasing the hunger-strikers in April, but said that 'we are gradually persuading the R.I.C. that they are being backed up, and will continue to be backed up.'[149]

The origin of reprisals

The critical problem for the R.I.C., and, though it did not see it, for the Government, was that the 're-establishment of the ordinary law' was at present a faint prospect. The law had, to all intents and purposes, broken down. The psychological effect of this, combined with the direct pressure on the police from the rebel campaign, was serious. For whereas the Army possessed, in military and if necessary in martial law,[150] the formalized means both of maintaining its own discipline in the face of provocation and of imposing order on the community at large, the police depended on the civil law. To make matters worse, the R.I.C. was now taking in an increasing number of British ex-soldiers, men with no mental habituation to the methods and restraints of a civil police force, and no affinity with the populace amongst whom they now found themselves. These were men who, as Macready's committee had said, would need 'the strictest discipline'. Tudor, however, saw the rebuilding of the R.I.C.'s shaken morale as the primary need, and elected to achieve this through 'backing up'. This was perhaps a reasonable expedient in the uncertain circumstances which prevailed at the time of his appointment, but in the long term both encouragement and discipline are necessary for the control of an armed force. Tudor was to prove unwilling to impose effective discipline even when his men resorted to the most blatant illegality in response to rebel provocation.

The system of 'unauthorized retaliation' or 'reprisal' was to become largely associated with the police in Ireland. The military authorities assiduously fostered the idea that 'the Army was practically free from

[147] Police Adviser to Sec. of State for War, 27 June 1920. S.I.C. 4, CAB.27 108.
[148] Ibid.
[149] Ibid.
[150] Military law being the code of discipline imposed by the Army Acts, not applicable outside the military services.

this taint',[151] and Macready asserted that only four military reprisals occurred during the whole conflict.[152] This was certainly untrue, though the facts about many instances will doubtless never be known. One incident, reported in the Dublin District records, provides a vivid illustration of the problems faced by military units. On 25 April 1920 a patrol of Lancashire Fusiliers in Arklow, Co. Wicklow, got into a scuffle with a crowd welcoming a released hunger-striker, and several of the soldiers were bruised or injured. After the patrol had returned to barracks the commanding officer of the detachment held a roll-call, and found that several men were absent. His report states that

About this time, 2220 hrs, firing was heard in the town. I sent out another picquet under an officer which returned about half an hour later. The officer brought with him two sergeants and about fifteen men. He had found them on the bridge crossing the river about half a mile from the camp. He reported that there had been firing, that one civilian had been killed, one wounded, and one soldier wounded.
   I interrogated the men, and found that when their friends had returned to camp, after being assaulted by the civilian population, and after the first picquet had returned, they had broken out of the camp through the barbed wire fence taking their rifles, and that whilst on the bridge one or more shots had been fired at them from the civilian population, wounding one of my men, and that they had opened fire without any orders.[153]

Officers clearly found it difficult to prevent such occurrences, and in the first half of 1920 there were, on a conservative count, military reprisals at Limerick, Fermoy, Tuam, and Tipperary.[154] *The Times* drew attention to the danger of military retaliation after the Fermoy incident in June (caused by the kidnapping of Brigadier-General Lucas).[155]

But the danger of police violence was far greater. To have overcome the weakness of constabulary discipline, the police authorities would have had to make efforts which they were not prepared to make. Few people doubted that the R.I.C. was responsible for the murder of the Lord Mayor of Cork, Tomás MacCurtáin, on 19 March, or that there was a grain of truth in the coroner's jury's extravagant verdict of murder against Lloyd George, French, Macpherson, T. J. Smith, Divisional Inspector [*sic*] Clayton, District Inspector Swanzy, and

[151] G.H.Q. Ireland, *Record*, i. 22.
[152] Macready, *Annals*, ii. 494. The four he admitted were Fermoy (omitting the 1919 incident), Queenstown, Mallow, and Ennistymon. In fact there were four other cases in the first six months of 1920 alone, leaving aside unverified instances.
[153] O.C. Minden Coy., 1st Lancs. Fusiliers, Arklow, to H.Q. D.D., 26 April 1920. D.D. War Diary 'D', W.O. 35 90/1.
[154] Cf. the list given in Street, *The Administration of Ireland 1920*, Ch. XI, which does not include the Arklow incident.
[155] *The Times*, 30 June 1920.

unknown members of the R.I.C.[156] Likewise few people believed the
denial of Colonel Smyth,[157] the Divisional Commissioner for Cork,
that he had told the R.I.C. in Listowel on 19 June, 'The more you
shoot, the better I will like you, and I assure you that no policeman will
get into trouble for shooting any man.'[158] (Smyth was assassinated
within a month.) In July a County Inspector told Macready 'in strict
secrecy that the R.I.C. were now half informers to Sinn Fein and the
other half prepared owing to the strain to become assassins'.[159] And,
amazingly enough, they were receiving encouragement in the latter
course from the very highest authority.

10. CONFLICTS IN BRITISH POLICY (May–August 1920)

Political groups and beliefs
By the summer of 1920 the threads of British policy had become so
complex that lines are hard to distinguish. Within the Governments in
London and Dublin there were different assumptions about the nature
of the Irish challenge and the methods of answering it. There were
some people who believed that the trouble was caused by a small
group of terrorists, and others who felt that the community (excluding,
of course, the vaguely defined group of 'loyalists' outside Ulster)[160]
was much more widely involved. At the 31 May Cabinet, as we have
seen, these views were propounded by Greenwood and French
respectively.[161] But whereas French drew from his premise the conclusion that the whole Sinn Féin–Volunteer movement must be destroyed, and that for this martial law, preferably coupled with a declaration of war, was essential,[162] others, notably Cope and William
Wylie,[163] who shared the same premise, concluded that military
measures could only worsen the chances of a final settlement. And
whereas Tudor, a proponent of the terrorist 'murder gang' theory,
agreed with French that full-scale treatment, including martial law,

[156] Report of Coroner's Verdict, 17 April 1920. Transcripts of Coroner's Inquest on
Lord Mayor of Cork, C.O. 904 47/2.
[157] Gerald Fergusson Smyth, 1882–1920. Royal Engineers, 1906; France, 1914–18,
wounded 6 times and lost left arm; Brig. Gen., 1918; Divisional Commissioner R.I.C.
and Police Commissioner for Munster, 1920; assassinated, July 1920.
[158] For the Republican version see Macardle, *The Irish Republic*, pp. 332–3; for Smyth's
version see *The Times*, 30 July 1920.
[159] Sir Warren Fisher to Prime Minister, 21 July 1920. Lloyd George papers, F/17/1/6;
cf. the absurdly optimistic official report of the same C.I. in R.I.C. Reports, C.I. Limerick,
August 1920, C.O. 904 112.
[160] For a survey of loyalists see Macready, *Annals*, ii. 554–6; Percival, Lecture 1, pp. 4–6.
[161] Jones, *Whitehall Diary*, iii. 17; see above, p. 88.
[162] Extract from a letter of Lord French, n.d. (June 1920). Cabinet Irish Situation Cttee.
Memoranda. S.I.C. 6, CAB.27 108.
[163] Hon. William Evelyn Wylie, 1881–1964. Barrister; Law Adviser, Irish Government, 1919; Judge, Supreme Court (Ireland), 1920; Judge, High Court (Irish Free State),
1924.

was necessary,[164] Greenwood, who was also committed to this theory, thought that ordinary justice, coupled with the Government of Ireland Act, would suffice.[165] Some of the Cabinet Liberals, like H. A. L. Fisher, accepted the murder gang theory but inclined instinctively to the sort of solution advocated by Cope, Wylie, and later Sturgis, who may be called the Castle group.[166]

The mainspring of the Castle group at this time was Wylie, the Law Adviser, who shaped the thinking of Macready and Anderson as well as Cope and Sturgis, though only the latter two followed his principles to the end. Wylie was loyal both to Ireland and to the legal system, and was torn between a hatred of coercion and a desire to uphold the sanctity of the law.[167] In May 1920 he wrote to Greenwood,

British law was framed for a constitutional people by a constitutional people. Its ultimate sanction is the people. In any democratic country that is so and the root reason why the present administration of Ireland is so difficult is that there is no body of people (or call it public opinion) behind the administration.[168]

Such vital support, Wylie declared, could only be won by a return to strictly constitutional government—dropping 'semi-martial' measures, and suppressing crime but 'not confusing crime with politics'.[169]

Macready's views at this time were close to Wylie's. He was a consistent Home Ruler, and though he came later to think that Cope's trust in the intentions of the rebel leaders was 'as pathetic as . . . it was misplaced',[170] he told Lloyd George in May 1920 that Sinn Féin contained many men of substance and deep feeling, and could not be dismissed as a party of murderers. Indeed, its programme for restoring law and order showed 'an energy and dispatch in favourable contrast to Government methods'.[171] He did not approve either of the new Home Rule Bill or of the way it was being fitted into Government policy, warning that

To introduce a Bill that is not acceptable to any party and then delay it till order is restored by force would, I am convinced, shake any remaining faith in the sincerity of the Government.[172]

Macready saw this policy as leading inevitably to martial law, an arid measure which could only create 'a state of comparative quietude',

[164] Riddell, *Diary of the Peace Conference*, p. 202 (6 June 1920).
[165] Jones, *Whitehall Diary*, iii. 18.
[166] Cabinet Irish Situation Cttee., 6th Meeting, 6 August 1920. S.I.C. 6th conclusions, CAB.27 107.
[167] Wheeler-Bennett, *Anderson*, p. 61.
[168] Law Adviser to C.S.I., May 1920. Anderson papers, C.O. 904 188/1.
[169] Ibid.
[170] Macready, *Annals*, ii. 493.
[171] Memo by G.O.C.-in-C. Ireland, 24 May, encl. in Macready to Frances Stevenson, 25 May 1920. Lloyd George papers, F/36/2/14.
[172] Ibid.

leaving the old bitterness festering. What was needed, he said, was a bold gesture of generosity, and he believed, as he put it to Miss Stevenson, that 'there is no man who could try such an experiment with such chances of success as our P.M.'[173] Macready's views remained constant during the summer of 1920. He was one of the few people who, in the debate on ends and means, stressed the importance of constructive steps such as the building or improvement of Irish harbours.[174]

In the last analysis, however, he was, like Anderson, a professional who would implement government policy without regard to his personal feelings. The moving spirit of the 'peace party' increasingly became that of the more unconventional Andy Cope, who, supported by Sir Warren Fisher, launched attacks in June 1920 on both the Government of Ireland Bill and a new coercive measure prepared by the Irish Chief Crown Solicitor, the 'Three Judges Bill', which proposed to suspend trial by jury in certain cases in favour of tribunals composed of three judges.[175] An instant counter-attack was led by Walter Long, who declared that any sign of weakness in the Government's stance could be disastrous. He told Lloyd George that

The Irishman is easily dealt with if you stand up to him, but he is the worst man in the world from whom to run away. . . . I hope with all my heart that we shall adopt Haig's motto when the days were blackest in France—'It's dogged that does it!'[176]

Notwithstanding this emotional appeal, Long was thwarted, at least over the Three Judges Bill. Greenwood, advised by Wylie and the Lord Chief Justice of Ireland, hoped that juries would 'do their duty' at the coming assizes, and explained to Long somewhat apologetically that he was postponing the Bill.[177] But Long's continuing influence was recognized when he became the chairman of a new Cabinet Committee on the Irish Situation, formed on 24 June to 'assist the Viceroy and Chief Secretary'.[178] This committee, which included three other 'hawks'—Balfour, Birkenhead, and Churchill—and only one 'dove'— H. A. L. Fisher—became a strong pressure group for tough action.

Two central figures, Greenwood and Lloyd George, were still not clearly committed to any course, and their ideas indicate further complexities in the threads of policy. Both 'peace' and 'war', and especially the latter, could be approached in many ways. Since April, Greenwood's policy had been to mix mild concession—Home Rule—with

[173] Macready to Frances Stevenson, loc. cit.
[174] Macready to Anderson, 28 May 1920. Anderson papers, C.O. 904 188/2.
[175] Cope to Warren Fisher, encl. in Warren Fisher to Prime Minister, 17 June 1920. Lloyd George papers, F/17/1/2.
[176] Long to Prime Minister, 18 June 1920. Lloyd George papers, F/33/2/27.
[177] Greenwood to Long, 20 June 1920. Bonar Law papers, 102/5/28.
[178] Cabinet, 24 June 1920. C.37(20), CAB.23 21; Cabinet Irish Situation (S.I.C.) Cttee. papers, CAB.27 107–8.

mild coercion. He evidently believed in the murder gang theory, but relied less on crushing the extremists than on weaning the moderates away from them (how this was to be done while the terrorists retained their power to terrorize, he does not appear to have considered too closely). Thus, as we have seen, he released suspects, cut back deportations, and retained trial by jury, while in June he favoured rescinding the original blanket proscription of Sinn Féin.[179] His attitude hardened noticeably in July, when the summer assizes failed humiliatingly, but he was never converted to the idea of formal military rule.

Lloyd George's approach is harder to analyse. He had not yet turned his full attention to Ireland, and while he was involved in the *sub rosa* efforts of Cope and others to explore possible lines of negotiation with Sinn Féin, in public he was a determined restorer of law and order, and made speeches which were highly prejudicial to the chances of settlement.[180] For a long time he saw the disarming of the I.R.A. as an essential condition of negotiations, ensuring in effect that the rebels would not talk until their physical power was broken. He showed little conception of the strength of anti-British feeling in Ireland, and even dismissed the notion of Irish nationality as 'a sham and a fraud'.[181] But his most fateful judgement in the summer of 1920 was his support for the methods of counter-terrorism which were increasingly being adopted by the police, and which were to become permanently associated with the name of the Black and Tans. He had a private meeting with Tudor on 6 June and assured him of full support:[182] just what he meant emerged next month. On 7 July Sir Henry Wilson, talking to Lloyd George at the international conference in Spa, found that he had an 'amazing theory that Tudor, or someone, was murdering 2 S.F.'s [Sinn Féiners] to every loyalist the S.F.'s murdered', and that counter-murder was the best answer to I.R.A. killings.[183] Wilson protested to Churchill that the idea was 'suicidal', only to find that he too had hopes of 'our "rough-handling" the Sinn Féins'.[184] Wilson was not squeamish about shooting Sinn Féiners—indeed his own scheme of shooting them 'by roster' was far too strong meat for the Cabinet.[185] What he, and the military authorities in Ireland, wanted was regularity

---

[179] C.S.I. to Ld. Privy Seal, 22 June 1920. S.I.C. 1st conclusions, 29 June 1920. CAB.27 107.
[180] Most notably at Caernarvon in October 1920, and in his 'murder by the throat' speech on 9 November.
[181] Boyce, 'How to Settle the Irish Question', p. 150.
[182] Riddell, *Diary of the Peace Conference*, p. 202; cf. Cabinet, 7 June 1920. C.33(20), CAB.23 21.
[183] Wilson's diary, 7 July 1920. Wilson papers.
[184] Ibid., 12 July 1920. It is noteworthy that Wilson at first blamed the rise of the Black and Tans on Macready, and only later transferred the blame to Tudor and Churchill. He still agreed with Churchill that 'Macready was very disappointing'. Diary, 19 July 1920.
[185] For the scheme, see Roskill, *Hankey*, ii. 153.

and public responsibility. Lloyd George preferred to let the police
have their heads and to observe the effect of 'unauthorized' reprisals.

The Cabinet Conference of 23 July

With such differences of approach a clash was inevitable. From May
onwards there was constant tension, which culminated at the first full-
scale conference between the Cabinet and the Irish Executive on 23
July. Three days before this, in a weighty memorandum to Greenwood, Anderson announced his adherence to the 'peace party'. After
summarizing the steps taken since May to clear up the 'really incredible' confusion in Dublin Castle, he went on to oppose coercion as
a future policy because 'we have not in my judgment the instruments
at command which would be essential to secure success.' 'To make the
attempt and fail', he declared, 'would be disastrous.'[186] On the other
side, the Irish Situation Committee met on 22 July to discuss the unsatisfactory military situation, and called on the Government 'actively
to assume the offensive in its Irish policy' and to introduce martial law
immediately.[187] On the middle ground, Bonar Law reiterated to the
Commons on 19 July that the Government's Irish policy was, 'by the
use of all the means in our power, to restore law and order in Ireland
and to carry into law the Government of Ireland Bill'.[188]

The Cabinet Conference on 23 July opened with a brilliant[189] speech
by Wylie, describing the breakdown of the legal system, and calling
for negotiations with Sinn Féin. He asked the Cabinet not to refuse to
talk to 'murderers', for the rebels

> were not committing outrages through blood-lust, but because they believed
> that they had been tricked by the British Government, and the only way to
> focus the eyes of Europe on their cause was by the adoption of (these)
> methods. . . .[190]

He declared that the R.I.C. would soon be little better than a mob,
capable only of terrorism, so that the Government would be unable to
restore the law. An Irish policeman now, he said, 'either saw white or
he saw red'.[191] Replying to this, Tudor candidly agreed that as a police
force the R.I.C. could not last much longer, but he said that 'they might
have a great effect as a military body.'[192] Following this extraordinary
remark (which, as time would show, did not imply the imposition of

---

[186] U.S. to C.S.I., 20 July 1920. Anderson papers, C.O. 904 188/1.
[187] S.I.C. 4th conclusions, 22 July 1920. CAB.27 107; C.P. 1672, CAB.24 109.
[188] Oral Answers, 19 July 1920. 132 H.C. Deb. 5s, col. 25.
[189] The judgement is that of H. A. L. Fisher. Diary, 23 July 1920. Fisher papers.
[190] Cabinet Conference, 23 July 1920. C.P. 1693, CAB.24 109. The official minute is
incomplete and needs to be read in conjunction with the likewise incomplete but fortunately complementary notes in Jones, *Whitehall Diary*, iii. 25–31.
[191] Speech of Law Adviser, C.P. 1693, CAB.24 109.
[192] Speech of Police Adviser, ibid.

military discipline), he announced that he was recruiting 500 ex-
officers, who 'formed a fine body of men', and said that the rebel
campaign could be defeated if martial law were declared, systems of
passports and identity cards instituted, changes of domicile restricted,
prisoners removed from Ireland to Britain, and the Post Office purged
of rebel sympathizers.[193] Macready also called for stronger measures,
including power to arrest members of Dáil Eireann, but sounded a
cautious note in warning the Cabinet not to 'lean too hard on the
Army', which, if the strain were doubled, would get 'near the danger
limit'.[194] By contrast, Anderson and Cope both attacked the ideas
expressed by Tudor, Anderson saying that he

could not help thinking that General Tudor, in stating that under certain
conditions he could restore order, must have been assuming the assistance of a
larger military force.[195]

He argued that in fact it would be impossible to restore order 'in the
time at their disposal' (the first mention of this vital factor); while Cope
declared roundly that 'any suppression now would come back like a
boomerang on the Government'.[196] In spite of this, Greenwood stated
that all the experts were agreed on the need for courts-martial and a
strengthening of the executive. Bonar Law drily corrected him, and
Churchill admitted that 'the unanimity of the experts, with the exception of General Tudor' was a 'formidable' feature of the debate.[197]

It is impossible here to deal with the whole of what H. A. L. Fisher
described as 'the first real discussion in his time' of the Irish Question.
In fact the conference reached no positive conclusions, and its aftermath saw nearly all the combatants firmly entrenched in their original
positions. Anderson submitted another strong memorandum in favour
of offering Dominion Home Rule, saying that 'it is at least a question
whether there is any alternative not foredoomed to failure.'[198] Wylie
decided that Irish support for Dominion Home Rule was even greater
than he had thought when addressing the Cabinet.[199] Against these,
Lord French (who had not spoken at the conference) wrote to Lloyd
George supporting Tudor's proposals, particularly the 'all-important'
one of identity cards, and drawing attention to the significance of one
of Wylie's remarks at the conference, 'I have got to live there.' This
consideration, French said, had 'coloured the opinions of many men of

[193] Ibid.
[194] Jones, *Whitehall Diary*, iii. 25–6.
[195] C.P. 1693, CAB.24 109.
[196] Ibid.
[197] Jones, *Whitehall Diary*, iii. 28.
[198] Irish Situation: Note by Sir John Anderson, 25 July 1920. C.P. 1689, CAB.24 109.
[199] Wylie to Anderson, 2 August 1920. Lloyd George papers, F/19/2/17; cf. Sturgis
diary, 28 July 1920. P.R.O. 30 59/1.

great ability' in Ireland.[200] Walter Long for his part remained confident
that, as he assured Lord Midleton, 'we have no intention of entering into
negotiations with . . . men who have been guilty of those awful
murders.'[201] His Irish Situation Committee resolved on 11 August that
no one in the Irish Government (a fairly explicit reference to Cope)
should have any communication with Sinn Féin except on the basis of
the Government's declared policy—the suppression of crime and
the implementation of the Government of Ireland Bill.[202] And Dublin
Castle found itself 'being urged quietly and persistently that reprisals
are the only thing to put down the gun men and hearten the police'—
even Sturgis almost began to believe it.[203]

The Restoration of Order Act and martial law
Practical policy, however, still rested with Greenwood (or, as the Castle
group hoped, with his wife). Undismayed by the disarray evident at
the conference, the Chief Secretary set about preparing a new Act to
extend the jurisdiction of courts martial, and he laid his proposals
before the Cabinet the very next day. Evidently his mind had been
made up before the conference, and was not changed by the mutiny of
Anderson and Cope. He described his new measure as a modification
of D.O.R.A. to make it possible for courts martial to try capital cases
(under D.O.R.A., they could only do so if the accused had assisted an
external enemy).[204] A short Bill was ready for parliament by 2 August
and was guillotined through in a week, receiving royal assent on the
9th as the Restoration of Order in Ireland Act. This Act, whose title
had long been the watchword of the Government's Irish policy, was in
essence a compromise. Although Dublin Castle described it as 'a strong
measure',[205] the Army was to find its legal procedures 'too slow and
cumbrous to be really effective against a whole population in
rebellion'.[206] The Government, of course, did not yet accept that Ireland was in such a state, and it is not certain that at that time the Army
fully realized it. Bu tin any case the Act was bound to prove awkward,
for while it re-involved the Army in some aspects of the judicial
system, it left others, notably the police, outside military hands; and the
efforts of the Army were often to be nullified in the general confusion.
The maintenance of divided authority under R.O.I.A. was presumably
intended to leave the police free to follow the course of counter-
terrorism approved by Lloyd George. Even later, when martial law

[200] French to Prime Minister, 27 July 1920. Lloyd George papers, F/48/6/37.
[201] Long to Midleton, 26 July 1920. Midleton papers, P.R.O. 30 67/43.
[202] S.I.C. 7th conclusions, 11 August 1920. CAB.27 107.
[203] Sturgis diary, 24 August 1920. P.R.O. 30 59/1.
[204] Memo by C.S.I., 24 July 1920. C.P. 1682, CAB.24 109.
[205] Note on Restoration of Order in Ireland Bill, 4 August 1920. Anderson papers,
C.O. 904 188/1.
[206] G.H.Q. Ireland, Record, ii. 10.

was finally declared, political dislike of overt military rule was to keep the police forces beyond the Army's control, and to maintain separate systems of administration and justice.

The attempt to maintain the primacy, or at least the existence, of the civil power in Ireland, was natural to a British government. Unfortunately in this case it was a matter of labels rather than realities. The Cabinet's belief that the Black and Tans, being nominally police, would be less offensive to public opinion than outright military administration, was a monumental act of self-deception, all the more remarkable after Tudor's statement that the R.I.C. could henceforth only hope to function 'as a military body'. Admittedly, the Cabinet was poorly advised on the subject of martial law. The concept was an alien one to British jurisprudence, there being no British parallel to the 'state of siege' often provided for in other countries. English law, as the 1914 War Office *Manual of Military Law* put it, 'never pre-supposes the possibility of civil war'.[207] All consideration of the use of force to maintain internal order lay in the shadow of Professor Dicey's theory of 'the common law right of the Crown and its servants to repel force by force'. Dicey's principle, a constitutional lawyer's dream but a peace officer's nightmare, was that all servants of the Crown, and indeed all citizens, had both the right and the duty to use exactly the degree of force that was necessitated by the situation, no more and no less.[208] He held, moreover, that the courts should subsequently judge whether the degree of force employed had been inadequate or excessive.[209] This doctrine, substantially similar to that of other nineteenth-century writers on martial law such as Clode and Finlason,[210] made it extremely difficult to decide at what point the ordinary process of the law should be superseded, and required the Crown as a practical matter to pass a generalized Act of Indemnity to shield the *bona fide* emergency actions of its servants from cold-blooded inquiry. This was not calculated to increase the democratic Englishman's liking for martial law, and its employment in England itself was generally regarded as unthinkable. No working precedents existed, except overseas examples like South Africa in the second Boer War and Germany in 1919—and the few months of martial law in Ireland in 1916, remembered, if at all, as the martyr-making reign of General Maxwell.

A major difficulty with the Irish guerrilla conflict of 1920 was that it was not an open riot or insurrection which plainly left the Army as 'the

[207] War Office, *Manual of Military Law*, 1914, with Amendments May 1919, pp. 3–4.
[208] A. V. Dicey, *Introduction to the Study of the Law of the Constitution* (London, 1885), Ch. VIII *passim.*
[209] And 'though a soldier is subject to special liabilities in his military capacity, he remains while in the ranks ... subject to all the liabilities of an ordinary citizen'. Ibid., p. 286.
[210] C. M. Clode, *Military and Martial Law* (London, 1872), esp. p. 165; W. F. Finlason. *Martial Law* (London, 1872), pp. 8, 26.

only remaining Force in the Community' capable of dealing with it.[211] In such an indefinite situation no definite remedy presented itself. None the less there is no doubt that the law as it stood permitted the rapid and effective supersession of the ordinary legal system once it had broken down (such as Lord French's idea of temporary and local use of martial law), and that very much depended on the energy and confidence of the executive. Such energy was little in evidence on the Cabinet's part, and confidence was not increased by uncertain advice about the means and effects of adopting martial law. Greenwood received a summary of the subject from the Judge Advocate General on 19 July which compared poorly in clarity and accuracy with the War Office *Manual of Military Law*, and which completely overlooked the accepted principle that martial law could come into effect without any formal proclamation: the Judge Advocate General, by contrast, advised that, if used, it should be brought into operation by legislation.[212] Macready can hardly have helped matters when he told Greenwood on 17 July 'I do not for one instant think that the British public would stand for Martial Law, as I understand it, for a week over here.'[213] Macready was not at this time in favour of the measure, but both he and the public were soon to find that the activities of the police were no easier to stand for than anything that might reasonably be expected from formal military rule. The Cabinet remained cautious and confused, however, as did the Judge Advocate General, with disabling consequences when, in December 1920, they were finally induced to take this last resort.

[211] Cf. Clode, *Military and Martial Law*, p. 165 (quotation from Sir James Mackintosh).
[212] J.A.G. to C.S.I., 19 July 1920. C.P. 1662; cf. memo by C.S.I., 24 July 1920. C.P. 1682, CAB.24 109.
[213] G.O.C.-in-C. Ireland to C.S.I., 17 July 1920. Lloyd George papers, F/19/2/12.

IV

VIOLENCE RESURGENT

'... the local police marked down certain SFs as in their opinion the actual murderers or instigators and then coolly went and shot them without question or trial.'

Sir Henry Wilson, September 1920

11. The Clash of Forces (August–October 1920)

Military courts

Under the Restoration of Order Act (R.O.I.A.) over 70 regulations (R.O.I.R.) were made, bringing most offences within the jurisdiction of courts martial, and even adding some new ones.[1] The main hope now was that a capital conviction could at last be achieved, for not a single murderer had been convicted since the shooting began in 1919.[2] Henceforth, in addition to their ordinary duties, regimental officers would have to spend many hours on military courts, and their labours in this direction were increased by a further provision of the Act substituting military Courts of Inquiry for coroners' inquests (which had generally, as in the MacCurtain case, become strongly Republican).[3] Critics of these 'Courts of Acquittal', as the Irish called them, regarded them as basically honest but led astray by the corrupt provision of evidence by the police.[4] The proceedings of the courts martial remain under 100 years' closure, but many of those of the Courts of Inquiry are now open,[5] and show clearly enough the problems caused by their members' lack of legal knowledge or aptitude, especially in the handling of evidence. Only courts martial trying capital cases were normally provided with qualified legal members,[6] and though all courts were supposed to be presided over by an officer of field rank, nearly all the Courts of Inquiry consisted only of a captain and two lieutenants.[7] They were instructed to make full investigations if a crime were suspected and not to limit their inquiries to 'the mere fact

[1] For the range of offences see the Epitome appended to D.D. Instructions for 26th(P) Bde., June 1921. W.O. 35 93(1)/4 (26th Bde. Instructions).
[2] Speech of Police Adviser, Cabinet Conference, 23 July 1920. C.P. 1693, CAB.24 109.
[3] Schedule, W.O. 35 146.
[4] e.g. Crozier, *Impressions and Recollections*, p. 255.
[5] 16 boxes in P.R.O., 7 having an 'A' suffix denoting material still withheld. W.O. 35 146–161A.
[6] Answer by Lloyd George, House of Commons, 14 April 1921. 140 H.C. Deb. 5s, col. 1275.
[7] G.H.Q. Ireland, Instructions Relating to Military Courts of Inquiry in Lieu of Inquest on Civilians, 17 December 1920, para. 3. W.O. 35 146.

of death', but they often failed to show even the minimum of 'ordinary diligence' enjoined on them, and returned very careless verdicts.

TABLE 3

Analysis of Findings of Military Courts of Inquiry in Lieu of Inquest on Civilians

A: Number of deaths inquired into:
Members of R.I.C. and A.D.R.I.C.	182
Other civilians	463
Total	645

B: Number of verdicts of:
(1) murder by John McKeown (Séan MacEoin) and others	2
(2) murder by person or persons unknown	342
(3) manslaughter by person or persons unknown	3
(4) death caused by Forces of the Crown in execution of their duty	233
(5) justifiable homicide by Crown Forces	4
(6) death caused accidentally by Crown Forces	6
(7) death caused feloniously by Crown Forces	2
(8) death by misadventure, accidental death, open verdicts, etc.	53
Total	645

C: Reasons for deaths caused by Forces of the Crown in execution of their duty (category 4 in B above)
(a) armed attack on Crown Forces or resisting arrest with arms	108
(b) attempting to escape	30
(c) failing to halt or evading arrest	78
(d) on streets after curfew	3
(e) misadventure during conflict with rebels	14
Total	233

Note. This Table has been derived by the present author from the records of the Military Courts of Inquiry; the categories and totals are not official.

An impression of their findings can be obtained from Table 3. The records are certainly incomplete, for less than two-thirds of the policemen (regarded as civilians for the purposes of the military courts) who died in this period are accounted for in them. But the tendency to exculpate Crown Forces for deaths caused 'in the execution of their duty' is, as one would expect, clear, and the finding that victims 'attempted to escape' or 'failed to halt' often covered culpable laxity in the use of weapons. The Adjutant General's department sometimes condemned failures to make even rudimentary investigations,[8] and the remarks of a senior Castle official on one verdict of murder 'by person or persons unknown' could be widely applied. On the evidence presented, he said,

[8] See, e.g., M.C.I., Patrick Donovan (W.O. 35 149A) and Michael Mullins (W.O. 35 155A).

the only possible verdict was murder by a member of the police force. I do not
say that would have been the correct verdict, but no attempt appears to have
been made by anyone to produce rebutting evidence, nor apparently did the
court think it necessary to suggest that such evidence might be produced.[9]

He felt that if the proceedings were ever reopened, an impartial
observer could only conclude that 'the court did not want to make a
full inquiry into the matter.'

In general, however, there was satisfaction at the first effects of
R.O.I.A. Criminal convictions began to mount up in August and
September, reaching 60 or 70 a week in October[10] (though a capital
conviction remained unforthcoming). Military and police morale was
felt to improve, along with the general level of guerrilla technique.[11]
Admittedly, an amateurish attitude was still evident, and remained
until after Bloody Sunday. In Dublin District, forms for reporting
raids and searches were not standardized until mid-August.[12] Searches
were everywhere unrewarding, and one regimental I.O. in the south
reached the conclusion that searches for arms were a waste of time.[13]
The real problem, however, seems to have been that little consistent
keenness and ability were yet being shown.[14] Rebel attacks on troops
became noticeably heavier towards the end of July,[15] and on 6 August
Macready admitted that although

The troops are certainly more experienced in the peculiar conditions of this
country ... this is discounted to some extent by the increased activity and
boldness of their opponents, who are daily becoming better armed, better
disciplined, and better established.[16]

This development forced the Army to concentrate on the defence of
installations and detachments, and went some way towards neutralizing
the increased powers provided by R.O.I.A.[17] The civil executive also
suffered a moral defeat on 9 August when the English civil servants
under Anderson moved from their exposed position in Kingstown into
the security of the Castle. Sturgis felt 'We shall lose all our power ...
with our own side, the rank and file of whom must stay out',[18] and the

[9] G. G. Whiskard to Col. J. B. Wroughton (D.A.G., G.H.Q. Ireland), 9 December
1920. M.C.I., James Coleman, W.O. 35 147A.
[10] See Appendix X below, p. 221.
[11] G.H.Q. Ireland, Record, i. 22; Hist. 5th Div., p. 68.
[12] D.D. Orders, 10 August 1920. D.D. H.Q. File, W.O. 35 70.
[13] Percival, Lecture I, p. 16.
[14] See especially 6th Div. Orders, 16 August 1920, complaining of erratic performance
of different units. W.O. 35 180(1)/3.
[15] G.O.C.-in-C. W.S.R., 27 July 1920. S.I.C. 22, CAB.27 108.
[16] Memo by G.O.C.-in-C. Ireland, 6 August 1920. C.P. 1750, CAB.24 110.
[17] Cf. D.D. General Plan for Defence Scheme, 7 September 1920. W.O. 35 71; 5th
Div. Standing Orders, June and September 1920.
[18] Sturgis diary, 9 and 13 August 1920. P.R.O. 30 59/1.

Cabinet even considered withdrawing them from Ireland altogether.[19]

The rebel campaign was still spreading. Their offensive against communications produced increasing disruption; by the end of August the Army had abandoned the Post Office entirely and set up its own system of couriers and air mail—a system which was inevitably overloaded from the start.[20] The railway embargo grew, and the policy of immobilizing trains by leaving parties of Crown Forces aboard them was an unimpressive reply, as G.H.Q. later admitted.

That it should be necessary for His Majesty's Forces to have recourse to such undignified methods in order to deal with the open defiance of constituted authority is eloquent testimony of the ineffectual powers that were given to the Commander-in-Chief for dealing with the situation.[21]

It is obvious now that, notwithstanding official denials, British policy aimed at 'blockading the railways' until the embargo ceased.[22] But Anderson had to tell the Cabinet on 26 July that the number of troops and police available was not sufficient to 'bring things to a standstill', and that at the present rate, 'we shall be broken sooner than the railway companies.'[23] That the railway embargo was a severe military handicap there can be no doubt, and disproportionate effort had to be directed into supply work. This was at a time when, owing to Wilson's fears of industrial crisis in Britain, ten of Irish Command's infantry battalions had to be concentrated for over two months (August–November) in readiness for possible despatch to the sister island.[24]

The R.I.C. and the creation of the Auxiliary Division

The condition of the police was still doubtful. The R.I.C.'s strength, as we have seen, fell to below 10,000, and though the mass breakdown of morale which its chiefs had feared did not occur, there were few signs of real confidence. Agitation was going on against the use of force and in favour of Dominion Home Rule. On 1 August Dublin Castle received a defeatist 'Manifesto' from the Connaught R.I.C., calling for the force to be wound up,[25] while the Representative of the Leinster R.I.C. was distributing pamphlets to the same effect. Sturgis wryly remarked in his diary, 'if it spreads, a bonny job to start coercion by having to coerce the R.I.C.'[26] According to a senior military

[19] Cabinet, 13 August 1920. C.48(20), CAB.23 22.
[20] D.D. Orders, 24 August 1920. D.D. War Diary 'D', W.O. 35 90/1.
[21] G.H.Q. Ireland, Record, i. 17; for a superb sketch encapsulating the railway hold-up see Briollay, Ireland in Rebellion, p. 67.
[22] A G.H.Q. press statement denying this appeared in the Irish Times, 16 July 1920.
[23] Cabinet Conference, 26 July 1920. Jones, Whitehall Diary, iii. 32.
[24] For the hampering effect of this immobility on operations see Macready, Annals, ii. 472; G.H.Q. Ireland, Record, i. 19.
[25] In Anderson papers, C.O. 904 188/1.
[26] Sturgis diary, 4 August 1920. P.R.O. 30 59/1.

intelligence officer, writing to Anderson on 6 August, the police force was paralysed:

Anyone passing by a police barrack with its locked doors and seeing the constables looking out through barred windows will at once realize that no body of men could preserve its morale under such conditions.[27]

The only solution, he said was either to stop murders or to punish them. Neither was likely to be achieved; and even though this assessment of the R.I.C.'s survival capacity was to prove exaggeratedly pessimistic, it was obvious that little rapid improvement was to be looked for.

But a very different development was taking place—the creation of a totally new force. The idea of a special 'gendarmerie' had been in the air since May, and though there is no record of any decision to raise it entirely from ex-officers, we have seen that Tudor told the Cabinet Conference on 23 July that he had 'obtained' 500 such recruits.[28] He said that they 'formed a fine body of men', but was otherwise vague about them, as well he might be, since, according to the Castle records, authority to recruit 500 ex-officers as 'Temporary Cadets' had not been sought until as late as 6 July, and for another 500 as 'Special Constables' five days later.[29] No appointments were made until 23 July, the very day on which Tudor was addressing the Cabinet,[30] and the new body was not officially inaugurated until the 27th.[31] It is hard to see to what 'fine body' Tudor could have been referring, but the Cabinet was not troubled by such vagueness. On 29 July the Irish Situation Committee, furnished doubtless with private information from Tudor about what he proposed to do with the force (though no such information was mentioned), enthusiastically called for an acceleration in the recruitment of ex-officers,[32] while on 5 August Lord Birkenhead made a public appeal for recruits, saying that there was 'no limit to the number we will take'.[33]

The force came into existence with a rapidity unexampled in Ireland. On 3 August Brigadier-General F. P. Crozier[34] was appointed its commander, and by September five companies ('A' to 'E') were

[27] Lt. Col. Toppin to U.S., 6 August 1920. Anderson papers, C.O. 904 188/1.
[28] Speech of Police Adviser, C.P. 1693, CAB.24 109.
[29] C.S.O. R.P. 18114(20), 18321(20). R.O.
[30] Auxiliary Division R.I.C., Journal No. 1. H.O. 184 50.
[31] Royal Irish Constabulary Auxiliary Division: Outline of Terms on which Cadets were engaged . . ., etc. Cmd. 1618, 1922 (xvii. 785), p. 1.
[32] S.I.C. 5th conclusions, 29 July 1920. C.P. 1703, CAB.24 110.
[33] Earl of Birkenhead, F.E.: The Life of F. E. Smith, 1st Earl of Birkenhead (London, 1959), p. 359.
[34] Frank Percy Crozier, 1879–1937. Raised W. Belfast Regiment, Ulster Volunteer Force, 1914; commanded 119th Bde., 1916; Insp. Gen., Lithuanian Army, 1919; Commandant, A.D.R.I.C., 1920–1.

operational, each with a strength of about 100. The number of companies doubled within two months, though companies 'in the field' were allowed to fall well below establishment so that new units could be formed at the main depot at Beggars Bush in Dublin.[35] The military committee in May had estimated that to build up the staff arrangements for a totally new force would take a year; here it was done in less than a month, but at the price of near-complete confusion and lack of control.[36] Even the title of the force remained uncertain until some time after its first units had gone into action. It was finally christened the Auxiliary Division, R.I.C. (A.D.R.I.C.), but its place in the command structure was never to be defined. There were no intermediate formations between company and division, and operational control of the companies was theoretically vested in R.I.C. Divisional Commissioners in co-operation with the military authorities. In practice they could be, outside Dublin at least, virtually independent. The divisional commandant was responsible only for training and administration.[37] Company commanders were usually ex-majors or captains, with the rank of 1st D.I. in the R.I.C., and had under them three platoon commanders called Section Leaders. The Temporary Cadets (T.C.s) enlisted for 6 months with the option of another 6.[38] After a brief instruction in the civil law, companies were despatched to the most disturbed areas of Ireland. They wore R.I.C. uniform distinguished by tam-o'-shanters with golden harp badges, and were given enough Crossley tenders to make them fully mobile. But what they were actually to do, no-one said.[39]

Here, then, was a force of immense potential, brought into action with the minimum of planning.[40] Given proper guerrilla warfare training it would very likely have achieved results out of proportion to its size,[41] but instead it was left to work out its own salvation in conditions where experience of the Great War was of limited relevance. The fundamental problem of the A.D.R.I.C., however, like that of the other Black and Tans (whose soubriquet it shared) was its police status. It lacked the military discipline essential to an armed force under constant stress, and the quality of A.D.R.I.C. companies depended entirely on the character of their officers.[42] Some became first-class

[35] See figures in Appendix II below, p. 210.
[36] Cf. 'Woman of No Importance', *As Others See Us*, p. 117.
[37] Crozier, *A Word to Gandhi*, p. 25.
[38] Cmd. 1618, 1922, p. 1.
[39] See the notable and chilling memoir, 'The Auxiliary's Story', in J. Gleeson, *Bloody Sunday*, pp. 56f.
[40] Sir Henry Wilson thought that 'This undoubtedly is the scheme which LG referred to in Spa when talking to me and later to Derby. It is an amazing and scandalous thing.' Diary, 30 August 1920. Wilson papers.
[41] Cf. G.H.Q. Ireland, *Record*, ii. 22.
[42] G.O.C. 6th Div. to G.O,C.-in-C. Ireland, 3 January 1921. W.O. 35 88(1).

fighting (if not police) units, but many succumbed to drunkenness[43] and gained a reputation as perpetrators of the most calculated and destructive reprisals.[44]

Military and police discipline

According to Macready it was in August that he 'began to be uneasy' about the behaviour of the new R.I.C. recruits, and to press the Castle to replace their khaki uniforms so that they could not be mistaken for soldiers.[45] Concern for the good name of the army led him to issue on 17 August a Special General Order warning that 'the severest disciplinary measures' would be taken against any sign of looting or retaliation (which, the Order pointed out, would merit the death penalty if the Army were on active service).[46] The Army could not control the police, but orders were issued later next month that if police who were operating with troops began to engage in reprisals, 'the Commander of the Troops will withdraw his men, *after giving* the Police due warning of his intention.'[47]

Macready admitted privately that the problem of discipline was a delicate one, because troops without enough spirit to retaliate when their comrades were attacked were 'not worth a damn', and harsh punishment might take the heart out of them.[48] But for him the honour of the Army outweighed everything else, including the success of the Government's policy and the survival of the Government itself.[49] Tudor, by contrast, could not free himself from the fear of disheartening his men. He was supposed to issue a parallel order to Macready's forbidding retaliation, but he kept delaying it because of increasing R.I.C. casualties.[50] On 13 August he began to publish a new police bulletin, the *Weekly Summary* (intended as a counter to Republican propaganda), which was generally regarded as an encouragement to retaliation rather than the reverse. And when he finally issued a call for tighter discipline on 9 November, it was in the form, not of an order, but of a 'memorandum' for the 'information and guidance' of the R.I.C.[51]

By that time Macready had given vent to his disgust at, among other things, the R.I.C.'s penchant for firing in the air as they drove

---

[43] At the Cabinet Conference on 29 December 1920 Tudor 'admitted that drink was the problem with the Auxiliary Divisions' [*sic*]. C.79A(20), CAB.23 23.

[44] *Report of the Labour Commission to Ireland* (London, 1921), p. 7.

[45] Macready, *Annals*, ii. 490.

[46] G.H.Q. Ireland, *Record*, i. App. III.

[47] D.D. Orders, 29 September 1920. D.D. War Diary 'D', W.O. 35 90/1.

[48] Sturgis diary, 19 August 1920. P.R.O. 30 59/1.

[49] Macready, *Annals*, ii. 502.

[50] Sturgis diary, 18 August and 4 September 1920. P.R.O. 30 59/1.

[51] Memo by Chief of Police, 9 November 1920. Hemming papers.

about,[52] a form of indiscipline which led to the much-publicized death of a young mother sitting with her child by a roadside in Co. Galway.[53] But Macready's attitude to the division of authority in Ireland had become one of sardonic resignation. (He wrote to Anderson privately, 'Coalition may be all very well in politics, but it don't work when active operations are required.')[54] The Castle group were surprisingly more alive to the need for structural reform, and Sturgis was a strong advocate of either a 'dictatorship' or at least a war council with overall authority.[55] Greenwood, however, was now clearly identifying himself with the concept of 'police war' as envisaged by Lloyd George and Churchill. Where he had once been blithely optimistic about winning over the moderates, he now became equally confident of crushing the murder gang. While Macready remained cautious, reporting on 18 September that although the Army was now more confident and successful, it would soon have to abandon outlying districts so as to concentrate in winter quarters,[56] and while Lloyd George was even considering abandoning the Irish hinterland and holding the ports,[57] Greenwood declared on 20 September, 'we'll win out quickly if we pursue our firm and consistent policy.'[58] He felt that his promotion of 'energetic young men full of fight' was instantly improving the R.I.C., and on the 25th he sent Bonar Law the impressive news that 'the tide has turned', 'the hostiles are growing frightened', and 'the mass of Irishmen are losing faith in the victory of Sinn Féin.'[59] The cause of this apocalypse was not, however, 'firm and consistent policy', but an explosion of police counter-terrorism which brought the name of Balbriggan to the attention of the world.

The I.R.A. and the creation of flying columns
Police reprisals, *pace* the Republican propagandists, were seldom premeditated acts of violence. The outburst of September 1920 can be associated with a noticeable change in the scale of the guerrilla campaign of the I.R.A., which applied a new level of provocation against the R.I.C. This development was in a sense an unplanned result of the Restoration of Order Act, for the increasing number of convictions by

[52] Macready to Anderson, 3 November 1920. Anderson papers. The Auxiliaries also had a way of hurling thunderflashes into crowds when excited. M.C.I., Michael O'Reilly. W.O. 35 157A.
[53] *Irish Independent*, 3 November 1920.
[54] Macready to Anderson, 11 October 1920. Anderson papers.
[55] Sturgis diary, 17, 19, 24 August, 20 September 1920. P.R.O. 30 59/1,2.
[56] G.O.C.-in-C. W.S.R., 18 September 1920. S.I.C. 38, CAB.27 108. This idea so alarmed the R.I.C. that its chiefs declared they could 'win' in two months if the troops were not withdrawn. Sturgis diary, 20 September 1920. P.R.O. 30 59/2.
[57] Hankey's diary, 18 September 1920. Roskill, *Hankey*, ii. 190.
[58] Greenwood to J. T. Davies (Secretary Prime Minister's Secretariat) 20 September 1920. Lloyd George papers, F/19/2/20.
[59] C.S.I. to Ld. Privy Seal, 25 September 1920. Bonar Law papers, 102/3/24.

courts martial persuaded many extremists to go 'on the run', in other words to leave their homes and jobs and become full-time rebels. The I.R.A. had hitherto been mostly a part-time army, and though it was never to find it easy to keep forces on operations away from their homes indefinitely,[60] during September and October the British authorities realized that these wanted men were forming into a number of full-time guerrilla groups, under the title 'Active Service Units', or, more notably, 'flying columns'.[61]

The East Limerick Brigade of the I.R.A. has claimed the invention of these units, formulating during the summer of 1920 the idea of an 'efficient, disciplined, compact and swift-moving body of men which would strike at the enemy when a suitable opportunity arose'.[62] I.R.A. headquarters issued general instructions to form flying columns late in August, and some of the most celebrated formations, those of the North and West Cork Brigades, began assembling in mid-September.[63] By the end of the year there were dozens of columns, some of them raised by individual battalions, but more usually by brigades. Most of them consisted of 20 to 30 men,[64] well provided with rifles and explosives (though seldom free from the endemic shortage of ammunition). They often travelled with bicycles or light country carts, billeting on friendly—or not so friendly—farmsteads.[65]

Their appearance was the signal for operations more dangerous than raids and night attacks, and the most significant of these were ambushes. Henceforth every Crown patrol and convoy that travelled by road was in danger of attack, and though comparatively few ambushes proved really destructive, the constant menace, and the necessity of strong escorts, was a definite additional strain on the already weakened system of communications. The mounting of ambushes called for considerable skill and nerve on the part of the rebels, as they often had to stay in position for a day or more until a suitable target appeared, and thereby risked betrayal or accidental discovery. The first ambush to display such preparation took place on 20 September in west Clare, when a police tender was attacked near

[60] I am indebted to Dr D. G. Boyce for drawing my attention to this problem. Irishmen no longer 'took to the hills' with the readiness which had been common in earlier, harder times, when large rural areas sometimes passed under the control of *banditti* for months on end. Cf., e.g., G. Broeker, *Rural Disorder and Police Reform in Ireland 1812–1836* (London, 1970), p. 10.

[61] Both G.H.Q. Ireland, *Record*, i. 24, and Percival, Lecture 2, p. 16, put the appearance of flying columns in mid-October, and Macready did not mention them until even later (W.S.R., 13 November 1920. S.I.C. 55, CAB.27 108.) They had perhaps failed to perceive what was going on.

[62] Col. J. M. MacCarthy (ed.), *Limerick's Fighting Story* (Tralee, 1949), p. 86.

[63] O'Donoghue, *No Other Law*, p. 97; Barry, *Guerrilla Days in Ireland*, new edn., p. 25.

[64] This number is something of a constant in the history of guerrilla bands. Cf. E. J. Hobsbawm, *Bandits* (London, 1972), p. 20.

[65] Percival, Lecture 1, p. 17. Percival papers.

Rineen, on the road between Ennistymon and Milltown Malbay, and a District Inspector was killed.[66]

On the same day two notable attacks occurred on the other side of the country. In Balbriggan, a small town in northern Co. Dublin, a capable R.I.C. Head Constable, due to be promoted to D.I., was assassinated.[67] In Dublin itself, at Patrick Monk's bakery in Church Street, a ration party of the Duke of Wellington's Regiment was called on to surrender by a group of 'armed civilians'. The lorry escort opened fire, and the civilians withdrew; but one was found to have taken refuge under the lorry, and was arrested with a loaded revolver— the first rebel to be taken in an armed attack.[68] He was a medical student by the name of Kevin Barry.

The coincidence of these three attacks was remarkable, and their consequences were, in the favourite adjective of the Irish press, sensational. *The Times* had that day condemned the reprisals which had so far occurred in the south-west, as creating 'permanent bitterness' and weakening 'to a dangerous degree any respect that survives in Ireland for the constitutional virtues of law and order'; moreover,

so long as reprisals are committed, the public is forced to infer one of two things—either that executive authority regards them with a certain leniency or that it is powerless to stop them.[69]

Such public criticism was now given a huge target. In Balbriggan on the night of 20 September a number of policemen broke into, looted, and burned four public houses, and went on to burn or damage 49 other houses and a hosiery factory. Two 'reputed Sinn Féiners' were killed,[70] allegedly by bayonet.[71] Even this outbreak was less serious than the reprisals which began next day in Clare when the R.I.C. patrol who found the results of the Rineen ambush went on a tour of the three nearest towns, Ennistymon, Lahinch, and Milltown Malbay, burning 26 buildings, including Lahinch Town Hall, and killing four people, among them a boy who was helping to put out one of the fires.[72]

The British press resounded with denunciations of these acts, which were widely alleged to have been planned by the Government. Only the Army was exonerated, the *Observer*'s respected Irish correspondent, Stephen Gwynn, remarking that the conduct of the troops after the

---

[66] For an account free of understatement see The Kerryman, *With the I.R.A. in the Fight for Freedom* (Tralee, 1955), pp. 67f.

[67] C.S.I. Weekly Survey, 20 September 1920. S.I.C. 39, CAB.27 108.

[68] 1st Lancs. Fusiliers to H.Q. D.D., 4 October 1920. D.D. H.Q. File, W.O. 35 70.

[69] *The Times*, 20 September 1920.

[70] C.S.I. Weekly Survey, 20 September 1920. S.I.C. 39, CAB.27 108.

[71] *Irish Independent*, 22 September 1920; Bennett, *The Black and Tans*, new edn., pp. 76–7.

[72] Ibid., pp. 77–8.

5

Monk's Bakery attack showed 'that reprisals are no part of the policy of the military command'; Gwynn even suggested that martial law would be 'less barbarous and brutal and far less demoralizing than the present anarchic and futile campaign of revenge'.[73] Dublin Castle was shaken by the events. Sturgis could not see 'any middle course between punishing someone and admitting that such a job is our war policy'.[74] Greenwood, however, found one without difficulty. In public he declared that these criminal acts could not be proved to have been committed by the R.I.C. (which, as few witnesses would testify in court against the Black and Tans, they could not). To the Cabinet he admitted that the upsurge of retaliation was 'unfortunate', but said that it needed

very delicate and sympathetic handling in view of the provocation which the police have received and the extreme tension of feeling which now prevails among all ranks.[75]

Plainly put, the R.I.C. was uncontrollable. On 23 September, Sir Henry Wilson recorded in his diary, 'Tudor made it very clear that the police and the Black and Tans and the 100 Intell: officers are all carrying out reprisal murders.'

At Balbriggan, Thurles and Galway yesterday the local police marked down certain SFs as in their opinion the actual murderers or instigators and then coolly went and shot them without question or trial.

Winston saw very little harm in this but it horrifies me.[76]

Publicity and propaganda

The upsurge of reprisals was a severe test of the Government's propaganda service, a department whose weakness was constantly blamed by the Army for much of the Government's loss of public support. The Army's attitude was somewhat simplistic: it was free, for instance, from the Government's disabling belief in the liberty of the press. But it is remarkable that whereas Macready soon after his arrival set up a G.H.Q. press section to deal with military publicity matters,[77] no equivalent Government department appeared until August 1920, and it was not until the end of September that Basil Clarke[78] was 'clearly established as the head of the news bureau', as Sturgis put it.[79] Even

---

[73] 'Ireland Week by Week', *The Observer*, 26 September 1920.
[74] Sturgis diary, 23 September 1920. P.R.O. 30 59/2.
[75] C.S.I. Weekly Surveys, 20 and 27 September 1920. S.I.C. 39, 40, CAB.27 108.
[76] Wilson's diary, 23 September 1920. Wilson papers.
[77] G.H.Q. Ireland, *Record*, ii. 14–15; Macready, *Annals*, ii. 456. The press section was headed by a G.S.O. 2, Maj. R. I. Marians (not, as Macready stated, Marions).
[78] Basil Clarke, 1879–1947. *Daily Mail* War Correspondent; Director, Special Intelligence, Min. of Reconstruction, 1918; Director, Public Information, Min. of Health 1920–3 (seconded to Irish Government, 1920–2); knighted, 1923.
[79] Sturgis diary, 29 September 1920. P.R.O. 30 59/2.

then, Clarke faced great difficulties. One of them was the poor supply of information from the Crown forces. As Anderson said in defending him against Macready's criticisms, 'I do not think that he or anyone ought to be expected to create propaganda out of his own inner consciousness.'[80] A still more serious handicap was, as usual, confusion and disagreement within Dublin Castle. Not until 1921 does the structure of the propaganda section appear to have become clearly established.[81] At the Chief Secretary's conference after Balbriggan it was evident that there was no agreed line for official publicity, and that the spheres of responsibility of Clarke and the other senior Irish Office publicity men, Loughnane and Power, were undefined. Greenwood favoured Clarke and disliked Loughnane, whom he accused of 'interference'; and while the Army thought that Power's communiqués were good, Wylie thought them 'tripe'.[82] On the vital question of reprisals, Sturgis and Clarke objected to Greenwood's 'no proof' approach, and wanted complete honesty. (Clarke later drew up a manifesto of his philosophy, which he called 'publicity by news' rather than concealment or false propaganda.)[83] Greenwood assured Clarke on this occasion that he could announce that reprisals were to stop, but only four days later there was a violent military outbreak at Mallow, Co. Cork, following a brilliant raid by the North Cork I.R.A. on the barracks of the 17th Lancers. Clarke protested that he had been let down, and Greenwood had to 'jolly him out of' resignation.[84]

The 24 September conference condemned the poor public handling of the Lynch case, which was one of the first cases in which an inquest on a man who had been shot by the police was transferred from the Dublin City Coroner to a Military Court of Inquiry. The Coroner protested, and the nationalist newspapers quickly took up the cry;[85] yet Greenwood apparently believed that the publication of the military court's verdict—that Lynch had been killed by the police 'in the execution of their duty'—had 'completely dispelled' the sinister mystery that the press had tried to create.[86] The editorial attitude of

[80] Anderson to Macready, 29 March 1921. Anderson papers, C.O. 904 188/2.
[81] The most substantial and interesting material on the aims, methods, and organization of the British information service (unfortunately not used by Boyce in his *Englishmen and Irish Troubles*) is the collection in C.O. 904 168; it concerns mainly the period after Clarke's emergence as acknowledged head of the service.
[82] Sturgis diary, 24 September 1920. P.R.O. 30 59/2.
[83] His view was that 'if after every care in the accumulation of plus results and the lessening of minus results, the balance result on public opinion is not plus, . . . It is a bad case and no propaganda will win a public sanction for it.' Memorandum, 4 April 1921. C.O 904 168/2/G.H.Q.
[84] Sturgis diary, 29 September 1920. P.R.O. 30 59/2.
[85] *Irish Independent*, 25 and 27 September 1920.
[86] C.S.I. Weekly Survey, 27 September 1920. S.I.C. 40, CAB.27 108. The Court of Inquiry had been held *in camera*, and the *Independent* branded this as 'hateful Star Chamber procedure'.

the major Irish papers inevitably raised the question of censorship, but the conference decided that, although the warning already issued by Anderson against sedition ('incitement to murder or disaffection') and misrepresentation ('spreading false reports') should be enforced, nothing was to be done about 'political' material.[87] The civil government never shared the military authorities' belief in the harm done by the hostile press, or at least it was compelled by its attachment to free speech to disregard it. The Army showed constant anxiety about the effect of hostile and untruthful reportage on military morale (especially the troops' self-control),[88] but Greenwood was able, after Balbriggan, to assure Bonar Law, 'Do not believe the *Man. Guardian*, the *Daily News*, the *Westminster Gazette* or the *Daily Herald*',[89] as if ignoring this formidable catalogue of critics was a sufficient answer.

When Macready took independent action by giving a press interview in which he explained police reprisals (ignoring those by the military) as resulting from the breakdown of the legal system,[90] he was 'properly wigged' for his pains.[91] And when on 1 October Arthur Griffith issued a counterblast declaring that reprisals were not a response to provocation but a calculated terrorist plan, the Army was ordered not to move against him. Dublin Castle itself started proceedings against the *Irish News* and the *Irish Independent* for publishing the Griffith interview, but was told over the telephone by Macready:

Macready: As for the Griffith interview I have been told not to go on—haute politique—and if I may not go for the man I suppose there's no sense in going for the papers.

Sturgis: Neither Cope, Wylie or I knew that Griffith was not to be proceeded against—this is news to us.[92]

When, in December, the *Freeman's Journal* was finally prosecuted for publishing a false report, and its owner and editor both received prison sentences, the Government ordered their immediate release.[93]

The republican propaganda campaign, by contrast, was not shackled by dogmas of freedom of the press, and did not hesitate to apply its own form of censorship by intimidating reporters. Reprisals were naturally a godsend to it, and from August 1920 onwards the *Irish*

---

[87] U.S. to Editors and Proprietors, various newspapers, 27 August 1920. C.O. 904 187; Sturgis diary, 24 September 1920. P.R.O. 30 59/2.

[88] See, e.g., G.O.C. D.D. to G.H.Q., 2 December 1920. D.D. H.Q. File, W.O. 35 70; Jones, *Whitehall Diary*, iii. 26.

[89] C.S.I. to Ld. Privy Seal, 25 September 1920. Bonar Law papers, 103/3/24.

[90] Interview, Associated Press of America, 10 September 1920, *Irish Times*, 7 October 1920.

[91] Sturgis diary, 12 November 1920. P.R.O. 30 59/2.

[92] Transcript of telephone conversation, October 1920. Anderson papers, C.O. 904 188/2. Cf. Clarke's communiqué denying Griffith's allegations, 2 October 1920. C.O. 904 168/1.

[93] See below, pp. 158–9.

Bulletin published a weekly 'List of the Acts of Aggression committed in Ireland by the Police and Military of the Usurping English Government', which gave statistics and descriptions of raids, arrests, assaults, court martial sentences, 'sabotage', 'murders', and so on.[94] On 29 September the *Bulletin* issued a list of 98 reprisals which had allegedly occurred in 1920, and the only effective reply was an investigation by Major Street which was not published until 1921, and then as part of a book.[95] Street pared the list of 98 down to 18, but this was alarming enough, especially since the most destructive of them had all occurred in September. He did make the point that over the whole period only 7 civilians had been killed in reprisals, while 84 police and 12 soldiers had been killed by the I.R.A. Such arithmetic was of doubtful value, however, for as the *Manchester Guardian*—which, as Basil Clarke said, 'Right or wrong . . . in political influence at home and abroad holds foremost place'[96]—thundered on 30 September,

of what use is it to tell us, as Sir Hamar Greenwood does, in extenuation of this savagery, that somebody else of the same nationality as these poor burnt-out people murdered a policeman or a hundred policemen? That is exactly what the German commanders in Belgium said. . . .[97]

The campaign of reprisals was crystallizing the issue into one not of killings and burnings, or even of illegality by the forces of the law, but of nationalism.

The policy of reprisals

Public pressure seemed now to compel some Government action. On 28 September *The Times* warned that by his 'perilous silence' on Irish policy Lloyd George was letting the Republican case go by default.[98] The Army too was making demands. It is not clear who originated the idea of 'official reprisals', but it is first mentioned in a letter from the D.M.O. at the War Office to Wilson on 23 September.

I think the only solution to this problem is to institute a system of *official* reprisals. . . . If there is a definite scheme of reprisals in force, and made known beforehand, it should be easy to get the troops to restrain their unofficial efforts, while the deterrent effect on the Sinn Fein [*sic*] cannot be inconsiderable.[99]

This dubious theme was taken up by Macready, who wrote to Greenwood on 27 September demanding the authorization of full-scale

---

[94] For instance, the weekly total of raids was 290 at the end of August and 3,197 at the end of November. In the same period alleged armed assaults increased from 26 to 46 a week.

[95] Street, *The Administration of Ireland 1920*, Ch. XI *passim*.

[96] Clarke to Loughnane, 17 September 1920. C.O. 904 168/2.

[97] *Manchester Guardian*, 30 September 1920.

[98] *The Times*, 28 September 1920.

[99] Maj. Gen. Radcliffe (D.M.O.) to C.I.G.S., 23 September 1920, W.O. 32 9537.

arrests of the I.R.A. (a notable reversion to French's ideas) in order to maintain the morale of the troops,[100] and to Wilson on the 28th outlining a plan for official reprisals. He argued that, whatever one felt about the indiscipline which had produced them, one could not ignore the fact that

> where reprisals have taken place, the whole atmosphere of the surrounding district has changed from one of hostility to one of cringing submission.[101]

People were even touching their caps to officers in Galway after a recent outbreak; and, more constructively, they were beginning to give information. What Macready now proposed was that houses from which shots were fired, or whose occupants 'must be well aware' of the presence of an ambush, should be destroyed 'as a military operation'.

On 29 September Wilson put this idea to Lloyd George, without undue refinement. The Prime Minister 'danced' and said that no Government could take such responsibility.[102] In fact, he disliked both responsibility and burnings, which too often affected landlords as much as rebels, and on 1 October the Cabinet ordered that reprisals 'by burning' should cease.[103] But Lloyd George made it clear to Macready that he still favoured 'gunning', and he evidently believed that the indiscipline of the R.I.C. could be discreetly channelled in this desirable direction. Sturgis was somewhat taken aback to learn from Lady Greenwood on 3 October that the Prime Minister was 'immensely pleased with the trend of events',[104] and if Greenwood's public condemnation of reprisals on 30 September was unconvincing,[105] the R.I.C. order on the subject on 4 October was positively ambiguous. 'Destruction of buildings' it deprecated as increasing 'want and disorder', but it declared that the use of weapons when threatened was 'only legitimate self-defence', and that the duty of the police was 'to hunt down murderers by every means in their power'.[106] In the circumstances, 'every legal means' might have been a more appropriate phrase.

The Government was now singleminded in its defence of R.I.C. activities, though Dublin Castle remained hesitant. When a big reprisal occurred at Tubbercurry, Co. Sligo, on 6 October, the Castle took the

[100] Memo by G.O.C.-in-C., in memo by C.S.I., 28 September 1920. Bonar Law papers, 103/3/27.
[101] G.O.C.-in-C. Ireland to C.I.G.S., 28 September 1920. Copy in Anderson papers, C.O. 904 188/1.
[102] Callwell, *Wilson*, ii. 263.
[103] Cabinet Conference, 1 October 1920. C.53A(20), CAB.23 23.
[104] Sturgis diary, 3 October 1920. P.R.O. 30 59/2.
[105] *Irish Independent*, 1 October 1920.
[106] R.I.C. Circular Orders by Deputy Inspector General, 4 October 1920. Published in *Irish Times*, 4 October 1920.

unusual step of issuing an explanatory communiqué, which stated that after a popular officer, D.I. Brady, had been killed with expanding ammunition his men 'broke out of hand', and

rushed out into the street calling on the Sinn Féiners to come out and fight them like men. Reprisals continued till early in the morning, despite the efforts of the officers. The men were eventually got into police lorries, and while final instructions were being given by the officer, the lorries moved off, and a creamery in the neighbourhood was burned.[107]

Republican propaganda alleged that there was a British campaign to destroy the creameries owned by the agricultural co-operative societies,[108] but up till now not a single instance had been admitted by the authorities.[109] Tubbercurry was thus a radical development. Even if it did not make the idea of a campaign seem much more likely, it was explosive political ammunition. And shortly afterwards Arthur Henderson[110] put down a motion of censure calling for an independent investigation into reprisals. The debate on this motion, on 20 October, strikingly demonstrated Greenwood's determination to battle against unpalatable facts, and his powers of histrionic oratory. He admitted that there had been some reprisals, but concentrated on describing the rebel provocation which had made the policemen 'see red'. He dealt with Balbriggan and Ennistymon, and, turning to Tubbercurry, described how the constables

saw Brady lying on the floor. They knew him. They loved him. Soldiers and policemen trained under the British flag love their officers. They so love them that they go to their death for them. I admit that when they saw Brady's form on the ground they saw red. I admit there was a reprisal.[111]

He would not admit that a creamery had been burned, however. Not only this, but he made the unequivocal declaration that he had 'never seen a tittle of evidence to prove' that Crown forces had destroyed any creamery.[112] His nerve was impressive, but, as H. A. L. Fisher noted, he 'skated on thin ice';[113] and it was breaking beneath him with every stride.

The military authorities were merely irritated by Greenwood's rhetorical protestations, and continued to press the idea of regularizing reprisals.[114] In order to stress the urgency of the matter they were even prepared to admit that

[107] Irish Government statement, *Irish Times*, 7 October 1920.
[108] Cf. e.g., George Russell ('Æ'), 'A Plea for Justice . . .', *Irish Homestead*, Dublin, 1920.
[109] Cf. Sturgis diary, 23 September 1920. P.R.O. 39 59/2.
[110] Deputy Laeder of the Labour Party; headed Labour Commission to Irelandat the end of 1920.
[111] Speech of C.S.I., 20 October 1920. 133 H.C. Deb. 5s, col. 943.
[112] Ibid., col. 948.
[113] H. A. L. Fisher's diary, 19 [sic] October 1920. Fisher papers.
[114] Macready, *Annals*, ii, 465; G.O.C.-in-C. Ireland to C.I.G.S., 17 October 1920. G.H.Q. Ireland, *Record*, i. 23.

the troops are getting out of control, taking the law into their own hands, and that besides clumsy and indiscriminate destruction, actual thieving and looting as well as drunkenness and gross disorder are occurring.[115]

Churchill reluctantly agreed to put the proposal to the Cabinet, but when it was discussed on 10 November the Cabinet concluded that the time was 'inopportune' for a decision: instead, the Chief Secretary was to 'do all in his power' to prevent troops and police from burning houses and creameries.[116] Unfortunately Greenwood had to report that week that 'violent counter-attacks on property' had caused extensive destruction in Nenagh, Thurles, Littleton, Granard, Athlone, and Longford.[117]

None the less the Army was encouraged by two other developments, the death of Terence MacSwiney and the execution of Kevin Barry. MacSwiney, the Lord Mayor of Cork and Commandant of the Cork No. 1 Brigade, I.R.A., had been on hunger-strike since his arrest on 12 August. In spite of the international attention focused on his long-drawn-out martyrdom, the Government refused to release him, and he died on 25 October. Two other men on a less publicized fast in Cork gaol also died,[118] and Arthur Griffith thereupon suspended the policy of hunger-striking.[119] The execution of Barry did not have such conclusive results, partly because of widespread sympathy aroused by his youth and his lack of political extremism.[120] He became a timeless symbol of the Irish rebel, 'a young lad of eighteen summers', as his still-popular ballad runs, 'who fought to free old Ireland on that bright September morn'.

A rebel of a more substantial sort, the dashing gunman Seán Treacy, had also died, in a gun battle in Talbot Street, Dublin, on 20 October; and the succession of deaths seems to have begun to have had a considerable moral effect on Michael Collins.[121] The I.R.A. at large, however, was in no great difficulties. Although the formation of flying columns was in theory an advantage to the Crown Forces, in that they provided definite targets for regular operations, the rebels remained able to move and disperse at will. Thus when a military patrol (30 strong) surprised an ambush of 60 rebels near Bandon, Co. Cork, on

[115] Memo by Sec. of State for War, (?)3 November 1920, holograph attachment to Cabinet, 10 November 1920. C.59A(20), CAB.23 23. For dating, see Jones, *Whitehall Diary*, iii. 41. These remarkable military admissions were never made elsewhere.
[116] Cabinet, 10 November 1920. C.59A(20), CAB.23 23.
[117] C.S.I. Weekly Survey, 8 November 1920. S.I.C. 52, CAB.27 108.
[118] Michael Fitzgerald and Joseph Murphy (not Murray, as Macardle states); cf. *Cork Examiner*, 29 October 1920.
[119] Macardle, *The Irish Republic*, p. 360.
[120] Barry had not wished to become involved in the fighting, and for this reason Michael Collins was particularly shaken by his capture and death. Cf. Forester, *Michael Collins*, p. 174.
[121] Ibid.

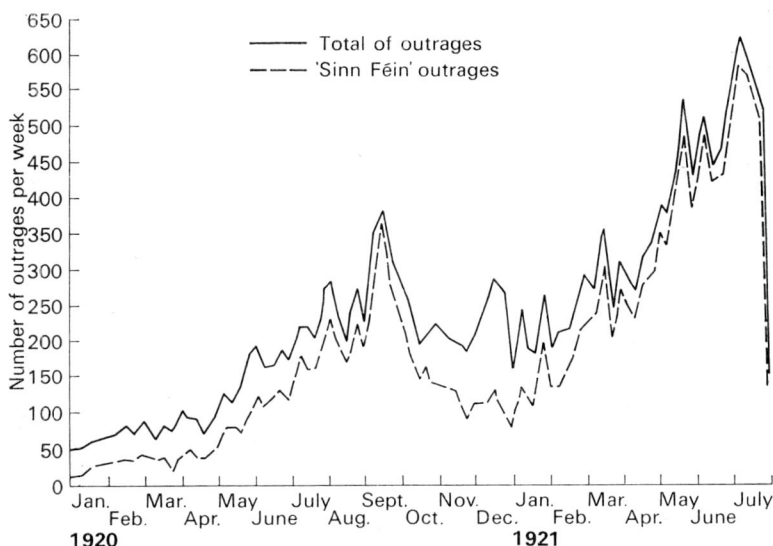

R.I.C. Statistics of Outrages (i.e. political crimes) 1920–21
(Based on figures in C.O. 904 150.)

4 October, it succeeded only in scattering them with a few losses;[122] and the I.R.A. struck back six days later by ambushing a patrol at Newcestown, killing an officer and wounding four men.[123] And although the overall total of I.R.A. operations fell from the prodigious peak of September (see graph, above), the proportion of serious attacks increased. November 1920 showed the lowest overall total since June, but it produced two of the most dramatic rebel successes of the whole conflict.

12. THE INTELLIGENCE GAP: BLOODY SUNDAY AND KILMICHAEL (October–November 1920)

Military planning and Government policy
None of the methods adopted since the spring of 1920 had prevented the military situation from worsening. In late September, when Macready announced the necessity of greater military control, he produced his only strategic plan to have survived. It was based on a four-stage sweep across Ireland: Macready proposed, by interning all members of the I.R.A. (not just those proven guilty of crimes), to

[122] G.O.C.-in-C. W.S.R., 9 October 1920. S.I.C. 45, CAB.27 108.
[123] The unit involved was the 1st Essex Regiment; for a first-hand account of the ambush see Percival, Lecture I, pp. 17–18.

'clear' first the major cities, second the main railway lines, third the worst areas of the south-west, and finally the remaining rural areas.[124] This plan can best be described as insubstantial. It did not discuss the critical problem of how such extensive clearances were to be mounted, let alone of how to keep the 'cleared' areas clear. It would certainly have depended on the creation of an effective system of identity checks, such as had been demanded by Tudor on 23 July, and the Cabinet did not bring itself to order even a preliminary investigation of such a scheme until 10 November, the day on which it shelved the proposal of regular military reprisals.[125]

The plan did none the less make the point that 'the first essential if we are to obtain success is to seize the initiative and assume the offensive', and that it was useless to limit the offensive to the rebel leaders, who could escape too easily. 'Our objective', Macready said, 'must be formations or units of the I.R.A.'[126] The Government was not yet ready for this return to Lord French's approach. Its policy was still defined in the Restoration of Order Act and the Government of Ireland Bill, and Lord Midleton's proposal that Balfour should be made British plenipotentiary to negotiate with all parties in Ireland was rejected by Bonar Law as 'another move in the direction of surrender'.[127] But, as Midleton wrote despairingly to Curzon on 4 November, there was 'hardly a line of the Bill with which Southerners, Nationalist or Unionist, Sinn Féin, Clerical or lay agree . . .'.[128] Partition, anathema to all these groups, was fast becoming a reality. In mid-September, to Sturgis's disappointment, a separate Under Secretary was placed in Belfast, 'another little king' standing in the way of unified command.[129] On 22 October, after much dissension, it was announced that a Special Constabulary would be recruited, theoretically from loyalists all over Ireland.[130] In practice the 'Specials' appeared only in Ulster, and their formation had been outspokenly opposed by the Castle group. Macready saw it as the 'raising of Carson's army from the grave'.[131]

The less public of the Government's methods remained. In October, Mark Sturgis was briefed by the Minister of Transport, Eric Geddes, on a plan to 'throttle the railway system' in response to the munitions embargo, and he became chairman of a special committee to ad-

[124] Military Appreciation of the Situation in Ireland on 26 September 1920. (G.O.C.-in-C. Ireland.) Bonar Law papers, 103/3/26.
[125] Cabinet, 10 November 1920, conclusion (a). C.59A(20), CAB.23 23.
[126] Military Appreciation, 26 September 1920. Loc. cit.
[127] Bonar Law to Lloyd George, 7 October 1920. Lloyd George papers, F/31/1/47.
[128] Midleton to Curzon, 4 November 1920. Midleton papers.
[129] Sturgis diary, 14 September 1920. P.R.O. 30 59/2.
[130] Classified as A, B, and C Specials according to terms of service. See Street, *The Administration of Ireland 1920*, 297–8.
[131] Macready to Anderson, 18 June 1920. Anderson papers.

minister it.[132] Though Sturgis himself was only anxious to restore normal working, there seems to have been some basis for the *Freeman's Journal's* cry that Ireland was being starved into submission by a 'Geddes–Greenwood plot'.[133] This impression was reinforced by the now frequent burning of factories and creameries, and by such reprisals as the 'blockade' of Tralee, when the R.I.C. cut the town's communications from 30 October to 10 November.[134]

The organization of intelligence

But in any case the fundamental handicap to an open offensive like that proposed by Macready was still the intelligence gap, a two-way mirror behind which the rebels moved with almost complete assurance. After the formation of flying columns I.R.A. terrorism became more stringent to cover their increased vulnerability, and the execution of 'spies and informers'—whose corpses were left, suitably placarded, in public view, to inspire a belief in the I.R.A.'s omniscience—became frequent occurrences.[135] The Irish Command manual 'Sinn Féin and the Irish Volunteers', issued in October 1920, paid ample tribute to the degree of popular co-operation achieved by the rebels. 'It may be taken for granted', it said,

that every move of military or police detachments on patrol, escorts, etc., and every guard are carefully watched at all times . . . and that the slightest slackness is detected and leads to attack.[136]

It was simple observation, carried out by countless Volunteers and sympathizers, that was at least as important to the I.R.A. as espionage. It put the Crown forces at a basic operational disadvantage which they could seldom overcome, for, as Dublin District's 1921 general instructions put it, 'a "bow wave" of suspicion precedes any but the most rapidly moving force.'[137] And even if a raid or search operation achieved surprise, the problem of distinguishing wanted men from innocent civilians proved almost insuperable.

The Crown intelligence system needed to be well-organized and expertly staffed. A single functional and effective intelligence service would have gone a long way towards overcoming the divisions between the military and police, and the creation of a joint intelligence chief in May 1920 should have led to this. A full explanation of why

[132] Sturgis diary, 11 October 1920. P.R.O. 30 59/2. The entries for 18 and 22 October, and 9 November, throw further light on this campaign.
[133] *Freeman's Journal*, 16 November 1920.
[134] *Irish Times*, 11 November 1920; Phillips, *The Revolution in Ireland*, p. 188.
[135] For a fairly candid account of these actions in the West Cork area see Barry, *Guerrilla Days in Ireland*, pp. 100–5.
[136] G.H.Q. Ireland, 'Sinn Féin and the Irish Volunteers', confidential manual issued October 1920. 79/Irish/708, W.O. 32 4308.
[137] 26th(P) Bde. Instructions, W.O. 35 93(1)/4.

Winter did not succeed is still impossible. From the evidence so far available, it appears that he failed to gain the approval of the military authorities or to win the complete allegiance of the secret service, and the reasons seem to have been partly personal: in this sphere, as G.H.Q. remarked, 'unfortunately personal considerations can rarely be left out of account.'[138] The main military objection to the police intelligence system had always been its reliance on personal knowledge and intuition rather than formal organization, and its shunning of the distinction between the intelligence functions 'Ia', 'Ib' and 'Ix'.[139] The Army thought that Winter was guilty of the same tendency to confuse the departments of intelligence work. In April 1921 Macready was to express to Anderson the opinion that Winter 'is, I fancy, a "born sleuth", but I doubt his organizing power, and that . . . is what is holding up the machine'.[140]

Winter's rather diffuse autobiography offers only a vague explanation of his delay in forming a central organization. He speaks of 'disruptive elements seeking to obtain some temporary advantage', and of the lack of office space until Tudor's H.Q. (of which Winter's organization was a part) moved into the Castle in October 1920.[141] The Army, however, saw this move as itself a serious mistake, leading Winter to

see Dublin out of all proportion and to act in some respects as a local centre,[142] in others as a County Inspector, rather than in his proper capacity.[143]

It also criticized his basic method as an attempt

to build up, bit by bit, a machine that will fit given circumstances, rather than adopting a sound machine and adjusting it so that it will suit circumstances. The result was an extraordinarily complex and involved organization.[144]

Winter himself was a figure to grace any spy thriller: a monocle sat in his eye and a cigarette hung from his lips; he was universally called by his adopted code-name 'O'. 'He looks like a wicked little white snake,' Sturgis wrote, 'is clever as paint, probably entirely non-moral, a first-class horseman, a card genius, knows several languages': all in all, 'a

[138] G.H.Q. Ireland, Record, ii. 19.
[139] Ibid., ii. 23. These are the main categories on which military intelligence organization is based: Ia, service of information; Ib, security (counter-intelligence); Ix, organization and administration.
[140] Macready to Anderson, 8 April 1921. Anderson papers, C.O. 904 188/2. Cf. p. 169 below.
[141] Winter, Winter's Tale, p. 302.
[142] Intelligence co-ordination units set up late in 1920.
[143] G.H.Q. Ireland, Record, ii. 20.
[144] Ibid., ii. 10. Cf. Brigadier Kitson's recent observation that it is 'much more difficult to turn an ineffective intelligence organization into an effective one at a later stage in the campaign than it is to build up a good one in the first place'. F. Kitson, Low Intensity Operations (London, 1971), p. 81.

most amazing original'.[145] But by mid-September Sturgis was wondering 'why "O" grouses so much about the jealousy of other branches', since according to Macready 'he has only to go ahead and make himself top dog.'[146] By late October it was clear that he was not doing so,[147] and in November an investigation of 'O's show' was begun by Cope, who was not pleased with what he found.[148] Eventually, on 17 December, a Castle conference decided to reduce Winter's responsibilities. Sturgis felt that he had not become 'enough of an idol to his people', and that they were not working as a loyal team.[149] Macready wrote to Anderson that 'the great point will be for O. to keep his finger off what may be called purely military intelligence and devote himself to the tracking of criminals.'[150] With this the idea of a single intelligence service disappeared.

All the means of obtaining or utilizing information suffered from this. Winter's overlordship did little to overcome the problems of the secret service, and the most effective unit, Dublin District Special Branch, naturally tended to associate with the Dublin military authorities. Its transference to Winter's direct control in 1921 (it became part of 'D' Branch, Chief of Police Office) was to produce a good deal of personal friction,[151] although it seems that in late 1920 its chief acknowledged his subordination to Winter 'courteously and clearly' enough.[152] In any case, however, owing to the exceptionally difficult circumstances in Ireland, secret service was, despite the often daring efforts of local officers and their men,[153] less significant as a source of information than regular raids and searches. The great mass of intelligence material came from prisoners and documents; interrogation of the former providing 'hot' information on which immediate operations could be based, and compilation of the latter building a framework for raid planning.[154] Raids had been curtailed in May 1920, but were again running at about 10 per day in Dublin by October.[155] A Central Raid Bureau (C.R.B.), created by Winter with clerical staff screened by Scotland Yard, began at last to function in November.[156] It aimed to compile and correlate all documents seized in raids, though it did not find it easy to induce raiding units to take documents which were not

[145] Sturgis diary, 1 September 1920. P.R.O. 30 59/2.
[146] Ibid., 15 September 1920.
[147] Ibid., 27 October 1920.
[148] Ibid., 19 November 1920.
[149] Ibid., 17 December 1920. P.R.O. 30 59/3.
[150] Macready to Anderson, 18 December 1920. Anderson papers, C.O. 904 188/2.
[151] G.H.Q. Ireland, Record, ii. 19.
[152] Sturgis diary, 21 November 1920. P.R.O. 30 59/2.
[153] Some cases can be seen in the medal citations of 12 July 1921, in W.O. 35 181. Cf. Macready, Annals, ii. 462.
[154] G.H.Q. Ireland, Record, ii. 26.
[155] Daily Raid Reports, D.D. H.Q. File, W.O. 35 70.
[156] Winter, Winter's Tale, p. 303; G.H.Q. Ireland, Record, ii. 10.

of local interest, or to send on to the C.R.B. those which were. Photo-copying machines were not provided until December, and then only at divisional level.[157] The C.R.B. made epitomes of all documents and circulated these to units, which could order full copies of originals. But even the epitomes often ran to one or two hundred foolscap pages, and G.H.Q. felt that 'with a proper I(x) branch for all intelligence, this procedure could have been simplified.'[158]

Raid technique
By October the difficulty of conducting raids had become noticeably greater. Wanted men were showing more determination in resisting arrest and in laying traps for raiders. On 19 October, raid parties were increased from 12 to 20, and were ordered to expect resistance.[159] Another problem, which could not be so easily solved, was that more ingenuity was being shown in concealing arms and documents in houses, and many hiding-places escaped discovery.[160] None the less the G.O.C. Dublin District felt able to claim on 5 November that

(a) Owing to the courtesy shown by troops, civilians are beginning to realize that, when innocent, they have nothing to fear from a military raid.
(b) Owing to the frequent Military and Police raids, the rebel leaders are continually on the run.
(c) Owing to experience gained from such affrays as at Fernside and Talbot St., and the sound tactical principles displayed by military raiding parties, ill-disposed civilians now hesitate to conceal dangerous rebels.[161]

This claim seems to have been generally justified, although the citing of the 'Fernside' incident as a success is rather peculiar. This raid on a Drumcondra house on the night of 11 October resulted in the escape of both wanted men involved, Seán Treacy and Dan Breen, and even if the slaughter of troops was not quite so heavy as suggested in Breen's own colourful account,[162] both the owner of the house and one of the

---

[157] G.H.Q.I. to D.D., 5th and 6th Divs., 6 December 1920. D.D. H.Q. File, W.O. 35 70; G.H.Q. Ireland, *Record*, ii. 11.
[158] G.H.Q. Ireland, *Record*, ii. 13.
[159] D.D. Orders, 19 October 1920; G.H.Q. I. to D.D., 5th and 6th Divs., 20 October 1920. D.D. H.Q. File, W.O. 35 70.
[160] Few regimental officers had any training in search methods; for instance, on 9 November 'an intelligence officer with a knowledge of searching' went over a house which had been pronounced clean after a raid, and found a revolver, a rifle, a rifle grenade, a stick of gelignite, a box of detonators, 56 rounds of ammunition, together with other equipment and a mass of documents, 'hidden in and around the door'. H.Q. D.D. to 24th and 25th(P) Bdes., 10 November 1920. D.D. H.Q. File, W.O. 35 70.
[161] Special Order by G.O.C. D.D., 5 November 1920. D.D. War Diary 'D', W.O. 35 90/1.
[162] Breen, *My Fight for Irish Freedom*, pp. 137–47, described how he and Treacy fought their way through a party of troops with grenades and an armoured car with machine guns.

officers in charge of the raid were killed. The former, moreover, did not die instantly, but made a deathbed statement in hospital that he had been deliberately shot by the raiding party.[163] The affair may well have discouraged people from sheltering rebels, but the general impression can hardly have been one of tactical skill on the part of the Army.

The arrival of the first A.D.R.I.C. companies in September and October promised to provide forces that were especially suited to mounting raids and rapid searches.[164] But the history of these units illustrated both the crippling effect of the poor Crown intelligence service and the inherent dangers of independence and weak discipline. Three companies were allotted to Dublin District, which proved more successful than other military divisions in maintaining operational control over them, partly because the Auxiliaries showed a greater inclination to obedience under the direct eye of Dublin Castle. Even so there was uneasiness about their arrogant conduct and their tendency to mount raids and patrols without reference to their nominal superiors.[165] In rural areas their virtual independence did little to discourage slackness and casual brutality, and though some companies, with strong and capable officers, did gain striking successes, in general the formidable potential of the force was seldom realized. During the last fortnight of November, Auxiliary slackness and indiscipline contributed to the dramatic events which led to the declaration of martial law.

Bloody Sunday and Kilmichael

The first of these events was the culmination of the long struggle of the two opposing intelligence services in Dublin, whose details are still shrouded by fear. On the morning of Sunday, 21 November 1920, groups formed from Michael Collins's 'Squad' (sometimes called the Dublin Brigade Active Service Unit) and the Dublin Brigade of the I.R.A. entered eight Dublin houses and shot dead 12 British officers, wounding several more.[166] According to Republican claims, all the victims were secret service agents, members of the notorious 'Cairo gang'.[167] Although this claim is undoubtedly exaggerated—several mistakes were made by the gunmen, owing partly to nervousness—the British counter-claim that they were ordinary regimental officers was

---

[163] Statement to a priest, reported in *Irish Independent*, 21 October 1920.

[164] Cf. note on Attachment of I and J Coys. A.D.R.I.C., D.D. Orders, 24 November 1920. D.D. War Diary 'D', W.O. 35 90/1.

[165] Note by H.Q. D.D., 6 November 1920; G.O.C. D.D. to O.s.C. I and F Coys. A.D.R.I.C., 20 December 1920. D.D. H.Q. File, W.O. 35 70.

[166] See the police reports, Cases A–H, in Street, *The Administration of Ireland 1920*, pp. 150–7; for list of casualties see *Freeman's Journal*, etc., 22 November 1920.

[167] See, e.g., R. Taylor, *Michael Collins* (London, 1958), p. 30.

even less justified,[168] and G.H.Q. later admitted that Dublin District Special Branch was 'temporarily paralysed' by the attacks.[169]

The news of the shootings created an electric atmosphere in the capital. The Irish Executive met at the Castle and, by a few brief decisions, put the whole counter-insurgency campaign on a new footing. Internment on suspicion was restored, curfews were extended, and a massive programme of road blocks, searches and arrests was set on foot.[170] Military personnel were at last prohibited from living outside barracks and the outside areas were declared no man's land.[171] Within a week 500 arrests were made. Arthur Griffith himself was arrested on Major-General Boyd's orders, and contrary to political instructions.[172] But the intensive searches did not produce many captures of weapons, and the Army recognized that unless pressure were kept up 'the rank and file of the I.R.A. will quickly reorganize.'[173] The spate of activity after 21 November overrode the Army's earlier intention of withdrawing detachments into winter quarters for training; it also channelled the tension of the Crown Forces away from illegal retaliation.

There were, remarkably, few reprisals for the 21 November attacks. Writers habitually refer to the Croke Park incident, which took place that afternoon and gave the whole day the name 'Bloody Sunday', as a reprisal, but this is to distort the term unacceptably. The incident began as a regular search operation based on the correct assumption that many I.R.A. men would be spending the afternoon at the big match at Croke Park football stadium. The idea that the rebels could actually be seized from the stadium was admittedly facile, and the operation became a fiasco when the A.D.R.I.C. search party drove up before the military cordon had been completed. Amid the welter of accusations about who started the shooting, it is perhaps wise to keep silence, except to say that the official account, which stated that warning shots were fired by I.R.A. scouts, is far from being the most improbable.[174] Confused allegations that the 'Black and Tans' fired rifles and even machine guns into the crowd at close range for ten minutes are hard to

---

[168] For the claim see Winter, *Winter's Tale*, p. 321; for first-hand contrary evidence see Mrs. Woodcock, *Experiences of an Officer's Wife in Ireland*, pp. 11, 68–9. The most thorough examination of the intelligence officers involved, with many interesting sidelights, is T. Bowden, 'Bloody Sunday—A Reappraisal', *European Studies Review*, ii. No. 1 (1972), pp. 25–42.

[169] G.H.Q. Ireland, *Record*, ii. 18.

[170] U.S. to C.S.I., 21 November 1920. Anderson papers.

[171] D.D. War Diary, 23 November 1920. W.O. 35 90/1.

[172] Lloyd George called this 'a piece of impertinence' by the military, and nearly countermanded it. Jones, *Whitehall Diary*, iii. 46.

[173] G.O.C.-in-C. W.S.R., 27 November 1920. S.I.C. 59, CAB.27 108.

[174] C.S.O. Report, C.O. 904 168; for Republican accounts see Macardle, *The Irish Republic*, p. 366; Younger, *Ireland's Civil War*, p. 113; Gleeson, *Bloody Sunday*, Ch. 9 passim.

reconcile with the total of 12 people killed and 11 seriously wounded, many not by gunshot but in the ensuing stampede. Even the official account, however, admitted that the police fired into the grandstand and ground for three minutes until 'the attackers' fire was silenced'.[175] At the very least this must be regarded as culpably dangerous use of weapons, and there is little reason to doubt that for a time the Auxiliaries were out of effective control. Croke Park was perhaps the most unfortunate of all the incidents which resulted from their general instability.

Somewhat different was the final dramatic event of November— the ambushing and annihilation of an A.D.R.I.C. patrol near Kilmichael, Co. Cork, a week after Bloody Sunday. It owed a good deal to their operational slackness, because the Macroom company had taken to sending patrols on almost fixed routes.[176] The slaughter of 16 Cadets in an area which had been quiet for some time, and which had come to look on the A.D.R.I.C. as, in Tom Barry's words, 'super-fighters and all but invincible',[177] was a notable triumph for Barry's West Cork flying column, and a comment upon the inefficacy of the measures so far taken against the rebels.[178] West Cork trembled in anticipation of Auxiliary reprisals. These did not come, however. The shock of Kilmichael numbed the police; and it was the Government which was to make the most significant response to this latest crisis.

[175] C.S.O. Report, C.O. 904 168. A neutral account which makes some use of the official view is Bennett, *The Black and Tans*, p. 127.
[176] 'The Auxiliary's Story', in Gleeson, *Bloody Sunday*, p. 70.
[177] Barry, *Guerrilla Days in Ireland*, p. 39; C.S.I. Weekly Survey, 29 November 1920. S.I.C. 58, CAB.27 108.
[178] For a good account of the action see Butler, *Barry's Flying Column*, pp. 63–7; see also the map of the ambush by Lt. and 3rd D.I. Fleming, C Coy. A.D.R.I.C., 25 January 1921. Hemming papers.

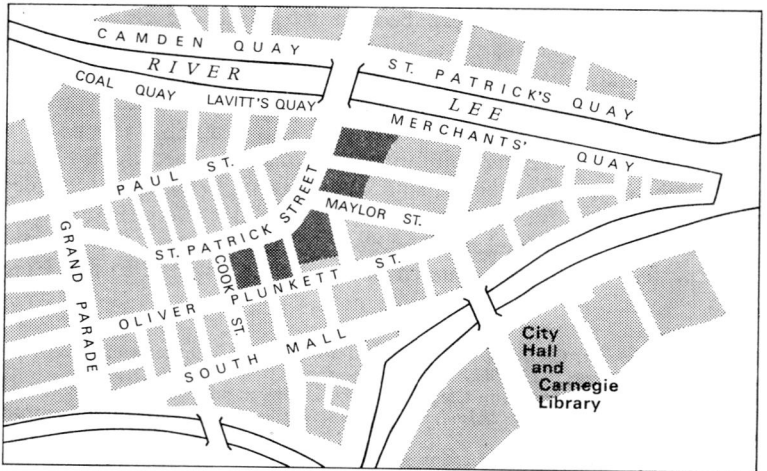

Map 4: The Burnings in Cork, 11 December 1920
(based on map in the *Irish Times*, 16 December 1920)

Areas of greatest destruction shaded between Cook Street and Merchants'
Quay. (See p. 138).

V

MARTIAL LAW

'Not only is the use of force not singly directed, but even as between the three
elements now existing there is little evidence of effective cooperation.'
Sir Warren Fisher, February 1921

13. MILITARY RULE CIRCUMSCRIBED (December 1920)

The proclamation of martial law

GENERAL MACREADY had been on leave in the south of France
since before Bloody Sunday—'a queer bad chance', Sturgis
reflected that day.[1] On 1 December after Kilmichael, he wrote
to Major-General Jeudwine, who had moved from the Curragh to
Dublin to take his place, that he could not understand 'Why on earth
they don't proclaim M.L. . . . unless it is that Hamar is afraid of losing
importance.'[2] That same day, however, the Cabinet was in fact
deciding, because of 'the recent outrage near Cork, which partook of a
more definitely military character than its predecessors', that the Chief
Secretary should apply martial law 'in such particular areas as he might
consider it necessary',[3] and Greenwood himself was already conferring
with Jeudwine in Dublin. Henry Wilson commented tartly,

Greenwood inferred that he had always been in favour of it and so did Winston
their only doubt being whether we had enough troops! What amazing liars.[4]

Greenwood appeared at first to have an open mind on the areas to
be considered. On 1 December, according to Jeudwine's report of their
meeting, Greenwood asked him

(a) Was I in favour of the application of Martial Law? To this I answered 'Yes'.
(b) If so, should martial law be proclaimed over the whole of Ireland? I answered
'Yes'.[5]

When Greenwood put further questions about what areas should be
brought under the 'full scope' of martial law, and what troops would be

---

[1] Sturgis diary, 21 November 1920. P.R.O. 30 59/3.
[2] Macready to Jeudwine, 1 December 1920. Jeudwine papers, I.W.M. 72/82/2.
[3] Cabinet, 1 December 1920. C.65A(20), CAB.23 23.
[4] Wilson's diary, 30 November 1920. Wilson papers. He added, 'My own opinion is
that we shall require less troops with Martial Law than under the present miserable
régime which is neither one thing nor another.'
[5] Acting G.O.C.-in-C. Ireland to C.I.G.S., 2 December 1920. Jeudwine papers.

needed to enforce it, Jeudwine reserved his answers until he had conferred with the other divisional commanders. Two days later he concluded that martial law was most required in the area of 6th Division, and that 6th Division would need four extra battalions in the first instance;[6] but he maintained the principle that martial law must be proclaimed, and thus usable if needed, over the whole country. In this, which was to become a major bone of contention between the Army and the Government, he was fully supported by Sir Henry Wilson, who warned him that 'It is quite in accordance with the usual practice of the "Frocks" to get a *locum tenens* to push off an enterprise without the knowledge and consent of his superior.'[7]

The Army expected many improvements to come with martial law. Jeudwine listed the attendant advantages as follows:

1. Unity of command (control of police, reprisals etc.).
2. Promptitude in action and administration.
3. Heavy sentences for carrying or being in possession of arms.
4. Heavy sentences for harbouring known rebels.
5. Restriction of movement.
6. Identification of individuals.
7. Control of the press.
8. Internment of *suspects* at discretion of Military Governor.
9. Moral effect.[8]

And when Major-General Boyd worried lest, in using martial law, 'our last reserve' was being committed prematurely, and might, if it failed, damage morale further, Jeudwine replied firmly that any drawbacks would be outweighed by one great advantage—unity of command.[9] But for the Government this military recipe was a good deal too unsubtle. Whatever he might say to Jeudwine, Greenwood had already decided against proclaiming the whole country, for Churchill told the Cabinet on 1 December that he and Greenwood had informed Wilson that such a course would 'wreck the scheme'.[10] The Cabinet did not inquire into their reasoning, nor did it pay much attention to the advice of Lord Milner—the only minister who had run a country under martial law—that 'unless you apply it to a sufficiently wide area your attempt to get arms will fail'.[11] When Greenwood and Jeudwine met again on 5 December, Jeudwine found that 'in spite of my reply to him when the subject was first mooted' the Chief Secretary now affected

[6] 'G' War Diary, G.H.Q. Ireland, 4 December 1920. W.O. 35 93(1)/1.
[7] C.I.G.S. to Acting G.O.C.-in-C. Ireland, 1 December 1920. Jeudwine papers.
[8] Holograph note, 1 December 1920. Jeudwine papers.
[9] Note by Maj. Gen. Boyd, n.d. (3/4 December 1920), and reply by Maj. Gen. Jeudwine, n.d. Ibid.
[10] Cabinet, 1 December 1920. Jones, *Whitehall Diary*, iii. 42.
[11] Ibid. Milner was High Commissioner for South Africa from 1897 to 1905.

surprise at the idea of proclaiming the whole country,[12] and 'exerted some pressure towards inducing a reconsideration'.[13]

Jeudwine held out, however, and felt that eventually 'our arguments told'; he gave Greenwood a memorandum agreeing to implement martial law on this condition and a number of others, including the introduction of press censorship, systems of passports and identity controls (compulsory lists of the occupants of buildings, and voluntary identity cards), greater assistance from the Navy, outlawry of certain rebels, and the internment of 5,000 or more members of the I.R.A.[14] Proclamations were then drawn up declaring that 'a state of armed insurrection' existed, and placing the Irish garrison on active service. But when the martial law schedules were printed, on 8 December, it transpired that the Government was limiting the measure to four counties, Cork, Kerry, Limerick, and Tipperary.[15] When he discovered this, Jeudwine was highly dissatisfied. He could do nothing, however, for Macready returned to London at this point and accepted the restriction. On 11 December Macready wrote apologetically to Jeudwine saying, 'I fully realize the difficulty this partial application of martial law means, but the "frocks" were firm not to impose it all over.' Instead,

I managed to extract from them a decision that in the event of my considering it necessary, after consultation with the civil authorities, to extend the area, I can do so at once without waiting for Cabinet sanction. This is good enough for me.[16]

When Lord French signed the Lord Lieutenant's proclamation of martial law on 10 December (it was published on the 11th[17]) he declared unequivocally that it was folly to leave Dublin outside the proclaimed area.[18] At that point the Irish Executive thought that the omission would soon be rectified, but within a few days it became clear how different the Government's plans were from those of the Army. On 14 December Sturgis remarked that while the soldiers were expecting 'to have full control of everything in two two's', and their watchword was 'No more damn civilians',

The P.M.'s idea, which they have not grasped, is to have martial law in the distant provinces, as a cloud on the horizon, leaving the seat of Government, Dublin, free for them as wants to negotiate—but it's tricky work. . . .[19]

[12] Acting G.O.C.-in-C. Ireland to C.I.G.S., 5 December 1920. Jeudwine papers.
[13] Jeudwine to Macready, 6 December 1920. Ibid.
[14] Memo for C.S.I. by Acting G.O.C.-in-C. Ireland, 5 December 1920. Lloyd George papers, F/19/2/28.
[15] Proclamations by Ld. Lt. and Military Governor of Ireland, pp. 207–8 in CAB.23 23.
[16] Macready to Jeudwine, 11 December 1920. Jeudwine papers.
[17] Irish Times, 11 December 1920.
[18] Sturgis diary, 10 December 1920. P.R.O. 30 59/3.
[19] Ibid., 14 December 1920.

Tricky work, indeed: anything less like the military idea that martial law would simplify the Army's position would be hard to imagine, and the absence of explanation and understanding had a dismal air of familiarity.

Democracy and military rule

The Government was not creating complications purely out of deviousness. Many of its members were simply at a loss to see how the measures which seemed necessary in Ireland could be reconciled with the normal British way of resolving conflicts. The problem of Anglo-Irish understanding has always been much more of a racial one than most people are prepared to admit,[20] and there was a great deal in one Frenchman's waspish observation that nothing could be more foreign to 'the everlasting spirit of compromise and bargaining so dear to the English' than Sinn Féin's idealism.[21] Few ministers were able to bring themselves to Bonar Law's conclusion that 'the Irish were an inferior race' and that a period of coercion followed by ten years of enforced calm was the best that could be expected from the present situation.[22] Most were bemused by the breakdown of legal authority in face of the methods of the I.R.A. Austen Chamberlain wrote after the 23 July conference, 'Most puzzling and most distressing. Can modern democracy handle such problems successfully?'[23]

The most obvious democratic problem was public opinion. Although there is little evidence of how the electorate really reacted to the use of coercion in Ireland, there is no doubt that the Cabinet was always apprehensive in this direction. In August 1920 it worried that if the Restoration of Order Act were fully enforced 'there might come a time when public opinion would desert the Government',[24] and even in May 1921 the Irish Situation Committee felt that to extend martial law to all the southern counties might open the Government to 'the reproach of undue severity'.[25] Yet it seems unlikely that in 1920 the British public found either the Irish Republic's political demands or the I.R.A.'s military methods acceptable, and it is possible that an appeal to the country would have produced a mandate for outright repression. But the Government could not be sure, and, itself divided, trod warily.

Its most fateful assumption was that public opinion would find the

[20] Cf. the almost unique racial–cultural study by L. P. Curtis, *Anglo-Saxons and Celts* (Connecticut, 1968).
[21] Briollay, *Ireland in Rebellion*, p. 19.
[22] Jones, *Whitehall Diary*, iii. 49–50 (30 January 1921).
[23] Austen Chamberlain to Hilda Chamberlain, 24 July 1920. Austen Chamberlain papers, 5/1/170. Sir C. Petrie, *The Life and Letters of Sir Austen Chamberlain* (London, 1940), ii. 150.
[24] Cabinet, 13 August 1920. C.48(20), CAB.23 22.
[25] Cabinet Irish Situation Cttee., 26 May 1921. C.P. 2983, CAB.24 123.

use of policemen, even though they were armed ex-soldiers, preferable
to that of the military in the suppression of disorder. This was due in
part to a failure to accept that the R.I.C.'s police capability had broken
down and could not be restored by pouring in ill-disciplined recruits;
and in part to a natural antipathy to military rule. When the Cabinet
discussed the proposal to extend the powers of military courts under
R.O.I.A. in July 1920, the view was put that

> it was a decision of the gravest moment to utilize machinery intended for time
> of war in time of peace, and considerable anxiety was expressed at thus handing
> over the whole administration of the law to soldiers.[26]

At the martial law discussion on 1 December, Chamberlain brought
forth one of his father's horror stories of military excesses in South
Africa, and said he wanted to be 'sure that the powers of martial law
shall not be exercised by junior officers without control'.[27] Macready
was probably not exaggerating unduly when he wrote later that
politicians either showed 'evident fear that the soldier once armed with
martial law powers would commit the most terrible atrocities', or
thought that 'the mere declaration . . . would bring about a mil-
lennium'.[28] In between the two, however, there was Anderson's
practical objection to martial law which was, according to Sturgis,
'not the imposition but the enormous difficulties of getting back to
Civil Govt. after the Army *pur et simple* have killed or cured the
situation'.[29]

There also remained confusion over what martial law would in fact
entail. In a ludicrous exchange in Cabinet on 1 December, Eric Geddes
said that Greenwood had told him that 'putting the country under
martial law involves feeding them', to which Lloyd George added, 'It
practically means no law.'[30] At a Chief Secretary's conference on the
implementation of martial law on 12 December, the Judge Advocate
General again showed a hesitant grasp of its principles, and warned that
Macready would have to await an Act of Indemnity to be cleared of
murder charges for executions carried out by military tribunals.[31] The
problem of responsibility, albeit not in this form, was to prove critical.
Although on 15 December, in answer to a parliamentary question
whether the military governors in the area under martial law were
'under the jurisdiction of the civil authorities', Bonar Law stated that

[26] Cabinet Conference, 26 July 1920. C.51(20) App. IV, CAB.23 22.
[27] Jones, *Whitehall Diary*, iii. 42.
[28] Macready, *Annals*, ii. 517; cf. G.O.C.-in-C. Ireland to C.S.I., 17 July 1920, quoted
p. 105 above.
[29] Sturgis diary, 30 November 1920. P.R.O. 30 59/3.
[30] Jones, *Whitehall Diary*, iii. 42.
[31] Sturgis diary, 12 December 1920.

martial law means that the rule is the rule of soldiers, and if the hon. and gallant gentleman [Captain Redmond] will carry it a little further he will find that ultimately it comes back to the rule of this House.[32]

this elegant formula was far too simple for a situation in which responsibility was divided between no less than three authorities, the civil, the military, and the police.

The Cork burnings

Macready was well aware that the R.I.C. was to remain independent, a 'foreign body' in the martial law system.[33] He warned Jeudwine on 10 December that

Strickland will have to watch the Police very carefully, for certainly Prescott-Decies[34] [sic] will think that martial law means that he can kill anybody he sees walking along the road whose appearance may be distasteful to him.[35]

Military distrust of the police was reinforced by dramatic events in Cork next day. On the night of 11 December, following an ambush some 200 yards from Victoria Barracks, the headquarters of 6th Division, a number of A.D.R.I.C. of K Company[36] went into the city centre, apparently under the command of their officers.[37] At 11.30 p.m., just after the curfew troops had gone into the city, a fire was seen in Patrick Street, the main thoroughfare (see Map 4, p. 132), followed by others an hour later.[38] The curfew officer called for reinforcements, which arrived at 1 a.m., but though he claimed to have told R.I.C. headquarters that his troops would fire on anyone found looting, he took no action. His brigadier later said that 'had the O.C. Curfew Troops arrested any of the police there is little doubt that there would have been a fight and considerable bloodshed would have ensued'.[39] By daybreak an extensive section of Patrick Street, together with the City Hall and Carnegie Library across the river, were in flames.

This was certainly the most spectacular reprisal that had yet occurred, even if its severity did not, as the map shows, live up to Republican hyperbole about the burning of half, or all, the city.[40] An immediate military inquiry placed all the blame for the destruction on the

[32] 133 H.C. Deb. 5s, col. 489.

[33] Note by G.O.C.-in-C., 11 December 1920. W.O. 35 88(1).

[34] Cyril Prescott-Decie, 1865–1953. Brig. Gen. Commanding 4th Div. Artillery, 1916; retd., 1920; D.C. R.I.C., 1920.

[35] Macready to Jeudwine, 10/11 December 1920. Jeudwine papers.

[36] Cf. note 3, Appendix II, below, p. 210.

[37] G.O.C.-in-C. to G.H.Q. Ireland, 22 December 1920. W.O. 35 88(1).

[38] 6th Div. to G.H.Q. Ireland, 13 December 1920. Ibid.

[39] Remarks of O.C. 17th Inf. Bde., 14 December 1920, attached to Finding of first Military Court of Inquiry, 13 December 1920. W.O. 35 88(1).

[40] The map, moreover, shows only the city centre. A recent writer who has perpetuated a Republican double distortion is Forester, *Michael Collins*, p. 175: 'In Cork martial law was celebrated by the destruction of the city by fire.'

A.D.R.I.C.—'disagreeable reading', as Anderson remarked after perusing its verdict.[41] Strickland was ordered to carry out a 'full and searching' inquiry, and was told that under martial law (which had not in fact been in force on 11 December) he had full powers and full responsibility.[42] The conclusion of the second inquiry on 21 December was substantially the same, exonerating the troops and laying blame on the A.D.R.I.C. together with some regular R.I.C. recruits who had masqueraded as officers;[43] but it also took upon itself to criticize 'the higher authority who ordered a unit in so raw a state to an area where active operations might be expected'.[44] This verdict, in one sense a part of the continuing military criticism of the conduct and discipline of the police, dumbfounded the Government, which had promised to publish the inquiry. It could not now bring itself to do this,[45] and the mysterious 'Strickland report' gained great notoriety in opposition circles. The 'higher authority' who had been criticized, Tudor, was incensed by the verdict, and held a counter-inquiry which shifted much of the blame from the police.[46]

At this time there occurred another incident, smaller but uglier than the Cork burnings. On 15 December an A.D.R.I.C. Cadet, Harte, killed a young man and a seventy-year-old priest on the roadside near Dunmanway, Co. Cork, in what was clearly a case of wanton murder. Although Harte was found insane,[47] the Cabinet recognized that this was 'particularly unfortunate' as the killer in the famous Sheehy–Skeffington case in 1916 had also been declared insane.[48] And in the privacy of his diary Sturgis fumed that, if Harte was insane, 'those who let him loose on the world in charge of a party armed to the teeth should take his place in the dock'.[49] Sturgis recorded that by 18 December G.H.Q. feared 'a real row between police and military', and was thinking of creating separate areas for troops and A.D.R.I.C.[50] Strickland unceremoniously expelled the Auxiliaries from Cork city, and Macready told Anderson that where police shared military barracks they would have to conform to military barrack discipline: 'I cannot

[41] U.S. to G.O.C.-in-C., 18 December 1920. W.O. 35 88(1).

[42] U.S. to G.O.C.-in-C., 14 December 1920. Ibid.

[43] It pointed out that the troops had had to consider the possibility of rebel action, and had not at first realized that the A.D.R.I.C. had 'broken from the control of their officers'; but it did find that two soldiers had committed highway robbery.

[44] Finding of Military Court of Inquiry at Victoria Barracks, Cork, 16–21 December 1920. W.O. 35 88(1).

[45] Cabinet, 14 February 1921. Jones, *Whitehall Diary*, iii. 50.

[46] This brave document can be found in C.O. 904 150. It at least convinced Lloyd George: see Jones, loc. cit.

[47] Only because Macready insisted on a proper trial. Lloyd George wanted Harte tried and hanged on the spot. Sturgis diary, 19 December 1920. P.R.O. 30 59/3.

[48] Cabinet, 30 December 1920. C.81(20), CAB.23 23. (The murderer then had been Captain Bowen-Colthurst.)

[49] Sturgis diary, 19 December 1920.

[50] Ibid., 18 December 1920.

run the risk of my troops being demoralized.' If Tudor did not like
this, he said, he would have to find somewhere else for the police to
live.[51]

The Cabinet was now sufficiently impressed by the explosive potential of military–police friction to count it as an argument in favour of
negotiations with Sinn Féin.[52] Such negotiations were in the air in
December, and made some progress, but the British demand for the
surrender of rebel arms was a stumbling-block, and as late as
20 December Lloyd George was still posing the fundamental question,

do we want peace or not? Are we to stamp out the very embers of rebellion or is
the policy a double one to crush murder and make peace with the moderates.?[53]

His own answer was 'We must hold the balance even. We must be
sternly just or we will not get Ireland back.'[54] This formula, elegant in
principle, had so far led to paralysing compromise for the forces in
Ireland. The seal was set on it when the Government of Ireland Act
finally became law on 23 December. The Act provided for two Irish
parliaments, a Northern, for the six counties of Ulster, and a Southern,
for the remainder, to be elected some time between January 1921 and
March 1922. British policy was now to 'crush murder' sufficiently to
allow these elections to take place in peace, and to convince Irish
opinion that the Act represented the limit of British concession, but to
reconcile the moderates who could, it was hoped, be persuaded to
accept the Southern parliament. 'Political' Sinn Féin was to be treated
with respect, and the Army was instructed to take no action against
de Valera when he returned to Ireland on 25 December.[55]

The timing of the elections obviously depended to a large extent on
the overall military situation, and to discuss this a Cabinet conference
met on 29 December. Any idea of a truce in the near future was decisively rejected, most tellingly by Anderson. Macready said that the
terror could be broken if martial law was spread over the whole
country, and Wilson rather wildly claimed that six months of military
government would bring 80–90 per cent of the population over to the
British side. Strickland, who—an advantage from the Cabinet's point
of view—did not seem to demand the extension of martial law across
the whole country, was even more optimistic, giving it as his opinion
that there would be 'definite and decisive results in four months'
time'.[56] Possibly euphoria after the declaration of martial law distorted

[51] Macready to Anderson, 18 December 1920. Anderson papers, C.O. 904 188/2.
[52] Cabinet, 24 December 1920. C.77(20), CAB.23 23.
[53] Cabinet, 20 December 1920. Jones, *Whitehall Diary*, iii. 46.
[54] Ibid.
[55] Ibid.; see D.D. H.Q. Note, 2 January 1921. W.O. 35 71.
[56] Cabinet Conference, 29 December 1920. C.79A(20), CAB.23 23.

military judgement. Certainly the onus which was put upon the military commanders to give a date by which order would be restored would have been more legitimate, and their predictions more realistic, if they had been given sole responsibility for the campaign that was to follow. But the Cabinet appears to have taken no account of this when it accepted Strickland's opinion and set the elections for May 1921;[57] and its agreement on 30 December to extend martial law to four more counties, Clare, Kilkenny, Waterford, and Wexford,[58] was a minimal concession to the military requirement for unified command.

14. Martial Law and Military Measures (December 1920–March 1921)

The command and strength of the forces
The extension of martial law to cover roughly the historic province of Munster (more relevantly the area of 6th Division: see Map 3, p. 86), proved to be its limit. Although Lord French once again declared, as he signed the new proclamations on 4 January, that it was vital to have martial law in the ports, above all in Dublin,[59] General Macready found that, no matter what had been said to him a month before, he could not obtain any further extension. On 10 January he began an attempt to get martial law imposed in Dublin, and kept this pressure up for a fortnight;[60] but on 28 January he was informed that the Chief Secretary was 'not convinced of its necessity at present'.[61] The Martial Law Area (M.L.A.) thus became another kingdom within a kingdom—a complication rather than a resolution of the command problem. The Army suffered the bitter disappointment of finding that even within this area its control was not to be complete. As far as the police were concerned, there was at first a theoretical improvement. Tudor went to G.H.Q. on 11 December and worked out joint instructions which placed the police 'under the orders' of Military Governors (i.e. brigade commanders and above) in martial law areas: such orders were to be issued via the highest police authority in a given area, and Military Governors were also instructed to 'hold Divisional Commissioners

[57] For the reliance which Lloyd George placed on this estimate see Cabinet, 8 March 1921. Jones, *Whitehall Diary*, iii. 54; cf. p. 174 below.
[58] Cabinet, 30 December 1920. C.81(20), CAB.23 23.
[59] Sturgis diary, 4 January 1921. P.R.O. 30 59/3.
[60] Macready to Anderson, 10 January (Anderson papers, C.O. 904 188/1), G.O.C.-in-C. W.S.R., 15 January (C.P. 2476) and 22 January 1921 (C.P. 2489, CAB.24 118); 'G' War Diary, G.H.Q. Ireland, 19 January 1921.
[61] 'G' War Diary, G.H.Q. Ireland, 28 January 1921. W.O. 35 93(1)/1. Macready later wrote that Greenwood, judging from his press interviews at the time, was 'in an optimistic frame of mind for which none of us living in Ireland could see any grounds'. *Annals*, ii. 538.

responsible for the discipline of the police in their areas'.[62] These in-instructions seemed at last to provide the military authorities with effective control over the R.I.C., but in practice the arrangements were vague, and left the police wide scope for independent action.

The A.D.R.I.C. excesses of December did not convince the Cabinet of the need for unity of command. In the House of Commons on 20 December, Greenwood struggled manfully to avoid answering a question on the overall authority for the M.L.A.: first he said that the question should be addressed to the Secretary for War; then, when it was pointed out that Bonar Law had recently declared that the Chief Secretary, not the Secretary for War, was responsible for all Irish matters, he said that he had been given notice of the question too late; only after further pressure did he give the answer that

all the Forces of the Crown in the Martial Law Area are under the command of General Strickland who is under the command of General Sir Nevil Macready.[63]

This seemed unequivocal, but it soon became clear that the word 'command' was at a discount in this case. At the Cabinet conference on 29 December it was stated that the police in the M.L.A. were under Strickland 'except as regards discipline', and, moreover, that the police carried out operations independently on special information, 'the area being a very large one'.[64]

These assertions went unquestioned, in spite of Tudor's admission that 'drink was the problem' with the A.D.R.I.C. The Cabinet seemed satisfied with his assertion that

men who came into the Police Force said that the discipline in it was stricter than the Army, and anyone who had seen the Black and Tans on parade must admit that their discipline was very fine; they were completely under the control of their officers.[65]

But it was not on the parade ground that the reputation of the Black and Tans was gained. In the Army's view at least, the general un-reliability of the R.I.C. in stations nullified Tudor's achievement in building the force up to its highest strength ever. The regular R.I.C. passed the 13,000 mark in mid-January, and was growing by about 200 per week at this stage, while the A.D.R.I.C. reached a strength of 1,300.[66] These totals were not achieved without a decline in standards: one interesting detail which irritated the older R.I.C. men was the

[62] G.H.Q. Ireland, 2/33227/G to 6th Div. and Police Adviser [sic, i.e. Chief of Police], 11 December 1920. W.O. 35 66. This document is given as Appendix XI below, p. 222.
[63] Oral Answers, 20 December 1920. 136 H.C. Deb. 5s, col. 1281.
[64] Cabinet Conference, 29 December 1920. C.79A(20), CAB.23 23.
[65] Ibid. It seems clear that by 'Black and Tans' Tudor was referring mainly to the A.D.R.I.C. (cf. his reference to the 'Black and Tan platoon' destroyed at Macroom).
[66] See Appendix III below, p. 211.

intake of men below the traditional height of 5 feet 8 inches.[67] Although it is no longer necessary to refute the Republican allegation that the new recruits were the sweepings of British gaols—an acceptable estimate is that of the Labour Commission, that perhaps one per cent were men of 'really bad character'[68]—there is no doubt that the selection process was less stringent than the Government thought, and that the actions of a few hundred wrongdoers were sufficient to destroy the reputation of the R.I.C.[69] It is harder to assess the military capability of the expanded force, because of the paucity of R.I.C. reports and records.[70] The Army's opinion was obviously prejudiced by the general military bias against the police, but it seems likely that the police were appreciably less capable in a tactical sense than were the troops. Perhaps more important, there were extreme local variations, especially with the A.D.R.I.C., which reduced their overall value: a typical military verdict was that 'a Regular company with five good officers, and provided with transport on the same scale as an Auxiliary company, would do as well'.[71]

The Army's problem was that there were far too few regular companies. It lacked sufficient strength to establish close control over the large rural areas in which the rebel forces operated. At the beginning of 1921 Irish Command disposed 51 infantry battalions (see Table 4, p. 144), most of which were very weak, and Macready drew attention to the strain on the young soldiers caused by long nights, incessant guard duties, and patrols under constant threat of ambush.[72] The provision of transport and armoured vehicles was still not up to expectations—in December 1920 Lloyd George himself criticized the Quartermaster General over this, though Churchill defended him by pointing out the difficulty of obtaining armour plate for lorries, and artificers to fit it.[73] Macready reported at that time that out of 154 sets of plate ordered for 'armoured' (rifle-proof) lorries, only 14 had been drilled

---

[67] Before the war, few of the R.I.C. had been less than 5 ft. 9 in. in height, according to the R.I.C. General Register; of the November 1920 intake of 985 men, 436 were 5 ft. 7 in. or under, and 6 were only 5 ft. 4 in. H.O. 184 38. Cf. L. Robinson (ed.), *Lady Gregory's Journals* (London, 1946), p. 144, which reports one of the old R.I.C. at Gort, Co. Galway, as castigating the Black and Tan recruits as 'little chaps of 5 foot 6—and with no character'.

[68] Labour Party, *Report of the Labour Commission to Ireland* (London, 1921), Part II, p. 7 (report of Gen. Thompson).

[69] On 14 April 1921 it was announced that 165 members of the Crown Forces had been tried for criminal offences since 1 January 1921, and 124 convicted. 140 H.C. Deb. 5s, col. 1272.

[70] The only substantial records are the R.I.C. Reports (I.G. and C.I.s), C.O. 904 108–15, and these record rebel outrages rather than police activities.

[71] Extract 2, Military Appreciations, in Macready to Frances Stevenson, 20 June 1921. Lloyd George papers, F/36/2/19.

[72] G.O.C.-in-C. W.S.R., 8 January 1921. C.P. 2456, CAB.24 118.

[73] Cabinet, 1 December 1920. Jones, *Whitehall Diary*, iii. 43; cf. Ordnance Summary, D.D. and 5th Div. W.O. 35 182(1)/1.

TABLE 4

Irish Command: Allotment of Battalions to Brigades January 1921*

1st DIVISION (10)

15th Brigade
1st Norfolk Regt.
1st Somerset L.I.
1st D.C.L.I.
1st K.R. Rifle Corps
2nd K.R. Rifle Corps

Londonderry Brigade
1st Queen's Regt.
1st Beds. and Herts. Regt.
1st Dorset Regt.
2nd K.O.Y.L.I.
2nd Rifle Brigade

5th DIVISION (9)

13th Brigade
2nd Suffolk Regt.
1st Leicestershire Regt.
1st E. Yorks. Regt.

14th Brigade
1st R. Scots Fusiliers
2nd K.S.L.I.
1st Cameronians
1st N. Staffs. Regt.

Galway Brigade
2nd Border Regt.
2nd Argyll and Sutherland Hlrs.

6th DIVISION (20)

16th Brigade
1st Buffs
1st Lincolnshire Regt.
1st Devonshire Regt.
1st Gloucestershire Regt.
1st R. Warwicks. Regt.

17th Brigade
1st. King's Regt.
2nd Hampshire Regt.
2nd S. Staffs. Regt.
1st Essex Regt.
1st Manchester Regt.
2nd Cameron Hlrs.
2nd K.O.S.B.

18th Brigade
2nd Green Howards
2nd R. Welsh Fusiliers
1st Oxon. and Bucks. L.I.
1st Northants. Regt.
2nd Royal Scots

Kerry Brigade
1st Royal Fusiliers
2nd Loyal Regt.
2nd E. Lancs. Regt.

DUBLIN DISTRICT (12)

24th (P) Brigade
1st Lancs. Fusiliers
1st S. Wales Borderers
2nd Worcestershire Regt.
2nd D. of Wellington's Regt.
1st Wiltshire Regt.
2nd E. Surrey Regt.

25th (P) Brigade
1st Prince of Wales' Volunteers
2nd R. Berks. Regt.
1st King's Own Regt.
2nd Welch Regt.
1st Cheshire Regt.
3rd Rifle Brigade.

* Source: G.O.C.-in-C. W.S.R., 8 January 1921. C.P. 2456, CAB.24 118.

and fitted, while only 6 out of 200 'protected' (pistol-proof) lorries were on the road.[74] At the end of the year only 25 armoured and 15 protected lorries were available for the whole of Irish Command. Armoured cars were in slightly better supply, though 5th Division

[74] G.O.C.-in-C. W.S.R., 4 December 1920. S.I.C. 61, CAB.27 108.

disposed only 14,[75] and many were obsolete Jeffrey Quad and Austin types, gradually becoming unserviceable through lack of spare parts. Apart from 5th Armoured Car Company in Dublin, there were no tank corps personnel. (In Dublin there were also a handful of Mk. V tanks.)[76] At the end of 1920 some 50 Peerless and 16 Rolls-Royce armoured cars arrived in Ireland, and further deliveries in mid-March 1921 brought these totals up to 70 and 34.[77] The 5th Armoured Car Company was re-equipped with Rolls-Royces, and the remainder were distributed among infantry battalions (the cavalry, of course, being still horse-mounted).

It is doubtful whether the shortage of armour was a real handicap. The slowness and excessive weight of armoured lorries, and all armoured cars except the Rolls-Royce (which was also the only vehicle whose approach could not be heard at a considerable distance),[78] effectively confined them to town or convoy use. For offensive operations the troops showed a universal preference for faster, unarmoured 15 and 30 cwt. vehicles, which at least had a chance of negotiating Irish minor roads.[79] Of the 60 lorries possessed by the Galway Brigade of 5th Division in June 1921, for instance, 27, being 3-tonners, were virtually unusable off the two main roads.[80] But in fact the most promising military development in 1921 was to come about not so much through the use of motor vehicles as through their abandonment in favour of movement on foot;[81] and the Army's real handicap seems to have been not material shortages but tactical unsureness and poor training. In the Irish conflict, such basic skills as marksmanship and fieldcraft were immensely more important than they had been in the Great War. When engagements occurred, targets were few and fleeting, while the troops were usually running hard in an attempt to outflank the rebels. Every soldier needed to be an expert skirmisher and sniper; few, of course, were.[82] As the *General Annual Report on the British Army* ruefully remarked in October 1920, 'the general standard of the men presenting themselves for enlistment has been poor'.[83] Ireland, still regarded as a major training area, received the bulk of these recruits, and little could be done to provide them with the intensive training they needed.

[75] 5th Div. War Diary, December 1920, App. XI. W.O. 35 93(1)/2.
[76] G.H.Q. Ireland, *Record*, i. 32.
[77] G.O.C.-in-C. W.S.R., 4 December 1920, loc. cit.; 'G' War Diary, G.H.Q. Ireland, 15 March 1921. W.O. 35 93(1)/1.
[78] The Peerless weighed 6½ tons and could reach only 20 m.p.h., compared with the 4½ tons and over 50 m.p.h. of the Rolls-Royce.
[79] Hist. 5th Div., pp. 88–9; Percival, Lecture 2, pp. 14–15.
[80] Hist. 5th Div., p. 89.
[81] See below, pp. 176–7.
[82] Percival, Lecture 2, pp. 13–14.
[83] *General Annual Report on the British Army*, 1919–20. 1922 Cmd. 1610 xii 611, p. 10; ibid., 1920–1. 1923 Cmd. 1941 xiv 665, p. 8.

The Army's winter concentration, which had been planned to permit such training, had been abandoned in the upsurge of military activity after Bloody Sunday. Subsequently the pressure of martial law made formal training impossible for 6th Division, and only 5th Division appears to have carried out any special guerrilla warfare training. Early in November it began a series of fortnightly courses at the Curragh, which continued through the winter.[84] Each lasted only three days: a typical programme being, first day, cycle patrols; second day, lorry convoys in ambush; third day, daylight lorry raids. In spite of their shortness these courses were undoubtedly useful, especially to those R.I.C. units which accepted invitations to attend.[85] All problems, however, were still overshadowed by that of intelligence, and here there were few signs of progress. Indeed, in one respect the advent of martial law was seen as a regression, for according to G.H.Q. it tended to make 6th Division 'an independent force and made any central control and co-ordination of intelligence more difficult than before'.[86] Elsewhere, the formation of 'local centres' for intelligence co-ordination at the H.Q.s of R.I.C Divisional Commissioners was a promising step, but the first of these was not in operation until January 1921, and others were established only slowly.[87]

Martial law measures

Martial law, or 'partial law' as applied in 1921, proved incapable of remedying these problems. Its distinctive theoretical feature, the supersession of the normal legal system by summary military tribunals, was blurred from the start. The martial law proclamation of 12 December introduced new capital offences—for carrying arms or harbouring rebels—enforceable by military courts, but authorized the ordinary civil courts to continue working.[88] A confusion of the two systems rapidly arose. On 15 January an appeal was lodged in the King's Bench Division of the High Court in Dublin on behalf of the first man, Joseph Murphy, to be sentenced to death by a martial law tribunal, and this was followed in early February by another on behalf of one John Allen. During these appeals, from 15 to 31 January in Murphy's case and from 9 to 24 February in Allen's case, the military authorities had to stay the execution of the sentences, though in both cases the high court accepted affidavits from Macready testifying that a state of war existed in the M.L.A., and ruled that appeals from military tribunals did not

[84] 5th Div. to 1st, 6th Divs. and D.D., 8 December 1920. W.O. 35 70; 5th Div. War Diary, December 1920, Apps. III, IV. W.O. 35 93(1)/2.
[85] Cf. Hist. 5th Div., p. 106.
[86] G.H.Q. Ireland, *Record*, ii. 12.
[87] Ibid., ii. 11, 21; the local centre in Cork was not created until April 1921.
[88] Proclamation No. 1 by G.O.C.-in-C. and Military Governor of Ireland, 12 December 1920. W.O. 35 169.

lie. The court could not, it declared on 24 February, '*durante bello*, control the military authorities, or question any sentence imposed in the exercise of martial law'.[89]

It might be thought that this unequivocal statement of principle would have closed the matter, and that all contact between the civil and military legal systems in the M.L.A. would have ceased. But on the very next day two brigade commanders (Military Governors) were served with writs in connection with damage caused by official punishments;[90] and though Macready immediately wired them orders to refuse the writs, this was, he later wrote, 'the thin end of the wedge'.[91] In March, on behalf of seven men sentenced to death after being captured in the Clonmult engagement, an appeal alleged that the military court had been improperly constituted, and the King's Bench issued conditional writs of certiorari and habeas corpus. These writs, along with yet another on behalf of Ronayne and Mulcahy, were not discharged until 25 April.[92] Further appeals continued to be lodged, and even to be carried to the House of Lords; and eventually, as will be seen, the confusion led to a legal crisis that was potentially disastrous for the power of the military authorities. In the meantime, the theory—maintained even by the cautious Judge Advocate General —that military courts could 'dispense with all formalities and technicalities and proceed in a very summary manner' had been rendered meaningless,[93] and a climate of 'delay and uncertainty' had been created which, in Macready's opinion, 'nullified the effect of martial law'.[94]

Turning from legal questions to the practical measures which were taken under martial law, it is noticeable that these too fell some way short of Jeudwine's original anticipations. An idea of what martial law meant to the troops who enforced it can be found in a list drawn up by a battalion intelligence officer in southern Cork.[95] The troops, he said, were now able to operate independently of the police, and the latter were confined to routine work; a new legal structure was set up, with local summary courts able to impose six-month sentences, a standing court martial in Cork for more serious offences, and drumhead

---

[89] *The King* v. *Murphy*, King's Bench, Ireland, 15, 17, 24, 25, 31 January 1921. *The Irish Reports* (Dublin, 1921), ii. 190–201; *The King* v. *Allen*, 9, 11, 12, 24 February 1921. Ibid., ii. 241–7. Cf. C.S.I. Weekly Surveys, 17, 31 January 1921. C.P. 2469, 2539, CAB.24 118–19.

[90] See below, p. 149.

[91] Macready, *Annals*, ii. 517.

[92] *The King (Garde and others)* v. *Strickland and others*, King's Bench, Ireland, 23 March, 20, 21, 25 April 1921; *The King (Ronayne and Mulcahy)* v. *Strickland and another*, 2, 25 April, 1921. *The Irish Reports*, 1921, ii. 317, 328, 333. Cf. C.S.I. Weekly Survey, 25 April 1921. C.P. 2892, CAB.24 122.

[93] Cf. J.A.G. to C.S.I., 19 July 1920. C.P. 1662, CAB.24 109.

[94] Macready, *Annals*, ii. 517.

[95] Percival, Lecture I, pp. 19–21.

6

courts to deal with rebels taken in arms; harbouring rebels, failing to give information, or giving a false name, became offences; internment without trial was introduced; fairs and markets were controlled; the use of cars and bicycles was restricted, to 'hamper the communications of the I.R.A.'; and curfew was gradually extended to the whole M.L.A., making it possible to arrest anyone moving at night.[96]

The interesting thing about this list is that some of these benefits were illusory, and others were not confined to the M.L.A. The police could not be got out of the way by any amount of wishful thinking, and, so far from being confined to 'routine' police work, they were being exhorted by Macready not to expose themselves to attack in that way.[97] Internment without trial was operative throughout Ireland after Bloody Sunday, and in fact until May 1921 more men were interned by Dublin District than by 6th Division.[98] Restrictions on vehicles derived from a Motor Permit Order effective across the whole country from 1 December 1920, which controlled the area and time in which vehicles could be used.[99] Prior to this there had been no registration of vehicles, so that the order was a considerable step forward for the civil government (it was naturally opposed by the Irish Automobile Drivers' and Mechanics' Union), but it did not succeed in preventing rebel movement by road. The restriction on fairs and markets, and the curfew, were widely used outside the M.L.A.

These facts suggest that the prime effect of martial law was moral rather than physical; and it is for this reason that the 'delay and uncertainty' of which Macready spoke had such damaging consequences. The physical effect of martial law might have been greater if certain of the measures demanded by Jeudwine at the start had been carried out. The long-postponed question of a system of identity checks, for instance, continued to evade practical solution. The records show no sign of the report on the subject which the Cabinet directed Tudor to prepare in November 1920, and inability to identify wanted men was a constant handicap to operations. No system of passports between Britain and Ireland was established, and a report in June 1921 described customs controls on the importation of arms as 'a farce'.[100] Moreover, naval assistance remained inadequate: in the seven months following 'bitter' military complaints on this subject noted by Greenwood in

---

[96] Ibid.
[97] G.O.C.-in-C. Ireland to Chief of Police, 24 February 1921 (copy). Anderson papers, C.O. 904 188/2.
[98] See Appendix XII below, p. 223, for the cumulative figures of internment. Cf. also p. 195 below.
[99] 5th Div. War Diary, 1 December 1920, App. II. W.O. 35 93(1)/2.
[100] Memo by Col. Comd. Tank Corps Centre, 24 June 1921. C.P. 3075, CAB.24 124; Winter had used exactly the same word the previous summer—see Sturgis diary, 31 August 1920. P.R.O. 30 59/1.

December,[101] little happened beyond a trifling scheme to supply four naval launches for patrol work on inland waters.[102]

In fact, the most striking feature of martial law proved to be one which had not been among Jeudwine's requirements. In the last week of December, Macready informed the Cabinet that Military Governors in the M.L.A. had been authorized to inflict punishments after rebel outrages, on the following conditions:

A. Punishments will only be carried out on the authority of the Infantry Brigadier, who before taking action will satisfy himself that the people concerned were, owing to their proximity to the outrage or their known political tendencies, implicated in the outrage, and will give specific instructions in writing or by telegram to the officer detailed to carry out the operation.
B. The punishment will be carried out as a Military Operation, and the reason why it is being done will be publicly proclaimed.[103]

This was clearly derived from the proposal which Macready had put forward in September 1920. The method of punishment was that the 'implicated' people were given an hour to remove 'any valuable foodstuffs hay or corn but not furniture'[104] from their houses, which were thereupon wrecked by explosives. In the case of terrace houses, where fires might spread, the furniture was removed and burned separately in the street. (The Limerick Corporation once claimed for damage to road asphalt after such a bonfire).[105]

The first of these revolutionary punishments, which soon became known as 'official reprisals', took place in Midleton, near Cork, on 29 December, when six houses were destroyed after an ambush in which three policemen had died.[106] The practice continued for five months, but no records survive of how many reprisals occurred: the total would seem to be in the region of 150.[107] Whatever the figures, the Government disliked the scheme, which, in taking public responsibility and in destroying property, reversed both its own preferences. In one way it was certainly right, for this was a very rough form of justice to receive official sanction (the investigations of 'complicity' which preceded reprisals were often cursory), and even when it punished the disloyal by ejecting them from their homes, the material loss of the buildings

---

[101] Greenwood to Lloyd George, 5 December 1920. Lloyd George papers, F/19/2/28.
[102] 'G' War Diary, G.H.Q. Ireland, 4 April, 25 May 1921. W.O. 35 93(1)/1. The launches did not arrive until June.
[103] G.O.C.-in-C. W.S.R., 1 January 1921. S.I.C.8, CAB. 627 108.
[104] The procedure employed can be observed in the cases and documents in W.O. File 79/Irish/753 (Claims Arising out of Official Reprisals in Ireland). W.O. 35 169.
[105] Ibid., claim of Limerick City Corporation, 9 April 1921.
[106] G.O.C.-in-C. W.S.R., loc. cit.; Irish Times, 3 January 1921.
[107] Estimated from instances in R.I.C. Reports, January–May 1921, which suggest an average of 4 reprisals per county per month. C.O. 904 114–15. Macready's reports (W.S.R.s) show far less, but they cannot be regarded as complete. Cf. also G.H.Q. Ireland, Record, i. 31.

usually fell on landlords. To stress this point, Lord Midleton testily informed Greenwood that the first reprisals in Midleton had cost him £1,500.[108]

The Military Governor of the M.L.A., Strickland, made it clear that the aim was to induce the public to co-operate with the Crown Forces in supplying information. An 'attitude of neutrality', he announced, was 'inconsistent with loyalty'.[109] He told the Lord Mayor of Cork in an open letter that 'citizens must co-operate in purging the streets of assassins if the burdens of martial law are to be lightened'.[110] In effect, as the *Westminster Gazette* put it, he was ordering

> the Irish people to risk their lives for an administration they have consistently opposed, and which has so far been unable to guarantee that ordinary well behaved people should be left unmolested. Technically, General Strickland is in the right, but in view of the circumstances . . . his order . . . exposes the people to an ordeal which is cruelly severe.[111]

And *The Times* pointed out after the first official reprisals that no attempt seemed to have been made to demonstrate that the victims could, even at risk of their lives, actually have given warning in time to prevent an ambush.[112] These were well-founded criticisms which the scheme never overcame. Another martial law scheme concerning civilians which caused some public doubt was the formation of 'civil guards'.[113] Even less is now known about these than about reprisals, though it appears that they were not pushed with much vigour. In some places the Crown Forces seem to have made serious efforts to form civilian groups to provide intelligence observation, but mostly it was a matter of herding out men to repair roads and bridges wrecked by the rebels.[114]

The first few weeks of martial law did little to substantiate Strickland's prediction of definite and decisive results in four months. None the less he remained optimistic, sending Macready a special progress report on 22 January in which he admitted that there had been 'a recrudescence of outrage' in the M.L.A., but put this down to a desperate reaction of the I.R.A. high command.[115] There was, he said,

---

[108] Midleton to Greenwood, 20 January 1921. Midleton papers, P.R.O. 30 67/44.

[109] *Irish Times*, 3 January 1921; cf. G.O.C. 6th Div., Proclamations Nos. 1, 2, and 3, 27 December and 7 January 1921. Hemming papers.

[110] *Cork Examiner*, 18 January 1921.

[111] *Westminster Gazette*, 4 January 1921.

[112] *The Times*, 3 January 1921.

[113] G.H.Q. Ireland to U.S. (Parliamentary Question), n.d. W.O. 35 66.

[114] See the account by Barry, *Guerrilla Days in Ireland*, p. 110, of the formation of a Civil Guard in Ballineen, Co. Cork. Robinson, *Lady Gregory's Journals*, 8 June 1921, has a first-hand account of a typical *ad hoc* labour squad.

[115] G.O.C. 6th Div. to G.O.C.-in-C. Ireland, 22 January 1921. E.P.S./1/G 6th Div., W.O. 35 88(1).

less sign of local initiative than in the past, and attacks requiring determination and courage, such as against R.I.C. barracks, were 'conspicuous by their absence'. As for official reprisals, he thought that 'in spite of the howls of condemnation' (and perhaps because of them), such actions 'must have a deterrent effect on those who may be detailed for future outrages'. The flow of information had noticeably increased and, though much of it was unreliable, several captures of arms had resulted. He concluded that

although on the surface there may be but few results visible yet, I think that we may safely say that the restrictions and increased activity allowable by Martial Law are having their effect, and that their continuance should give us tangible results in the future.[116]

The military situation
There is certainly some evidence of a decline in rebel determination in 1921, though much of it is conflicting.[117] The reduction in serious attacks on R.I.C. barracks was striking. Up to the end of 1920, 54 had been damaged and 26 destroyed. In 1921, while 213 were damaged— often by only a few sniping shots—only 2 were destroyed.[118] At the same time there arose new spheres of rebel activity involving no fighting, notably the 'offensive against communications', manifested in the blocking of roads with trees or trenches and the breaking of bridges. This habit became noticeable in Kildare and Meath in January 1921, and thereafter spread rapidly.[119] There was also an I.R.A. order for attacks on transport, with the aim of making it 'impossible for it to move unescorted in town or country',[120] which resulted in the shooting of a number of mules and horses.[121] Raids on mails increased, and, more unpleasantly, there was a reversion to the practice of assassinating individual, and sometimes unarmed, troops and policemen.

These changes were reflected in I.R.A. tactical doctrine. On 17 February, I.R.A. G.H.Q. wrote to the Mid-Clare Brigade, 'A little action wisely and well done must be our motto at present',[122] and later *An tÓglách* enunciated the principle that 'In guerrilla warfare, it is the number and distribution of actions that counts, more than their magnitude.'[123] Certainly the overall total of outrages rose and went on

[116] Ibid.
[117] For instance, in Tipperary in April 1921 the North Riding R.I.C. reported a decline in serious outrages, while the South Riding found them increasing in number and seriousness. C.O. 904 114.
[118] See Appendix V below, p. 214.
[119] G.O.C.-in-C. W.S.R., 29 January 1921. C.P. 2520, CAB.24 119.
[120] I.R.A. Operation Memo No. 1, 1921, attached to I. Summary, D.D. War Diary, April 1921. W.O. 35 90/2.
[121] Ibid., 17 April 1921; on 26 April, Boyd provided all animals with armed escorts, who 'will defend them to the utmost'.
[122] Hist. 5th Div., p. 76.
[123] *An tÓglách*, vol. iii, No. 6, 1 May 1921.

rising, with great political effect.[124] The I.R.A. did not show symptoms
of the desperate terrorism which often marks guerrilla movements in
decline. It continued to wage urban and rural war on roughly the same
lines, without resorting to indiscriminate attacks. A small but sufficient
proportion of its flying columns had become ruggedly professional,
and these inflicted regular punishment on military and police patrols.
Admittedly there were bad patches during the winter. In January the
R.I.C. captured a flying column report which recounted a succession
of abortive attempts at ambushes, 'a bad week for the men as they had
to stay in a position from dark to dark', and were not welcomed in the
farms where they billeted.[125] But rebel units crushed police patrols at
Sixmilebridge in Clare on 20 January, Tureengarriffe Glen in Kerry
(where the R.I.C. Divisional Commissioner for Munster was killed)
on 28 January, and Drumkeen, Co. Limerick, on 3 February.[126] On
2 February at Ballinalee, Co. Longford, where Seán MacEoin's Longford Column had fought a noted engagement in November 1920,
MacEoin struck again with a brilliant ambush in which 18 Auxiliaries
were pinned down until they surrendered through lack of ammunition.[127] On 5 March the Military Governor of Kerry, Colonel-
Commandant Cumming, was killed in an ambush at Clonbanin, Co.
Cork, and a fortnight later the West Cork flying column achieved the
most celebrated rebel success of the period when it escaped and dis-
located a major search operation by 17th Brigade around Crossbarry.[128]
Macready called this engagement 'the nearest approach to actual
warfare, as contrasted with ambushes, that has yet occurred'.[129]

In response, the strength of police patrols in Cork was raised to 25–50
in February: the reason given was to create uncertainty about the
number of vehicles that might enter a rebel ambush, thereby inducing
the I.R.A. to deploy larger forces, which in turn would provide better
targets for counter-attack.[130] Self-preservation was probably also a
motive. The I.R.A. could easily ignore patrols that were too big for
their taste, as they 'completely dominated' large areas, where the effect
of patrols was transient.[131] The road-cutting campaign posed increasing
problems in the south-west, and was taken far more seriously than military reports from less critical areas may suggest.[132] By February a

[124] See Graph, p. 123 above.
[125] Cork 2nd Brigade to Brigade H.Q. 22 January 1921. In R.I.C. Reports, C.I. Cork,
January 1921. C.O. 904 114.
[126] G.O.C.-in-C. W.S.R., 29 January, 5 February 1921. C.P. 2520, 2568, CAB.24 119.
[127] Hist. 5th Div., p. 98.
[128] For rival first-hand accounts see Barry, *Guerrilla Days in Ireland*, pp. 116–22;
Percival, Lecture 1, pp. 25–6.
[129] G.O.C.-in-C. W.S.R., 19 March 1921. C.P. 2764, CAB.24 121.
[130] R.I.C. Reports, C.I. Cork, February 1921. C.O. 904 114.
[131] Ibid.; cf. G.H.Q. Ireland, *Record*, ii. 32.
[132] For instance 5th Division: Hist. 5th Div., p. 80.

ten-mile journey in Kerry often took four or five hours, and only one main road was open.[133] An intelligence officer in southern Cork concluded that 'it is really impossible in warfare of this nature to keep the road communications open if the enemy are determined to deny you the use of the roads'.[134] Every possible remedy was tried: bridges were carried on patrol lorries, but the rebels widened the trenches; forced labour was used to fill them in, but by next day they were re-excavated. A number of successful military operations did occur, but they were due to chance rather than calculation. When the 1st Manchesters surprised an ambush on 28 January, killing two men and capturing ten, it was because information had been provided by a courageous old lady, Mrs. Lindsay, who was kidnapped and shot by the I.R.A. (out of 'the stern necessity to protect our forces').[135] And when a patrol of the 2nd Hampshires trapped a group of 21 rebels in a farmhouse near Clonmult on 20 February, killing 13 and capturing 8, it was because the rebels had inexplicably opened fire and revealed their position.[136]

The situation in Dublin naturally differed from that in the provinces. In the city itself road-cutting was impossible, and though ambushes were frequent the proximity of reinforcements kept them short and sharp. Often they consisted only of a grenade hurled into a patrol lorry. Dublin District recorded complacently on 18 January that

The long threatened and much boomed attack on cars and lorries carrying military and police has been launched, resulting in little damage to the personnel of the Crown Forces and considerable loss of prestige to the attackers, whose markmanship has proved to be incredibly bad and their bombs [i.e. grenades] in most cases defective.[137]

Even so, for a few days the remarkable step was taken of carrying I.R.A. prisoners as hostages against attacks on patrols,[138] but for most of the time wire mesh and quick reactions sufficed. Dublin District's most effective response was a system of 'intensive patrolling', something which was never possible in rural areas. It began after 26 January, when 'loitering on the streets' was made an offence under R.O.I.R., and within two months loitering had been almost eliminated, further reducing the I.R.A.'s chance of mounting prepared attacks.[139]

Dublin District was the first military command to attempt large-scale area searches. The earliest one, wryly codenamed 'Optimist', and ostensibly aimed at capturing Michael Collins himself, was certainly a

[133] R.I.C. Reports, C.I. Kerry, February 1921. C.O. 904 114.
[134] Percival, Lecture 1, p. 27.
[135] Col. H. C. Wylly, *History of the Manchester Regiment* (London, 1925), pp. 209–10.
[136] G.O.C.-in-C. W.S.R., 19 February 1921. C.P. 2625, CAB.24 120.
[137] I. Summary, 18 January 1921. D.D. War Diary, W.O. 35 90/2.
[138] D.D. Orders, 26 January (cancelled 4 February) 1921. W.O. 35 66.
[139] D.D. Proclamation, 26 January, and Orders, 27 January 1921. W.O. 35 66; I. Summary, 20 March 1921. D.D. War Diary, W.O. 35 90/2.

Linen Hall Barracks

BRUNSWICK ST. NORTH LISBURN ST.

HENRIETTA PLACE

BOLTON ST.

E D C B A

KING ST. NORTH

STIRRUP LA.

ANNE ST. NORTH

HALSTON ST.

GREEN ST.

LITTLE BRITAIN ST.

GT. BRITAIN ST.

BERESFORD ST.

CHURCH STREET

CAPEL STREET

MARY ST.

MARY'S LANE

GREEK ST.

Fish Market

BOOT LANE

ARRAN ST. EAST

Bridewell

PILL LANE

MARY'S ABBEY

Four Courts

KING'S INN QUAY

ORMOND QUAY UPR.

RIVER LIFFEY

Cordon
○ 20–man section
△ 12–man section
King St.N. } 1st Lancs. Fslrs
Church St. }
Quays } 1st Wilts. Regt.
Capel St. }
Total 396 O.R.

Search
⇐ Search group sectors
A 1st King's Own Regt.
B 1st Pr. of Wales Volunteers
C 2nd Welch Regt.
D 3rd Rifle Brigade
E 2nd Royal Berks.Regt.
Total 300 O.R.

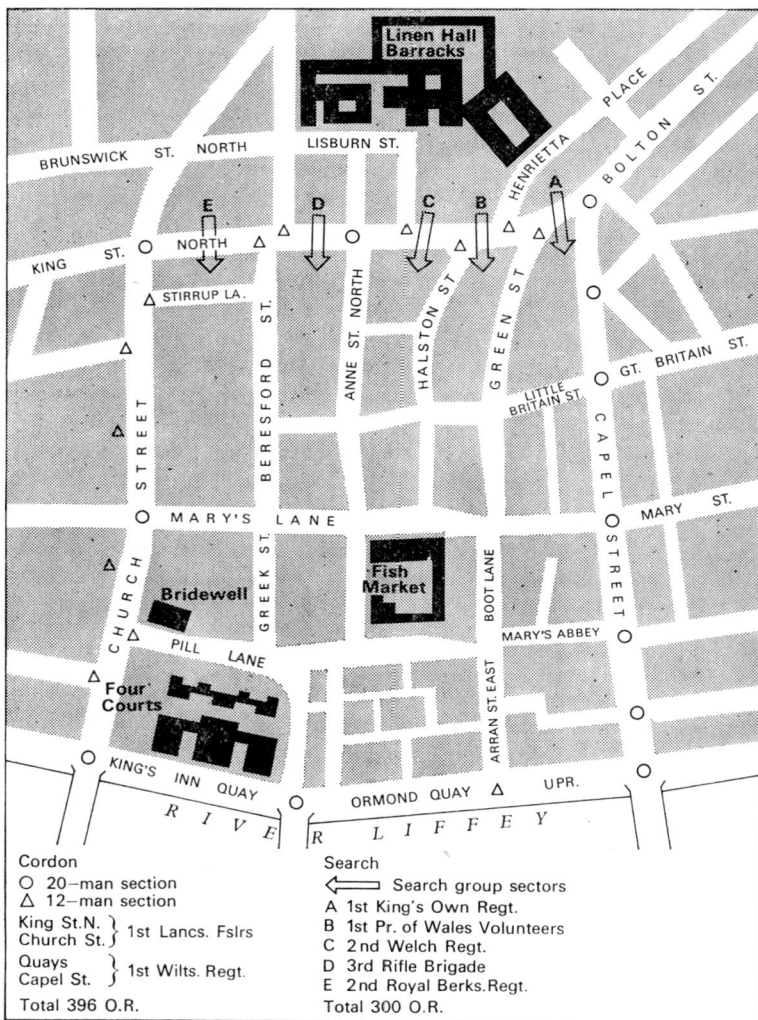

Map 5: Dublin Area Searches I: Operation 'Optimist', January 1921

technical experiment as much as anything else.[140] On the night of
Saturday, 15 January, over 600 troops were concentrated to seal off
and search an area of the city centre between North King St. and
the Liffey (see Map 5).[141] About half of them formed the cordon,
wiring the outer sides of the surrounding streets and setting up sand-
bagged machine-gun emplacements on the bridges over the river.[142]
The area was searched block by block for the next two days, though
the original schedule was disrupted by the apparently unforeseen need
to clear the Four Courts and the Fish Market before the working week
began on 17 January.[143] The whole operation caused considerable
public wonderment, with the *Freeman's Journal* asking what this
'amazing military move' could mean, and greeting the withdrawal of
the troops on 17 January with the headline 'Dublin Siege Raised';[144]
but its effect was problematical. Although no important arrests were
made, Dublin District H.Q. judged that it had been 'of great military
value, and of deterrent importance in so far as the hostile population is
concerned'.[145] The brigade conferences which analysed it had more
reservations, especially concerning the failure of the searches, and the
penetrability of the cordon. The arrangements for entry and exit, food
supplies to the area, and so on, had been poor, and the soldiers had
shown an obvious willingness to let 'friendly' people pass in and out.[146]
The opinion of 24th Brigade was that the I.R.A. warning system was too
efficient to permit the capture of important rebels by such cumbrous
operations, and that the disappointment inevitably resulting among
the troops cast doubt on the whole idea.[147] None the less, Dublin
District drew up a set of instructions for the mounting of area
searches,[148] and another big operation was carried out around Mountjoy Square in February (Map 6, p. 156). Its results were not much
different. Later evidence shows that at least one group of rebels caught
within the cordon (which included tank and armoured car patrols)
had little difficulty in escaping, while the equipment they left behind
was not found.[149] Once again, 24th Brigade concluded, the area had
proved too large and the cordon too penetrable. 'Young soldiers', it

---

[140] Efforts were made, however, to mount road blocks and search trains leaving Dublin
for the south, in case Collins was flushed out by the operation. H.Q. D.D. to 25th Bde.,
18 January, and to F Coy. A.D.R.I.C., 19 January 1921. D.D. H.Q. File, W.O. 35 71.
[141] D.D. Orders, 15, 16 January 1921. Ibid.
[142] O.C. Cordon Troops to H.Q. D.D., 17 January 1921. Ibid.
[143] D.D. Orders, 16, 17 January 1921. Ibid.
[144] *Freeman's Journal*, 17, 18 January 1921.
[145] D.D. War Diary, January 1921. W.O. 35 90/2.
[146] Reports of 24th and 25th(P) Bde. Conferences, 21 January 1921. D.D. H.Q. File,
W.O. 35 71.
[147] Report of 24th(P) Bde. Conference, ibid.
[148] D.D. S/G1, 'Instructions for Raiding and Searching an Extended Area of Houses in
Dublin', 29 January 1921. D.D. H.Q. File, W.O. 35 71.
[149] C. Dalton, *With the Dublin Brigade 1917–1921* (London, 1929), p. 142.

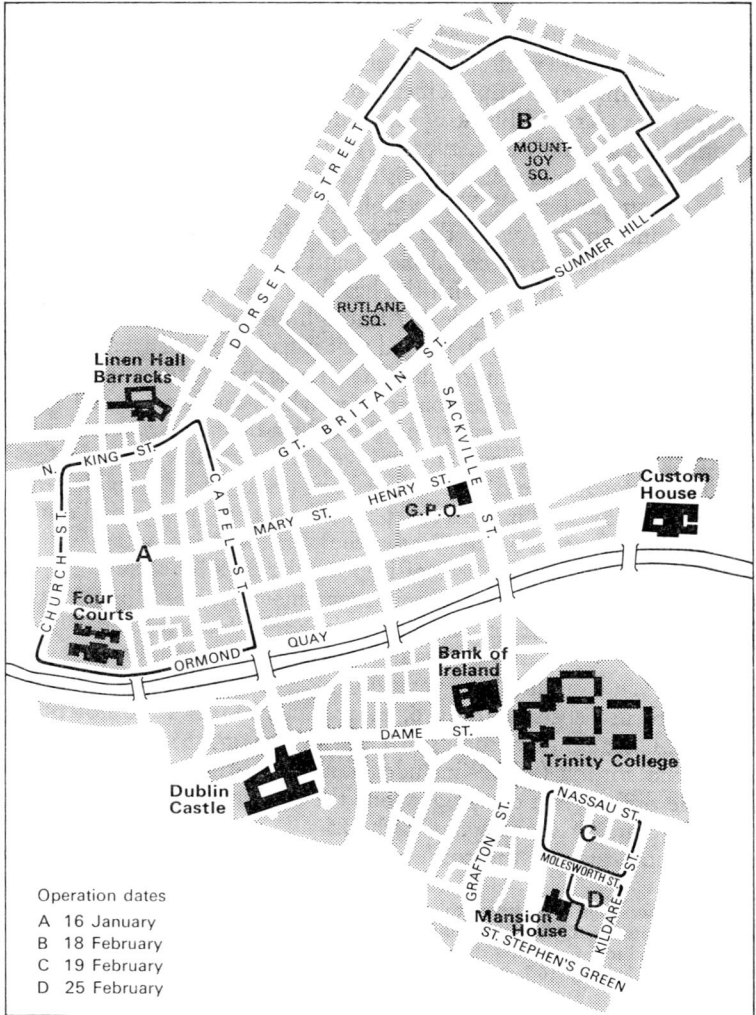

Map 6: Dublin Area Searches II: Four Courts, Mountjoy, and Molesworth Street

said, 'must be taught to harden their hearts while on duty.'[150] The scale of searches after this was more modest. Cordons were often applied round one or two blocks in conjunction with multiple raids rather than full-scale searches.

The more ordinary business of raiding was also depressingly unproductive in the first three months of 1921. Dublin District Intelligence attributed this to a growing popular reluctance to keep arms or even documents in the house.[151] This was an equivocal development unless the new dumps proved easier to discover, and at present they did not seem to be. A document drawn up on 31 January, a 'search history' of Cullenswood House (once the home of Pearse's Irish School, St. Enda's; now often used as a rebel H.Q., and often raided—but never at the same moment) summed up the cat-and-mouse game in which the I.R.A. seemed always just half a step ahead.[152] In mid-March, because of persistent rumours that the I.R.A. had 'munition factories' in bicycle workshops, no less than 69 such establishments were raided in two days. Only one Mills bomb and two bullets were found.[153] Captured I.R.A. reports left no doubt that raids often failed to find concealed arms, and G.H.Q. exhorted troops to take more care:

When opposed to such people as we are at present, nothing but the most careful, methodical and lengthy investigation will achieve success. The searchers must have as much imagination as the other side.[154]

But when Dublin District, following this sermon, told its units to be more thorough, it received the sharp reply,

if you order a list [of raids] as long as your arm to be carried out by say next morning, Units must have several raids allotted to them to exhaust the list, and get through them as best they can.[155]

Clearly the long period of military frustration was beginning to strain tempers.

Military and public opinion
The period following the setbacks of November 1920 had seen a considerable and very necessary increase in the professionalism with which the Army tackled the Irish conflict, but military involvement remained ill-defined. As Irish Command later wrote, 'There was no objective for operations, there was no defined theatre of war, there

[150] 24th(P) Bde. to H.Q. D.D., 24 February 1921. D.D. H.Q. File, W.O. 35 71.
[151] I. Summary, 1 February 1921. D.D. War Diary, W.O. 35 90/2.
[152] I. Summary, 13 March 1921. D.D. War Diary, W.O. 35 90/2.
[153] H.Q. D.D. to 24th and 25th(P) Bdes., XV Hussars, and C.R.E., 18 March 1921. D.D. H.Q. File, W.O. 35 71.
[154] G.H.Q. Ireland to 1st, 5th, 6th Divs., and D.D., 7 March 1921. Ibid.
[155] 24th(P) Bde. to H.Q. D.D., 26 March 1921. Ibid.

was no "front line".'[156] The difficulty which has been observed in forming effective cordons for area searches was symptomatic of an easy-going attitude on the part of the ordinary soldiers; it was very hard to convince them of 'the necessity for regarding every civilian with suspicion as a potential enemy'.[157] This was a remarkable tribute to their forbearance, a priceless characteristic, but not on its own likely to bring success.

As regards the officers, there is no doubt that many were depressed by the widespread hostility of public opinion as reflected in the newspapers, and by the lack of clarity and determination of the Government's policy. In February the G.O.C. 5th Division, Jeudwine, submitted a memorandum analysing the chances of attaining the Government's aim (which he took to be the establishment of a self-governing Ireland in close federation with Britain). He pointed out that

military measures alone can have no lasting effect, and their employment can only be effective when they are directed as the expression of a determined policy towards the foundation of a sound and practical political structure.[158]

It was vital, he said, to convince the Irish people of the Government's determination, and to try to drive a wedge between the majority of the population and the 'extremists committed to the gun'. These things could now only be done by applying martial law over the whole country; this

would substitute for the present divided control by military and police, which is enforced by different authorities in different ways, according to very diverse standards, and often with more than questionable justice or even advantage, a unified and codified control with definite aims, regulations and penalties.[159]

This view of the Army's capacity to work out effective aims and methods was perhaps not entirely borne out by experience, but it was by no means confined to the Army.

Public opinion was becoming increasingly critical of the Government's Irish policy, and in particular of the police. In Ireland itself, of course, most of the nationalist press had for some time been apparently irreconcilable, and in December 1920 even the cautious Castle administration had agreed to the prosecution of the *Freeman's Journal* for 'spreading a false report'. The editor and proprietor both received six-month prison sentences; but the reaction of the British press speedily convinced the Government of the need to order their release 'on

[156] G.H.Q. Ireland, *Record*, i. 33.
[157] Ibid. Macready reported in the spring that 'The troops remain in good heart, easy to handle, and keen in participating in operations. . . . They appear to treat the civilians as they did the Germans—"a thing apart".' *Annals*, i . 554.
[158] G.O.C. 5th Div. to G.O.C.-in-C. Ireland, 14 February 1921. Jeudwine papers, I.W.M. 72/82/2.
[159] Ibid.

medical grounds'. Anderson disliked this surrender sufficiently to procrastinate, and Greenwood had to issue a direct order—'this decision to release is final', he announced on 6 January, and 'must not be contingent on payment of fines'.[160] Macready reserved one of his bitterest comments for this affair, which, he said, 'aroused disgust and contempt in the hearts of those who were risking their lives for the policy of the Government'.[161] Two months later he tried to obtain the suppression of the *Freeman* and the *Independent*, which he described as 'nothing less than daily propaganda of rebellion', but was told that the reaction of the British press would make such a step impossible.[162]

The opposition of the press in Ireland played, as Macready suggested, a great part in stiffening resistance among Irish moderates, while public criticism in Britain undermined the assurance of the Government. A strong attack was launched at this time with the publication of the report of the Labour Commission to Ireland, which struck at almost every aspect of the coercive policy. Brigadier-General C. B. Thomson,[163] the Commission's military adviser, described the Army in Ireland as raw and ill-trained, with most of its officers 'ignorant of their professional duties'.[164] The Auxiliaries were portrayed as the most potent, and also the most vicious, of the Crown forces. They did not 'seem to recognize even the authority of Dublin Castle', and the Commission put the crucial question 'Under whom do they serve?'[165] It concluded that, in creating the Black and Tans, the Government had 'liberated forces which it is not at present able to dominate'.[166] This sinister note was well-judged. An attack from a different quarter came in an article published by General Sir Hubert Gough[167] in February, which argued that

it is impossible to come to any other honest opinion (whether you excuse them or not, on account of the provocation they have received) but that the police in many cases and the soldiers in some, have been guilty of gross acts of violence,

[160] C.S.I. to U.S., 6 January 1921. Lloyd George papers, F/19/3/1.

[161] Macready, *Annals*, ii. 476.

[162] G.H.Q. Ireland, *Record*, i. 34; cf. Macready to Anderson, 7 March 1921. Anderson papers, C.O. 904 188/2; and to Frances Stevenson, same date. Lloyd George papers, F/36/2/17.

[163] Later Secretary of State for Air in the Labour Governments of 1924 and 1929. Macready's reaction to Thomson and the Commission was, 'Is C. B. Thompson [*sic*] on the active list? If so what is he doing with the Labour Deputation? Arthur Henderson cannot be trusted a yard—nor C.B.T.!' Macready to Jeudwine, 4 December 1920. Jeudwine papers.

[164] Labour Party, *Report of the Labour Commission to Ireland*, Part II, p. 6. Macready later pointed out that 53·3 per cent of subalterns had been through the R.M.A. *Annals*, ii. 530–2.

[165] *Report of the Labour Commission*, p. 7.

[166] Ibid., pp. 53–4.

[167] Leader of the 'Curragh mutiny' in 1914; commander of the ill-fated 5th Army on the Western Front, 1917–18.

without even a semblance of military order and discipline, and that these acts are not only never adequately punished, but no steps are taken to prevent their recurrence.[168]

In fact, Gough pointed out, the R.I.C. *Weekly Summary* seemed actually to encourage them; and, he added, 'we may well stand aghast' at Tudor's order of 14 December deprecating reprisals by burning—'It is not an order, it is merely an "appeal".' Such a police force, Gough said, was 'a danger to its own superiors'.[169] The question now was whether these strong criticisms of the structure of authority in Ireland, added to those which were being heard closer to the Government, would be sufficient to produce a change.

15. DIVIDED COMMAND (February–April 1921)

The Civil Government, the Army, and the Police
The legal confusion which grew up around the martial law courts in January and February threw into sharper relief the general problem of relations between the civil and military authorities. While Macready's reaction was to call for the suspension of all civil courts in the M.L.A., Anderson felt that the King's Bench judgement in Allen's case was

an enormous asset and puts us in an infinitely stronger position than if we had somehow contrived to dodge the issue. . . . From the House of Commons point of view also the continuance of the civil courts guards one obvious line of attack.[170]

Macready's view was that, however democratically reassuring this might be, it had little point if it prevented martial law from operating effectively. The King's Bench had done no more than state the law, which should have been known anyway, yet it had failed to close the issue. In Macready's opinion the issue should not have been 'dodged', but should never have been allowed to arise.

His desire to suspend the civil courts (an eventuality which had been implicit in the original martial law proclamation),[171] became more urgent in March, when the threatening case of *The King* (*Garde*) v. *Strickland* arose. The threat here was in the principle on which the appeal was urged, namely that R.O.I.A. had made it impossible to proclaim martial law except by statute.[172] If upheld, this principle would mean that the powers of the Crown had been curtailed rather

---

[168] Gen. Sir Hubert Gough, 'The Situation in Ireland', *Review of Reviews*, lxiii (February 1921), p. 35.
[169] Ibid., p. 36.
[170] Anderson to Macready, 26 February 1921. Anderson papers, C.O. 904 188/2.
[171] See above, p. 146.
[172] See App. to C.S.I. Weekly Survey, 25 April 1921. C.P. 2892, CAB.24 122.

than increased by R.O.I.A. Over this appeal, Anderson argued that since it was made in the High Court, it could not be prevented unless Dublin were also under martial law.[173] Macready replied on 7 April,

I do not think that I have ever agreed, except under pressure, to Civil Courts functioning in a Martial Law Area. I always thought it an anomaly, and I think so now. If Civil Courts did not function at all . . . writs by the High Court . . . could not run, and we should have been saved all this trouble.[174]

Finally, on 14 April, he took independent action, and issued a proclamation ordering that

within the areas in which Martial Law has been declared the jurisdiction of all Courts of Justice in all matters whatsoever relating to any claims whatsoever in respect of any damage or injury alleged to have been done by the Forces of the Crown . . . is hereby suspended.[175]

According to Sturgis he thereby 'raised a storm', with Hamar Greenwood doubly furious because he had not been consulted. Macready was forced to explain that he meant the suspension to apply only to official reprisals, but, as Sturgis noted, 'it certainly doesn't say so'.[176]

Meanwhile the basic problem of divided authority had once more been brought into the foreground. When the legal dispute was still in its infancy, Sir Warren Fisher made a second inspection of the Dublin administration, and his verdict was perhaps even more crushing than that of his first, nine months before. He held that Greenwood, on his trips to Ireland,[177] remained isolated at the Chief Secretary's Lodge in Phoenix Park, out of touch with public feeling. Much worse, the civil, police, and military authorities had developed into separate, almost rival powers.

Not only is the use of force not singly directed, but even as between the three elements now existing there is little evidence of effective cooperation. On the contrary there are to my mind undoubted signs of an untimely lack of sympathy and uncomprehension in attitude and liaison in working.[178]

Fisher paid lip-service to the 'cordiality' of relations at high level, and laid the blame on a general adherence to rigid old procedures, in a 'wholly abnormal emergency'. He reserved his most astringent

---

[173] Anderson to Macready, 29 March 1921. Anderson papers, C.O. 904 188/2.
[174] Macready to Anderson, 7 April 1921. Ibid.
[175] Proclamation No. 3 by G.O.C.-in-C. and Military Governor-General of Ireland, 14 April 1921. W.O. 35 169.
[176] Sturgis diary, 19 April 1921. P.R.O. 30 59/4.
[177] Macready criticized Greenwood as 'somewhat of a mythical personage', rarely seen in Ireland (*Annals*, ii. 492), but the latter's correspondence with Lloyd George shows that he went over quite often and always tried to stay as long as possible, in face of pressure to return to parliament.
[178] Report of a Visit to Ireland by Sir Warren Fisher, 11 February 1921. Lloyd George papers, F/17/1/9.

criticism for the dogged maintenance of the R.I.C.'s independence. Old ideas and present circumstances, he said, 'including their present composition', led them to 'regard themselves as their own masters'. Nor did they compensate for this by great achievements, for

That the police themselves thus on their own are engaged on really thinking out and organizing some concerted plan of campaign is a proposition which even an ostrich could hardly entertain.[179]

He declared that the shock effect of 'brute and blind' reprisals had now worn off, and that the police were 'getting fully as much as they give'. Independent patrolling by the police he dismissed as a 'shibboleth'. (It is clear that even now there was little in the way of joint military-police patrols.)[180] He endorsed the Army's belief that the relative decline in rebel attacks on troops as against those on police was due to the superiority of military methods, not, as the police alleged, to the fact that the troops were less active.[181] Fisher concluded that the need for unified command was incontrovertible. The G.O.C.-in-C. should be given complete power, with or without full martial law—though 'the real fact is that Martial Law everywhere is an intelligible policy, or Martial Law nowhere'.[182]

This reasoning did not recommend itself to the Cabinet. Lady Greenwood told Sturgis that Macready was 'somewhat out of favour' at this time, and that Lloyd George was more likely to remove martial law than to extend it.[183] Sturgis was mystified that Lloyd George, who had been the apostle of unified command on the Western Front, could not see 'the absolute necessity for it here'.[184] In fact, of course, Lloyd George had seen unity of command as a matter not of principle but of politics. In France it had served to control generals he did not trust, but in Ireland it would have a different effect, exalting the military over the police, whose methods he approved.[185]

The control of the R.I.C.
The facts so far known do not permit a satisfactory analysis of the part played by the Chief of Police in the development of these methods. Sturgis regarded Tudor as a likeable man of 'almost childlike simplicity', out of his depth in the subtlety of Lloyd George's policy:

[179] Ibid.
[180] Cf. Macready to Anderson, 5 February 1921. Anderson papers.
[181] The police also had a theory that the rebels were purposely refraining from attacks on troops so as to foment friction between the Crown Forces. Fisher's Report, 11 February 1921.
[182] Ibid.
[183] Sturgis diary, 23 February 1921. P.R.O. 30 59/4.
[184] Ibid., 28 February 1921.
[185] In June he 'expressed his strong resentment at the animus against the police constantly shewn by Macready'. Jones, *Whitehall Diary*, iii. 73.

He does not consciously deceive, but his belief in all that's good of his Black and Tans and his inability to believe a word against them is superhuman.[186]

Undoubtedly Tudor's passivity in matters of discipline was itself important, but it seems clear that he also played a more positive role. Sturgis, reflecting in February on 'the spoiling of what might have been a first-rate force', wrote that the Black and Tans 'could have been ideal for the job if some of them hadn't taken a completely wrong view of their functions from the stupid tone of their heads';[187] and Anderson, talking to Tom Jones on 15 February, expressed the view 'that when Tudor came over to Ireland he was not unfriendly to the Irish cause but that the murdering of his men had embittered him'.[188] Anderson also felt, significantly, that 'whenever Tudor came over to see the P.M. he returned very much strengthened in his policy'.[189]

These remarks were made at a time when Tudor had suddenly come under considerable pressure. The immediate reasons for this were two crimes committed by Auxiliaries on 9 February. At Balbraddagh, near Trim, Co. Meath, an A.D.R.I.C. search party stole £325 worth of liquor and food from a shop which they later burned.[190] In Republican mythology this became 'the notorious looting of Trim'. That same night a far uglier event took place in Dublin: two prisoners held by F. Company, A.D.R.I.C. at Dublin Castle, were taken out and shot in a field; in the suburb of Drumcondra. Shortly afterwards the military authorities arrested the commander of F. Company, Captain King,[191] and two of his men. Crozier, the head of the A.D.R.I.C., meanwhile hastened to Trim where he summarily tried 26 Cadets of N Company, dismissing 21 and placing 5 under arrest pending court-martial. Tudor, who had curtailed Crozier's disciplinary powers the previous year, promptly reversed these proceedings and reinstated the 21 until a full inquiry was made. On 19 February Crozier resigned amidst a barrage of public recrimination (a godsend to Republican propaganda), alleging that the authorities had surrendered to threats from the dismissed men to reveal the black deeds of the police in Ireland.[192]

---

[186] Sturgis diary, 13 January 1921. P.R.O. 30 59/3.
[187] Ibid., 11 February 1921.
[188] Jones, *Whitehall Diary*, iii. 53.
[189] Ibid.
[190] Bennett, *The Black and Tans*, p. 146.
[191] Capt./1st D.I. W. L. King, M.C. For allegations regarding his torture of prisoners see the American edition of O'Malley's book, *Army Without Banners* (Boston, 1937), pp. 288f.
[192] Crozier's account (see *Impressions and Recollections*, pp. 265–6) was naturally accepted unreservedly by opponents of the Government, but it should be treated with some caution. Macready, no staunch supporter of Tudor, thought that Crozier's record was 'hardly a recommendation as an administrator of discipline in any capacity whatsoever' (Macready to Anderson, 25 February 1921. C.O. 904 188/2). Basil Clarke wrote privately (C.O. 904 168), in an idiom suited to the situation, a wry ballad which began:

In fact Crozier had acted precipitately, as the eventual conclusion of the official courts-martial undoubtedly showed. Of the 8 Cadets finally convicted, 4 had not been suspected by Crozier, while no *prima facie* case could be found against 18 of the 21 he had dismissed.[193] Yet it is obvious that these courts-martial, which did not take place until July, lacked the deterrent effect of Crozier's summary action. Tudor could certainly with benefit have employed some of Crozier's dispatch. His part in the Drumcondra case was still more doubtful. On 15 February Macready wrote to Anderson that 'every effort is being made to prove alibis and such like in the case of Major [sic] King', and that 'Tudor of course has a cock and bull story about the two men who were killed being rabid S.F.'s', but he hoped to 'circumvent' all this and see justice done.[194] The only other known fact about the affair is that King and his two men were acquitted by a court-martial on 15 April.[195]

Tudor's position may have weakened slightly on 13 February when Churchill left the War Office and was replaced by Sir Laming Worthington-Evans. Long also left the Government at this time through ill-health. Tudor certainly received 'an awful doing' from Anderson,[196] and was summoned to London to 'listen to a good many plain words' from Lloyd George on 14 February.[197] (He was justifiably confused, as he had been strongly encouraged a week before.)[198] Anderson had at last become convinced of the need to impose discipline on the R.I.C., and of the fact that, while Tudor would agree in private that some tightening-up was necessary, 'he took another line when he met his men'.[199] Even Lloyd George was impelled to notify Greenwood that he was 'not at all satisfied with the state of discipline of the Royal Irish Constabulary and its auxiliary force'. He referred to

increasing evidence that in certain sections of the Irish police there are certain men who are no longer the guardians of the law, but are themselves guilty of unlawful acts against the population it is their duty to protect.[200]

Brigadier General C	Brigadier General C
Was Head of the Auxiliaree	Was right at the top of the tree
When skies were serene	Everything that they did
You couldn't have seen	They did as *he* bid—
A bucko more lordly than he.	A towzer for discipline he! . . .

The implication that Crozier himself had been an instigator of reprisals is widespread in Castle sources.

[193] C.S.I. Weekly Survey, 11 July 1921. C.P. 3130, CAB.24 124.
[194] Macready to Anderson, 15 February 1921. Anderson papers. C.O. 904 188/2.
[195] Sturgis diary, 15 April 1921. P.R.O. 30 59/4. Cf. Crozier, *Impressions and Recollections*, p. 269.
[196] Sturgis diary, 13 February 1921. P.R.O. 30 59/3.
[197] Anderson to Macready, 17 February 1921. Anderson papers, C.O. 904 188/2.
[198] Sturgis diary, 8 and 14 February 1921.
[199] Anderson's conversation with Jones, 15 February 1921. Jones, *Whitehall Diary*, iii. 52.
[200] Prime Minister to C.S.I., 25 February 1921. Lloyd George papers, F/19/3/4.

After this summary of what had in effect been his policy for eight months, he complained that violence and indiscipline would lead an 'already unhappy' public opinion to 'swing round and withdraw its support' from the Government.[201]

The situation therefore looked favourable for a renewed assault by Macready on the bastions of police independence. He began with the Martial Law Area, demanding full powers for General Strickland and the placing of a special R.I.C. officer on Strickland's staff. In a memorandum to the Castle on 14 February he warned that

until the whole of the police in the Martial Law Area look to the Military Governor as their immediate and only superior in everything except Police routine of administration and interior economy, Martial Law will not only be ineffective, but friction will occur between the Military and Police Authorities.[202]

He wrote privately to Anderson at the same time of police 'wild men treating the Martial Law Area as a special game reserve for their own amusement'.[203] In answer to his demands, Brigadier-General Prescott-Decie—the R.I.C. D.C. about whom Macready had been so scathing in December 1920[204]—was appointed Strickland's 'Police Adviser' (though yet again his powers were unclear).[205] Macready soon had bigger targets in sight. On 15 February he advised Anderson to make sure that, since Churchill had left the War Office, Tudor had 'no connection of any kind with him'.[206] He then set about trying to modify Tudor's own staff by the addition of a 'discipline officer' nominated by G.H.Q. He achieved this transplant early in March, but the officer concerned, Colonel Ralph Umfreville, faced a stormy future in a hostile environment.

After Umfreville's appointment Sturgis remarked in his diary, 'As far as I can make out, this is the only step that has been taken to "win the war"!'[207] Military control over the police proved tenuous. In the M.L.A. the situation remained unsatisfactory, largely owing to the weakness of the R.I.C.'s own authority. Macready paid one of his rare visits to Cork between 16 and 18 March, and found that there was 'no love lost' between the R.I.C. D.C.s and the A.D.R.I.C. companies except where the latter were 'thoroughly in hand'.[208] He reported severe shortages of Head Constables and District Inspectors, especially

[201] Ibid.
[202] G.O.C.-in-C. Ireland to U.S., 14 February 1921. Anderson papers, C.O. 904 188/2
[203] Macready to Anderson, 14 February 1921. Ibid.
[204] See p. 138 above.
[205] G.O.C.-in-C. Ireland to Chief of Police, 24 February 1921. Copy, Anderson papers, C.O. 904 188/2.
[206] Macready to Anderson, 15 February 1921. Ibid.
[207] Sturgis diary, 6 March 1921. P.R.O. 30 59/4.
[208] Macready to Anderson, 18 March 1921. Anderson papers, C.O. 904 188/2.

for staff work. He was also infuriated to meet a blatant instance of an A.D.R.I.C. commander ignoring the Military Governor and sending an important report direct to Tudor in Dublin,[209] and he warned that any officer doing this again would be suspended and removed from the M.L.A.[210]

Almost everywhere outside Dublin city the independence of the R.I.C. was manifest. Even the basic principle that a military officer must be in command of any mixed force, first enunciated at the beginning of 1920, seems to have been often ignored.[211] The commander of 24th Brigade reported on 31 March that the R.I.C. were still carrying out unofficial raids and looting, with men from the Gormanstown depot ranging as far afield as Drogheda.[212] And, amazingly, in late March the R.I.C. D.C. at Galway, regardless of the fact that his area was not under martial law, began to carry out 'official' police reprisals. At first, Macready thought that these were further manifestations of indiscipline, and threatened to withdraw military detachments from places where they occurred.[213] When it became clear that the D.C. was taking responsibility, the Castle showed some alarm (even under martial law, reprisals could only be authorized by brigade commanders), but Tudor supported him.[214] There is no indication of how the matter ended.[215]

The Castleconnell incident

To obtain a vivid impression of police operations at this time it is worth turning in detail to an incident which took place on 19 April 1921, and which, though it caused a stir at the time, has since been almost completely ignored. This was a raid carried out by G. Company A.D.R.I.C. (Killaloe) on the Shannon Hotel, Castleconnell, some six miles up-river from Limerick, where suspicious characters had been reported to be meeting. The raiding force, commanded by Captain/2nd D.I. Wood, was divided into two parties. Two officers and 12 Cadets in plain clothes were ordered to filter unobtrusively into the hotel bar to look for suspects, while a uniformed party of an officer and 20 Cadets with

---

[209] Macready to Anderson, 20 March 1921. Ibid. The report concerned a threatened 'rising' in Kerry: the warning was received in Dublin two days before it reached Strickland in Cork.

[210] Macready to Anderson, 21 March 1921. Ibid. The officer was Major McKinnon, the 'tyrant Major' of the ballad 'The Shooting of Major McKinnon'. He was assassinated less than a month later on Tralee golf links.

[211] See 1st S.W.B. to H.Q. D.D., and note, 29 March 1921. W.O. 35 71.

[212] G.O.C. 24th(P) Bde. to H.Q. D.D., 31 March 1921. W.O. 35 66.

[213] Macready to Anderson, 28 March 1921. Anderson papers, C.O. 904 188/2.

[214] Sturgis diary, 31 March 1921. P.R.O. 30 59/4.

[215] An official statement of 4 May 1921 declared that 'outside the Martial Law area there is no power under which acts of official punishment . . . can be carried out. No such acts have at any time been executed at the direction of the Government.' Hemming papers.

two Lewis guns surrounded the area. As they drove up to Castle-connell, however, a number of men were seen running across the fields, and the Auxiliaries promptly forgot their plan.[216] The plain-clothes party, on reaching the hotel, rushed straight into the bar, shouting 'Hands up!' In the bar were three off-duty R.I.C. men, who took the intruders to be rebels, opened fire on them, and drove them out. A brisk exchange followed in which an R.I.C. sergeant in the bar and a Cadet in the courtyard outside were killed. Eventually the arrival of the uniformed party led the two remaining R.I.C. men in the bar to realize the mistake, and they, together with the landlord, Denis O'Donovan, ran out to surrender. The Auxiliaries continued to fire, wounding one of the R.I.C. and killing O'Donovan, who was hit by six bullets.[217] Captain Wood then ordered fire to cease.

So, at least, the official story went.[218] The problem was that one of the hotel guests, an eminent surgeon by the name of Cripps, alleged that the A.D.R.I.C. had not stopped firing but had rampaged around the hotel 'like demented Red Indians'. On 26 April his brother, Lord Parmoor,[219] rose to read this testimony to the House of Lords—accompanied by a dum-dum cartridge which had been picked up in the hotel after the A.D.R.I.C. had left, and which was passed round for examination by the peers—and to demand a full public inquiry.[220] Even the best courtroom tactics, however, failed to embarrass the Government, which calmly ignored the allegations of violence and indiscipline and said that a full inquiry—the Military Court of Inquiry in Lieu of Inquest—was already in progress. Parmoor's evidence was effectively disregarded. On 5 May the military court's verdict was presented to the Lords with all the skill of Birkenhead himself. He subtly discounted Cripps's testimony as that of 'a man of peace sud-denly and unexpectedly introduced into a terrible scene of war'.[221] He stated that the A.D.R.I.C. had ceased firing when ordered to, and that the military authorities had found no evidence of indiscipline: 'notwithstanding the very great excitement which naturally prevailed, the Cadets were under complete control'.[222] In fact, however, the

[216] Note by G.O.C.-in-C., Proceedings of Mil. Ct. of Inquiry in Lieu of Inquest on Denis O'Donovan, Sgt. William Hughes, R.I.C., and T./C. Donald Pringle, A.D.R.I.C. W.O. 35 157A.

[217] He received 3 wounds in front, 1 in the side, and 2 in the back. This suggests that he ran right through the surrounding A.D.R.I.C. There was unsupported evidence from a chambermaid that he had been deliberately shot against a wall.

[218] Narrative taken from M.C.I. (case of O'Donovan and others), W.O. 35 157A, and statement by Lord Chancellor, House of Lords, 5 May 1921. 45 H.L. Deb. 5s, cols 257–8.

[219] Lord President of the Council in the Labour Governments of 1924 and 1929; Barrister; father of Stafford Cripps.

[220] 45 H.L. Deb. 5s, cols. 16–19.

[221] 45 H.L. Deb. 5s, col. 262.

[222] Ibid.

view of the military authorities was quite different. Macready, commenting on the proceedings of the military court, condemned both the conception and execution of the raid, and neither he nor the Deputy Adjutant General seems to have doubted that the A.D.R.I.C. had run amok.[223] The Lord Chancellor might think it natural for 'very great excitement' not only to occur, but to prevail, amongst the police, but military opinion was less indulgent. The Deputy Adjutant General wrote,

They all had the wind up, blood up, and did what they used to do in the trenches in France. In the circumstances you cannot hold them criminally responsible, but they are not fit to be policemen—but are any Auxiliaries?[224]

Propaganda and Intelligence
Returning to the wider problem of divided authority in Ireland, one can see that this had a distinct effect in the vital spheres of propaganda and intelligence. Military dissatisfaction with the handling of Government publicity became if anything more acute in 1921 than before, and on 7 March Macready, conveying to Anderson General Strickland's complaints on this subject, declared that 'Until this question of propaganda is properly tackled by someone far more able than Basil Clarke we shall never get right.'[225] It is evident that within the Castle there was also a great lack of confidence. Loughnane, for instance, made an 'impassioned' complaint to Anderson in February that

the police reports from the country are on the face of it false in the main, and that he feels he is being employed creating a smoke screen for the CS's parliamentary answers, under cover of which these things can continue.[226]

Loughnane disliked the covering-up of reprisals, but the Army was most concerned at the lack of energy in countering Republican propaganda. The most serious example of this was when the Judge Advocate General produced a set of memoranda on the legal questions of the war, the most important being 'why captured Irish rebels are not treated as prisoners of war', a demolition of the I.R.A.'s claim to belligerent rights.[227] Macready thought it vital that these be given the strongest possible publicity, but the actual press release was so poorly managed that he did not notice it.[228] Anderson explained that the piece

[223] M.C.I. (O'Donovan and others): Note by G.O.C.-in-C. Ireland, 1 May 1921. W.O. 35 157A.
[224] Ibid.: Note by D.A.G. Ireland, 3 May 1921.
[225] Macready to Anderson, 7 March 1921. Anderson papers, C.O. 904 188/2.
[226] Sturgis diary, 12 February 1921. P.R.O. 30 59/3.
[227] Memo by J.A.G. (1. Trial and Punishment by Military Courts; 2. Reprisals; 3. Hostages; 4. Illegitimate Ammunition), 17 March 1921. Hemming papers.
[228] Macready to Anderson, 4 April 1921. Anderson papers, C.O. 904 188/2. Cf. J.A.G. to C.S.I., 6 April 1921. Ibid., C.O. 904 188/1.

had been 'crowded out by more immediately interesting material'.[229]

In the still more critical sphere of intelligence, the Army maintained its opposition to the overall Director of Intelligence, Winter. Macready wrote to Anderson on 4 April that, in the opinion of G.H.Q.,

> Winter has not got the right method, and we here doubt very much whether he will ever get it. He is, I fancy, a 'born sleuth', but I doubt his organizing power, and that, so far as I can see, is what is holding up the machine.[230]

Counsels were divided in the Castle too, for on 15 March Sturgis recorded that there was nearly 'a three-cornered fight' between Anderson, Cope, and Winter 'about O's show, responsibility for raids, etc.'.[231] A picture of Crown intelligence in 1921 cannot better be conveyed than by quoting from an order of 7 March, concerning documents captured in raids.

(a) Documents which do not actually form part of the evidence against an individual.

All documents captured by the troops are forwarded to the Brigade headquarters. All documents captured by the police are forwarded to the local centre at the Divisional Commissioner's office.

(b) The military intelligence service is responsible for dealing with all documents relating to the operations, armament, training, and organization (including the order of battle and the names of commanders and officers) of the IRA. After duplication of such documents they are passed in original to the police intelligence service as signatures, handwriting, typing of such papers may often be important links in a chain of evidence.

The military intelligence service transfers to the 'Local Centre' of police intelligence all documents referred to in (c) below.

(c) The police intelligence service is responsible for passing through to the military intelligence service all documents referred to in (b) above and for dealing with all documents relating to individuals, addresses, Sinn Fein police, Sinn Fein courts, Sinn Fein organization in Great Britain and abroad, propaganda, etc., etc., and for working up cases against individuals.

(d) In cases where documents form the evidence against an individual or individuals charged with possession of seditious documents, the documents are forwarded by the local CMA through the usual military channels to GHQ, except in the martial law area where they are dealt with by 'the Military Governor.[232]

The awkward separation of 'military' and 'criminal' or 'political' aspects of the Republican campaign demonstrated the failure to integrate the intelligence services into a single, efficient system.[233]

[229] Anderson to Macready, 5 April 1921. Ibid., C.O. 904 188/2.
[230] Macready to Anderson, 4 April 1921. Ibid.
[231] Sturgis diary, 15 March 1921. P.R.O. 30 59/4.
[232] G.H.Q. Ireland, *Record*, ii. 13.
[233] For a recent discussion, based on experience, of the principle of unity in intelligence services for counter-insurgency work, see Kitson, *Low Intensity Operations*, pp. 74–5.

Air co-operation

A final sphere of divided command worthy of mention was in the employment of air power. Though not productive of such acrimony as the police issue, the ineffectiveness of air operations in the Irish theatre was puzzling to many people. The matter had been raised in Cabinet in April 1920, and Lord Midleton brought it up again in March 1921—finding no sign of development in the meantime.[233a] On 21 February a question was put in the House of Commons on the control and use of aircraft in Ireland, to which Worthington-Evans replied,

The aircraft in Ireland is employed in carrying out important work in connexion with military operations. Their value in dealing with ambushes is fully realized by the C-in-C, and when it is considered advisable to employ them in this way they are so utilized. The military authorities have full control over the use of aeroplanes.[234]

This statement was very misleading. No real operational role had yet been found for aircraft, nor was their employment under purely military control

Great hopes had at first, been placed in the air arm. On his appointment as Viceroy in 1918, Lord French had told Lloyd George that the 'essence' of his plan was the use of aircraft, based on 'strongly entrenched "Air Camps"'.[235] Air patrolling with bombs and machine guns ought, he thought, 'to put the fear of God into these playful young Sinn Féiners'. Shaw expressed the same opinion to Sir Frederick Sykes, Chief of the Air Staff.[236] The Government, however, did not permit the aircraft to use bombs or machine guns, and the young Sinn Féiners soon learned to treat them with disdain. Two squadrons, totalling 7 flights, mainly of Bristol fighters, were allotted to Irish Command, but nothing was done to create 'Air Camps' or to increase the small number of landing grounds.[237] Even the number of aircraft declined. Churchill complained to Trenchard on 24 September 1920 that a mere 18 serviceable machines were available, and called for this **total** to be trebled.

The presence of aeroplanes in the air is a great protection to armoured car work on the road and a great deterrent to illegal drilling and rebel gatherings.[238]

[233a] Cabinet Conversation, 30 April 1920, CAB.23 20; Cabinet Conference, 8 March 1921. Jones, *Whitehall Diary*, iii, 55.

[234] 138 H.C. Deb. 5s, col. 573.

[235] Ld. Lt. to Prime Minister, 18 April 1918. Lloyd George papers, F/48/6/7.

[236] G.O.C.-in-C. Ireland to Chief of Air Staff, 16 April 1918. W.O. 35 173.

[237] G.O.C.-in-C. W.S.R., 10 August 1920. S.I.C. 28, CAB.27 108; G.O.C. 5th Div. to G.O.C.-in-C. Ireland, 23 July 1920. Jeudwine papers.

[238] Sec. of State for War and Air to Chief of Air Staff, 24 September 1920. Churchill papers.

Churchill's intentions were laudable but bore little relation to reality. Aircraft flew regular observation patrols, especially in the abandoned areas of the south-west, and later they were used for observation during searches and drives. But even here their utility was limited by lack of radio communication with base or ground forces. For more positive functions they were useless. Worthington-Evans's implication that they could 'deal with' ambushes was absurd as long as they remained unarmed. There was little military contact with the R.A.F. and little development of ideas: the future Field-Marshal Montgomery, then Brigade Major of the 17th Brigade in Cork, said that the aircrews 'knew nothing whatever about the war, or the conditions under which it was being fought'.[239] But this was perhaps not entirely their fault, and a more imaginative approach by the Army might have yielded different results.

The only real use which the Army found for the R.A.F. was in transporting senior officers and in running an air mail service once the roads and ordinary mails had become dangerous and slow to use.[240] Macready tried to get Cabinet permission for the arming of aircraft in September 1920, but was refused, and not until 24 March (a month *after* Worthington-Evans's statement) was authority given.[241] Even then, the Cabinet, worried by incidents on the North-West Frontier of India, stressed

the great risk of death and injury to innocent people, owing to the extreme difficulty of distinguishing innocent from guilty from an aeroplane summoned possibly from a great distance by telephone, and necessarily proceeding at high speed and operating at a considerable height.[242]

This caution in fact underlined the fundamental handicap in using aircraft in Ireland. For if identification was difficult for the troops on the ground, it was all but impossible from the air. The remaining months of the war were to show that while political restraints existed (as in this case they must), the potential of air power could not begin to be applied.

[239] Montgomery to Percival, 14 October 1923. Percival papers. Cf. also Percival Lecture 2, p. 15.
[240] Air mails began during the summer of 1920 in the south-west. G.O.C.-in-C. W.S.R., 10 August 1920; they ran later across 5th Division area and D.D.—3 times a week between Oranmore (Galway Bde.), Athlone (13th Bde.), the Curragh, and Baldonnell (G.H.Q.). 5th Div. War Diary, W.O. 35 93(1)/2.
[241] Cf. Macready, *Annals*, ii. 547. The reason for the sanction was the threatened Kerry 'rising'—see note 209, p. 166 above.
[242] Cabinet, 24 March 1921. C.15(21), CAB.23 24; Irish Command received the authorization on 29 March. 'G' War Diary, G.H.Q. Ireland. W.O. 35 93(1)/1.

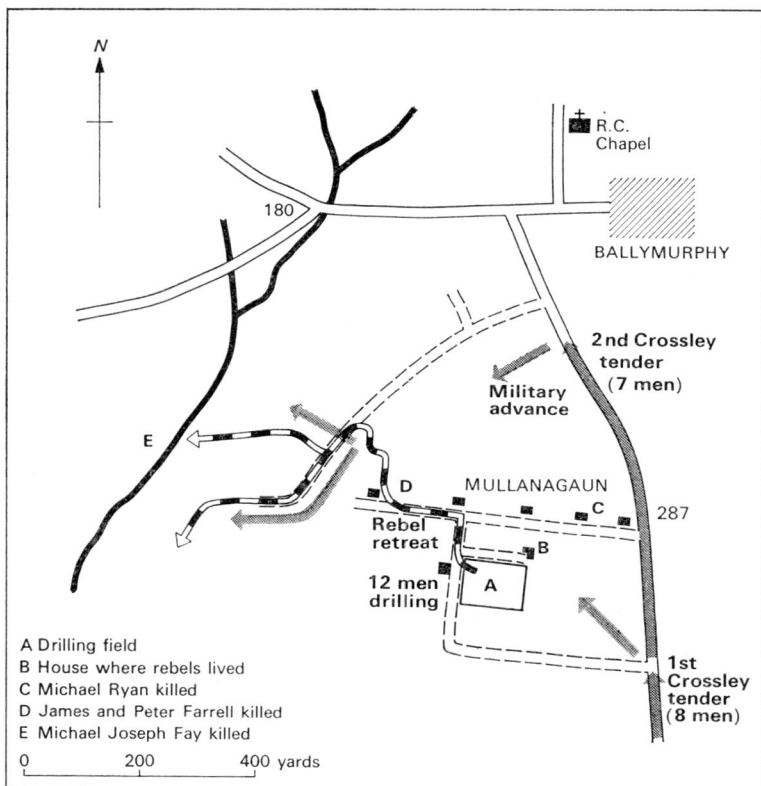

Map 7: A typical small patrol action: Ballymurphy, Co. Carlow, 18 April 1921 taken from a sketch by Lt. J. E. Grundy, R.G.A., attached 1st North Staffs. Regt.)

Note: 8 rebels were captured and 1 (Fay) killed; Ryan and the Farrell brothers were killed accidentally in the engagement. 11 rifles and 4 revolvers with 500 rounds of ammunition (including 16 dum-dum) were taken. (Military Court of Inquiry, case of Michael Fay and others, W.O. 35 150.)

VI

DEADLOCK

'... the history of the last three months is the history of the failure of our
military methods to keep pace with, and to overcome, the military methods
which have been taken by our opponents.'

Lord Birkenhead, June 1921

16. WARFARE AND ELECTIONS (March–May 1921)

Political changes

BY MARCH 1921, when Macready was battling with the police
over discipline and with the civil authorities over martial law,
and the general military situation was not one to encourage
optimism, the Government had to begin preparing for the implementation of the Government of Ireland Act. It was evident that the military
promises somewhat recklessly given in December could not be fulfilled.
On 8 March, Lord Midleton taxed Lloyd George with the fact that,
'Whatever any soldier has said to the contrary, no civilian that I have
met will admit that we have gained in the last six months': he estimated
that, taking rebel resistance in July 1920 as 100, it was now 300.[1] In
reply Lloyd George complained that the Army had said 'that by May
we should have the rebellion sufficiently under to justify going on
with the elections', but now

> General Macready's view was that progress was certainly being made, but the
> situation was bad at the moment because the desperate men were being driven
> to the hills. He was confident they could be subdued, but would not give a
> date.[2]

From now on the signs multiplied that the Cabinet was finding the
cost of military victory too high, and that it was beginning to think of
a settlement as a means to, rather than a consequence of, the restoration
of order (as Macready had urged in May 1920). Lord French, still a
symbol of coercion, was retired from the Lord Lieutenancy much
against his will,[3] and took an emotional farewell from Dublin at the
end of April.[4] He was succeeded by the first Roman Catholic to hold

---

[1] Conference of Midleton, Lloyd George, and Greenwood, 8 March 1921. Jones'
Whitehall Diary, iii. 54.
[2] Ibid.
[3] Sturgis diary, 11 March 1921. Part of his distress was due to the fact that the Viceregal
Lodge was virtually his only home.
[4] Ibid., 29 April 1921; Macready, *Annals*, ii. 553.

the post, Viscount Fitzalan,[5] a solid Unionist but, like Midleton, very unhappy with the violence of the coercive policy.[6] Meanwhile the announcement of Bonar Law's retirement on 17 March caused widespread speculation that the 'die-hard' party was losing ground (Law was especially loathed by Irish nationalists for his opposition to Asquith's Home Rule Bill). And though health, not Irish politics, was the cause of his departure, Sturgis heard from inner Cabinet circles shortly afterwards that Lloyd George was 'in a much more yielding mood' over concessions to Ireland.[7]

In fact a gradual change was coming over the attitude both of politicians and of public opinion. When the conflict began, British opinion had probably been no more prepared than the Government to take Republican pretensions seriously. As time went by the British people began, as Hancock put it, 'to realize that they were facing Machiavelli's terrible dilemma; things had come to such a pass that they must either exterminate the Irish or satisfy them'.[8] It was with a still more painful slowness that this realization dawned upon the Government; but towards the end of March 1921, as the weekly totals of Crown casualties became higher than they had ever been since Easter 1916, even Greenwood could not keep a note of depression out of his reports.[9] Although in public the Government maintained an uncompromising attitude, it saw that the prospects for its present policy were grim. On 21 March, Birkenhead confessed to a deputation at the House of Lords that

we cannot say that murder is throttled, and continued outrages on the part of the Irish Republican Army seem to call for increasing and more drastic measures of repression on ours.[10]

Significantly, too, he all but disowned the policy of reprisals, saying that it was doubtful whether they affected the I.R.A. 'one way or the other'.[11]

Development of the guerrilla conflict

One reason for the persistence of stalemate—or worse—was the somewhat surprising fact that British military strength in Ireland was declining. Although Macready declared it his intention on 28 March to 'increase the activities of the troops . . . to the utmost' during the

[5] Edmund Bernard Fitzalan-Howard, 1855–1947. Unionist M.P., 1894–1921. Chief Whip, 1913–21; Viscount, 1921; Ld. Lt., Ireland, 1921–2.
[6] Cf. Fitzalan to Midleton, 10 May 1921. Midleton papers, P.R.O. 30 67/44.
[7] Sturgis diary, 27 March 1921. P.R.O. 30 59/4.
[8] W. K. Hancock, *Problems of Nationality 1918–1936* (Survey of British Commonwealth Affairs, vol. i) (London, 1937), p. 126.
[9] C.S.I. Weekly Surveys, 21, 28 March 1921. C.P. 2772, 2782, CAB.24 121. (The totals were 45 (3rd week) and 46 (4th week).)
[10] Deputation to Lord Chancellor, C.P. 2807, CAB.24 122.
[11] Ibid.

summer, 'in the hope that by constant harrying the rebel forces may be exhausted before Autumn sets in', he pointed out that only 39,961 men (of all arms) were available, which was 7,849 below establishment.[12] In April Greenwood reported that in the last six months Irish Command had lost no less than 9,000 experienced troops, through drafts ten demobilization; and he added that this 'great depletion' had been emphasized by a check on recruitment designed to 'make a show' in the Army estimates.[13] A suggestion from Macready that a quick and economical reinforcement could be achieved by transferring I.R.A. internees to Britain, thus freeing the 5 battalions guarding them, went the way of similar proposals in the past. In fact, far from being re-inforced, Irish Command was ordered on 1 April to earmark ten infantry battalions for use in Britain,[14] where the industrial crisis was once more allowing Sir Henry Wilson to prepare a crusade against Bolshevism.[15] Between 6 and 9 April, four of these battalions were sent to Liverpool, and two more were concentrated on 12-hour stand-by.[16] They were not released for about a month, and not until the end of May were any fresh units sent to Ireland.[17]

In spite of this, it seemed in April that the Army's operations were at last having a significant, perhaps even decisive, effect. In Dublin there was a sudden change in the depressing pattern of unsuccessful raids. On 24 March, in Mountjoy Square, an arms dump including 6 rifles and 35 revolvers, a 'veritable arsenal' by previous standards, was found.[18] Six days later this was eclipsed by the discovery in Harcourt Street of a Lewis gun, a German machine-gun, and nearly 6,000 rounds of ammunition.[19] On 3 April the office of the Dáil Ministry of Home Affairs was raided at 11 Molesworth Street, and several tons of docu-ments were seized.[20] Collins's own office in Mespil Road was found at about the same time.[21] By 25 April, Major-General Boyd was able to congratulate his command on having captured, since 22 March, 3 machine-guns, 16 rifles, 97 revolvers, 305 grenades, and over 10,000 rounds of ammunition.[22] Impressive though this was, the total was almost doubled at a stroke two days later by the discovery in some stables in Baggot Lane of a dump which was clearly an I.R.A.

[12] G.H.Q. Ireland to Army Council, 28 March 1921. Anderson papers, C.O. 904 188/2.
[13] C.S.I. to Prime Minister, 3 April 1921. Lloyd George papers, F/19/3/7.
[14] 'G' War Diary, G.H.Q. Ireland, 1 April 1921. W.O. 35 93(1)/1.
[15] Cf. B. Ash, The Lost Dictator (London, 1968), p. 269.
[16] 'G' War Diary, G.H.Q. Ireland, 6, 7, 9 April 1921. W.O. 35 93(1)/1.
[17] G.H.Q. Ireland, Record, i. 40.
[18] I. Summary, 27 March 1921. D.D. War Diary, W.O. 35 90/2.
[19] G.O.C.-in-C. W.S.R., 2 April 1921. C.P. 2800, CAB.24 121.
[20] I. Summary, 3 April 1921. D.D. War Diary, W.O. 35 90/2.
[21] Forester, Michael Collins, p. 193. Collins's next office, at 29 Mary Street, fell not long afterwards.
[22] H.Q. D.D. to 24th and 25th(P) Bdes., 25 April 1921. D.D. H.Q. File, W.O. 35 71.

provincial distribution centre. Account books found there showed the following turnover of arms in the previous quarter:

	Rifles	Revolvers and Autos.	Rifle Ammunition	Revolver Ammunition	Explosives
Receipts	60	89	4,488	27,489	682
Issues	61	73	7,980	5,560	960

Actual seizures at the dump included a machine-gun, 14 rifles, 54 revolvers, and 12,442 rounds of ammunition.[23]

These captures were a staggering blow at I.R.A. supplies. It would perhaps be unwise to think that the I.R.A. at large was entirely dependent on supplies from Dublin, because the Director of Purchases for I.R.A. G.H.Q., Liam Mellows, often found his procurements disrupted by independent agents from the more active local units.[24] But such losses would never be easy to make good; and, equally importantly, they showed that military intelligence was no longer condemned to being half a step behind the rebels. On 29 April a raid on Blackhall Place even succeeded in capturing 40 men of the Dublin Brigade, a more elusive—if less functional—prize than weapons.[25]

In the M.L.A., too, military confidence grew. Strickland made another vague and optimistic report in mid-April, in which he claimed, not very logically, that the dying-away of the intensified campaign with which the I.R.A. had reacted to martial law was proof that martial law had justified itself. Some of the points in this report hardly seemed to warrant Strickland's optimism, for though the rebels had been stopped from moving around so freely, their new wariness made it even harder to get information about them, and the people at large were inclined to blame the Crown Forces for all the inconveniences caused by the conflict and by the martial law restrictions. Only the attitude of the press, 'thanks to firm control', had noticeably improved.[26]

It was not martial law so much as tactical flexibility which held out the hope of real success in the rural areas. The intelligence service in the M.L.A. was improving, but it always remained better in Cork city than in the country,[27] and the front-line troops seem to have realized that it could never turn big motorized patrols into an effective counter to rebel forces. In other words, mechanical mobility, in which such faith had been placed by Macready, was found to be of limited use:

[23] D.D. War Diary, 28 April 1921. W.O. 35 90/2.
[24] Greaves, *Liam Mellows and the Irish Revolution*, p. 231.
[25] Ibid., p. 243.
[26] Report of G.O.C. 6th Div., quoted in G.O.C.-in-C. W.S.R., 23 April 1921. C.P. 2872, CAB.24 122.
[27] G.H.Q. Ireland, *Record*, ii. 20–1; cf. 6th Div. I Report, App. to G.O.C.-in-C. W.S.R., 30 April 1921. C.P. 2911, CAB.24 123.

motor patrols were simply too obvious, too noisy, and too dependent on usable roads. In their place the idea grew up of 'playing the enemy at his own game' by creating forces which could move across country on foot, and which would be, in the ironic words of an R.I.C. officer, 'unhampered by transport'.[28] Under the new system, at least as adopted in the Essex Regiment area (southern Cork), two or three foot columns, usually of two platoons each, with a cooker and two carts to carry food and packs, and including two cyclist sections, would be dropped at various points in the country by motor transport, and would then operate in random directions for several days, eventually converging by night marches on an area frequented by a rebel group.[29] Alternatively, concealed patrols would establish themselves in positions where they could observe rebel movements or ambush small rebel parties.

This attempt to secure the degree of surprise and secrecy which had hitherto been the monopoly of the I.R.A. was a dramatic, if long overdue, development. It was perhaps the only true counter-guerrilla tactic employed during the whole conflict. Yet it is not mentioned in any official source, even Irish Command's *Record of the Rebellion*. This might lead one to think that it was either ineffective or not widely employed, were it not for the fact that detailed instructions for very similar patrols can be found in Dublin District's instructions drawn up for the newly-created 26th Brigade in June 1921,[30] and that ample tribute to the efficiency of the new method in north Cork was paid by Liam Lynch's biographer, O'Donoghue.[31] It seems in fact that its true value was not appreciated by the higher military authorities, who were more attracted by the idea of area searches and 'drives' on a large scale. A small number of the latter operations had been tried in February and March, with little success;[32] and, as the next chapter will show, they were to increase greatly in size in the following months, though without corresponding increase in effect.

Oddly enough, the I.R.A. was also at this time experimenting with larger forms, with equal lack of success. It was not a matter of large operations, for rebel operations were becoming less impressive. Even the West Cork flying column, though it mounted a successful attack on Rosscarbery R.I.C. barrack on 31 March, managed no big action thereafter. The I.R.A.'s increase in scale was in the sphere of organization, for in April 1921 it attempted to override its brigade areas—which, being defined by county boundaries, sometimes made little

[28] R.I.C. Reports, C.I. Tipperary N.R., May 1921. C.O. 904 115.
[29] Percival, Lecture 2, pp. 1–2.
[30] 26th(P) Bde. Instructions, W.O. 35 93(1)/4.
[31] O'Donoghue, *No Other Law*, pp. 166–7. The tactic, he said, threatened communications and restored a sense of perpetual danger in 'safe' areas.
[32] Hist. 5th Div., p. 87.

military sense—by the formation of divisions. This move caused a stormy debate in the south, where Tom Barry made clear his dislike of the proposed divisional commanders, Liam Lynch and Ernie O'Malley, and his conviction that

> It was absurd to speak in terms of a division when the three Cork brigades could hardly muster 300 rifles between them, were without automatic weapons, artillery or transport, had no signalling equipment and no proper staff arrangements.[33]

In spite of these well-founded objections, especially over the staff question,[34] the creation of divisions went ahead. Eventually 16 were formed across the whole of Ireland, but, in the south at least, their commanders were not able to secure effective control of operations.[35]

The British approach to the elections

This was the military situation in which the new Irish constitution was finally to come into being. The elections to the Northern and Southern parliaments under the Government of Ireland Act were due in mid-May 1921, and in the preceding month the Cabinet lucubrated over whether to offer a truce for their duration. Otherwise it was obvious that no candidates would dare to stand against the Republicans. The alternative of postponing the elections was rejected on 21 April,[36] and six days later, after a long discussion, a truce was also rejected. Of the former 'war party' only Churchill favoured a truce, and then only because he believed it would not worsen the military situation, and that if necessary 'we can break up this Irish parliament and revert to coercion'.[37] But early next month the Irish military and police authorities cast a wet blanket over this belief, declaring that a truce would definitely alter the military balance in favour of the rebels, particularly in the intelligence sphere.[38] For once these authorities agreed with each other and with Greenwood that any relaxation of pressure could only reduce the chances of a peace on terms acceptable to Britain.[39] Admittedly, Macready, with his now habitual sardonic detachment, remarked that he was consoled by the reflection that 'Whatever we do we are sure to be wrong.'[40]

The Cabinet's reasons for pressing on with the fight were varied.

---

[33] Quoted in Butler, *Barry's Flying Column*, p. 140.

[34] In April the Crown Force captured an I.R.A. document in which O'Malley admitted that the Cork area was 'badly hit for staff officers'. G.H.Q. Ireland, *Record*, ii. 21.

[35] See O'Donoghue, *No Other Law*, pp. 150f., and map.

[36] Cabinet, 21 April 1921. C.27(21), CAB.23 25.

[37] Cabinet, 27 April 1921. Jones, *Whitehall Diary*, iii. 56.

[38] Memos by G.O.C.-in-C. Ireland, 27 April, and Deputy Chief of Police, 11 May 1921. Encl. in C.S.I. to Prime Minister, 11 May 1921. Lloyd George papers, F/19/4/10.

[39] C.S.I. to Prime Minister, 11 May 1921. Ibid.

[40] Memo by G.O.C.-in-C. Ireland, 27 April 1921. Ibid.

Balfour, who suddenly made his authority felt over this issue, as he had over partition in February 1920, objected to any sign of truckling to, or negotiating with, murderers. Chamberlain, on the other hand, saw the danger that a 'wartime' election would renew Sinn Féin's declared commitment to the Republic and thus make negotiation more difficult. As late as the last-minute discussion held on 12 May he hoped for a truce, but he was, as he put it, 'driven to it because I rather felt we were failing' (militarily); and he was converted by testimony from Anderson to the growing success of military operations—testimony which impressed him 'much more than if it came from Hamar Greenwood'.[41] Anderson had clearly been influenced by the striking run of military successes in Dublin, which thus had a direct bearing on policy. As for Lloyd George himself, Frances Stevenson admitted to Sturgis on 11 May that he still hoped 'in his inmost heart that Southern Ireland might still be forced to work his Act without any additions whatsoever'.[42]

The Republic and the elections

Sinn Féin was hard at work removing what grounds remained for such a hope. The election results were declared on 25 May and surprised no one, though G.H.Q. professed to find the Unionist majority in the carefully-engineered province of Northern Ireland 'unexpectedly large'.[43] In Southern Ireland, Republicans were returned unopposed in all but the four seats allotted to the Unionist stronghold of Trinity College.[44] Sinn Féin treated the election as constituting the second Dáil, and there was no likelihood of the M.P.s assembling as the Southern Parliament. Most importantly, the I.R.A. survived. A document captured at the time of the elections showed its active strength as over 5,000, of whom 3,386 were in Munster.[45] Basil Thomson's out-of-touch intelligence service thought these figures 'far smaller than was supposed',[46] but they were fully adequate for a campaign which was directed towards producing an ever-increasing number of minor raids and attacks. During the election period only one notable operation showed both inspiration and careful planning—the seizure of an armoured car in Dublin on 14 May and its use in an attempt to rescue Seán MacEoin from Mountjoy gaol.[47] The burning of the Custom

---

[41] Cabinet, 12 May 1921. Jones, *Whitehall Diary*, iii. 70.

[42] Sturgis diary, 11 May 1921. P.R.O. 30 59/4.

[43] G.H.Q. Ireland, *Record*, i. 42.

[44] Most of the Republicans were, as Macready put it, 'leading gunmen and high officials of the I.R.A.'. Macready to Anderson, 14 May 1921. Anderson papers, C.O. 904 188/2.

[45] G.O.C.-in-C. W.S.R., 14 May 1921. C.P. 2948, CAB.24 123.

[46] Home Office Report on Revolutionary Organizations in the U.K., No. 106, 19 May 1921. C.P. 2952, CAB.24 123.

[47] The vehicle involved has been variously described as a Rolls-Royce, a Peerless, and even a Whippet. The best inside accounts of the operation are Dalton, *With the Dublin Brigade*, pp. 156–60, and *With the I.R.A.*, pp. 214f.

7

House on 25 May was a disastrously mismanaged stroke. Over 100 men of the Dublin Brigade, many of them unarmed and inexperienced, were captured,[48] and the destruction of the building removed many property records of ordinary individuals.[49] This operation was the first fruit of de Valera's belated declaration that Dáil Eireann was responsible for the actions of the I.R.A.,[50] and it certainly reflected a sacrificial approach appropriate to the only surviving commandant of the 1916 Rising.

It may be that Collins, as his most recent biographer says, agreed with de Valera that only a move on this scale 'could keep Sinn Féin in a position to negotiate at all'.[51] But if the conflict had been prolonged, the repetition of such operations would have been catastrophic. And in fact the British were not impressed by the military achievement of burning an undefended building, perhaps the most beautiful in Ireland: the 'incredible vandalism' of the action may have had a psychological effect,[52] but in practical terms the loss of tax records was an irrelevance. Far more effective was the inexorable rise in small outrages, especially assassinations. Military and police casualties had fallen to 30 per week or less in late March and during the period of British success in April, but in May they rose to new record levels—55 in the second week of May,[53] 67 in the first week of June,[54] with 23 and 24 fatalities respectively. The overall total of outrages, which had fallen below 300 per week in April, topped 500 at the end of May.[55] On 6 June Greenwood had to admit that there was 'a very marked increase in rebel military activity throughout the whole country'.[56]

Behind the scenes, moreover, the I.R.A. was preparing to add a new sting to its tail. In Dublin on 24 May Michael Collins showed Tom Barry an American weapon which had only just gone into production, the Thompson sub-machine-gun.[57] Nearly the whole of the April and May output of these guns at the Colt factory had been secured by the Irish-American organization Clan-na-Gael.[58] In spite of the efforts of the U.S. Department of Justice, some 25 to 50 of them were shipped to Ireland in May, and a few examples appeared in action next month.

[48] Macready gave the number arrested as 111, Greenwood as 127; Republican historians have preferred 80–90.
[49] C.S.I. Weekly Survey, 28 May 1921. C.P. 3019, CAB.24 124.
[50] Made on 30 March. See Macardle, *The Irish Republic*, p. 402.
[51] Forester, *Michael Collins*, p. 196.
[52] The phrase is Greenwood's (Weekly Survey, 28 May 1921).
[53] C.S.I. Weekly Survey, 16 May 1921. C.P. 2945, CAB.24 123.
[54] C.S.I. Weekly Survey, 6 June 1921. C.P. 3027. CAB.24 124.
[55] See graph, p. 123 above.
[56] C.S.I. Weekly Survey, 6 June 1921.
[57] Barry, *Guerrilla Days in Ireland*, pp. 177–8.
[58] For an account of early production and purchases, and probable deliveries to the I.R.A., see J. Bowyer Bell, 'The Thompson Submachine Gun in Ireland, 1921', *Irish Sword*, viii, No. 31 (1967), pp. 98–108.

They were not ideal from a guerrilla point of view, as they used heavy and bulky ·45 ammunition, and had a slow rate of fire and limited range. None the less, 'the rattle of the Thompson gun' was to become a much-loved sound among rebels; while the British military authorities acknowledged that 'such a weapon cannot be ignored', and that its possession 'undoubtedly makes the I.R.A. a more formidable organization from the military point of view'.[59]

17. MILITARY UNCERTAINTIES (May–June 1921)

Macready's memorandum of 24 May
The failure of the Southern Parliament to assemble would lead, by the terms of the Government of Ireland Act, to the imposition of Crown Colony government on the 26 counties (which would otherwise be left in a constitutional vacuum). This eventuality, which Montagu called 'an awful irony',[60] now seemed unavoidable unless a settlement could be reached with Sinn Féin. The Cabinet faced a dilemma largely of its own making. On the one hand it had always maintained that no settlement was possible until the extremists had been crushed; yet on the other hand it had tried to keep open the doors to negotiation, and in so doing it had hamstrung the efforts of its military forces to crush those extremists. The resulting situation was unattractive. Crown Colony government, presumably accompanied by full martial law, was in any case a daunting prospect, and it was unthinkable unless it could ensure victory over the forces of the Republic and make possible a settlement on British terms. The alternative was immediate negotiation on the basis of some form of Dominion Home Rule, a solution which many of the Cabinet still disliked. On this issue Lloyd George lagged behind British public opinion. As late as 12 May he declared that the Dominion idea would be used to exact too many concessions from Britain, and he was emphatically not prepared to give Ireland the degree of independence enjoyed by Canada and Australia.[61] One reason for his caution may have been doubt about whether the Conservative party would tolerate more than minimal concessions.[62]

The Army could not provide the clear answers which the Cabinet needed as a basis for decision. It could not say, 'Crown Colony rule with full martial law will bring victory', whether in three, six, or

---

[59] App. C to C.I.G.S. to Sec. of State for War, 11 October 1921. Worthington-Evans papers.
[60] At the Cabinet of 27 April 1921. Jones, *Whitehall Diary*, iii. 62.
[61] Cabinet, 12 May 1921. Jones, *Whitehall Diary*, iii. 68.
[62] Cf. D. G. Boyce, 'How to Settle the Irish Question: Lloyd George and Ireland 1916–1921', in A. J. P. Taylor (ed.), *Lloyd George: Twelve Essays* (London, 1971), pp. 154–6.

twelve months. The military attitude in May 1921 was ambiguous, and reflected a deep uncertainty. The upsurge of rebel attacks that month undoubtedly punctured the optimism of April, and though regular military reports maintained a tone of unconcern, one document was more than sufficient to destroy this routine impression. This was General Macready's memorandum of 24 May. This major appreciation was presented in two parts. The first dealt with general military policy, in fairly uninspiring terms. Macready pointed out that even if Irish Command were strongly reinforced, the new troops would need special training for Irish conditions, and he also said that in future they would not be put out in detachments of less than a company.[63] At present, he wrote, military activity was limited to 'countering the pressure of the Irish Republican Army wherever that becomes prominent'.

Apart from little expeditions of a couple of subaltern officers and from 12 to 20 men, extending over from 24 to 48 hours, and directed against a spot where information has been received of a collection of rebels . . . the only possibility of offensive action lies with the Cavalry. . . .[64]

His plan of action was based on his continuing faith in the effect of 'showing the flag' in inducing 'people who "sit on the fence" ', as he put it, to come down on the British side. Disregarding experience, he still hoped to use 'mobile columns to act against rebels who have been located', and to mount large-scale 'movements' with the three cavalry brigades which were available.[65]

The second part of the memorandum followed up these vague prospects with a survey of the Army itself. Macready underlined, as he had before, the stress and strain which the nature of the Irish conflict imposed on both officers and men. Many of the former, he said, though they would not admit it, would soon be unfit to go on serving in Ireland 'without a release for a very considerable period'. The physical strain also told seriously on the men, who were mostly very young and 'fine drawn'. His conclusion was dramatic.

Unless I am entirely mistaken, the present state of affairs in Ireland, so far as regards the troops serving there, must be brought to a conclusion by October, or steps must be taken to relieve practically the whole of the troops together with the great majority of the commanders and their staffs. I am quite aware that troops do not exist to do this, but this does not alter in any way the opinion I have formed in regard to the officers and troops for whom I am responsible.[66]

This opinion was later castigated by Churchill as 'baseless and

[63] Memo 'A' by G.O.C.-in-C. Ireland, 23 May 1921, in memo by C.I.G.S., 24 May 1921. C.P. 2965, CAB.24 123.
[64] Ibid.
[65] Ibid.
[66] Memo 'B' by G.O.C.-in-C. Ireland, loc. c .

alarmist'[67] (though Churchill himself had made similar points in the previous summer to explain the ill-success of the troops).[68] But no one disputed it at the time, and it was presented to the Secretary of State for War with the bluntness of which Sir Henry Wilson was a master. Worthington-Evans was 'really impressed and frightened' (or so Wilson thought),[69] and in a memorandum the same day he conveyed to the Cabinet a warning still more direct than Macready's.

There is [he wrote] a risk that a position of virtual stalemate may continue throughout the summer and that winter will be a time of decisive advantage to the rebels.[70]

This went far beyond the written statements of Macready and Wilson. Worthington-Evans said that unless full advantage was taken of the summer weather to intensify military activity there was a 'grave risk of failure'; and he proposed to strip the British garrison to 17 infantry battalions and 6 cavalry regiments—well below the bare minimum—in order to reinforce Irish Command as soon as possible (if 'things have settled down and there is peace at home').[71]

Plans for martial law

The Army's motive in thus speaking in terms not just of stalemate but of defeat (which had hitherto seemed, militarily at least, an unimaginable eventuality) was to impel the Cabinet either to make terms with the rebels or to stop compromising over coercion. Macready and Wilson differed over which of these options would be preferable, but they were both determined that a decision should be made. The choice of October as the deadline gave the Cabinet the chance of 'going all out', as Wilson put it, during the summer, while protecting the Army from the ordeal of another winter in detachments. And at first the Cabinet, fresh from its decision not to call an election truce, seemed inclined to accept the inevitability of outright military action. The Irish Situation Committee, which had not sat since August 1920, was reconstituted with Chamberlain as chairman,[72] and met on 26 May, expanded by many extra advisers, to discuss the extension of martial law.[73]

The arguments put forward at this discussion in favour of extending

---

[67] W. S. Churchill, *The Aftermath* (London, 1941), p. 288.
[68] See above, p. 169.
[69] Callwell, *Wilson*, ii. 192.
[70] 'Ireland and the General Military Situation', memo by Sec. of State for War, 24 May 1921. C.P. 2964, CAB.24 123.
[71] Ibid.
[72] Cabinet Note, 26 May 1921. CAB.23 25.
[73] The committee members present were Chamberlain, Worthington-Evans, Greenwood, Balfour, Shortt and Fisher; the others were Macready, Wilson, Guest (Sec. of State for Air), Trenchard (Chief of Air Staff), and Brook (Deputy Chief of Naval Staff).

martial law to all 26 'Southern' counties were numerous: it would, it was said, produce unity of command, unity of legal administration, control of the press, an end to official reprisals (a curious idea), and would demonstrate the benefits which had accrued to 'Ulster' through acceptance of the Government of Ireland Act.[74] Arguments against it were more or less confined to the feeling that 'the English people generally were against resort to martial law except in extreme cases'.[75] (What constituted an extreme case was not said.) The committee concluded that martial law should be extended on 12 July if the Southern parliament failed to function. The Army should be reinforced by 16 or more battalions, and full naval assistance should be arranged.[76]

On 2 June the Cabinet agreed to these recommendations, and Worthington-Evans undertook to begin the reinforcement immediately with two battalions per week.[77] But a general lack of conviction could be sensed. Lloyd George was resentful of Macready's attitude towards the R.I.C., and chose this moment to enunciate a principle which he might helpfully have vouchsafed twelve or eighteen months earlier, that 'The Irish job . . . was a policeman's job supported by the military and not vice versa. So long as it becomes a military job only it will fail.'[78] Churchill went further, suggesting that 'on balance Tudor and his men were . . . getting to the root of the matter quicker than the military', a suggestion to which Lloyd George assented. The question of military responsibility was also raised: under universal martial law, would Wilson, or Greenwood, be Macready's direct superior? Lloyd George complained that Wilson's approach to the Irish issue was so emotional that he 'could never get a sane discussion with him' on it.[79] Predictably, it was arranged that Macready, as Military Governor, would be put directly under Greenwood—an arrangement which, because of their personalities, Sturgis rightly described as unworkable.[80]

The end of official reprisals
During the renewed debate on martial law the argument was put forward that

Martial law will be a substitute for authorized reprisals, which are disliked by the military, but which could not be abandoned without something to take their place.[81]

[74] S.I.C. 8th conclusions, 26 May 1921. CAB.27 107.
[75] Ibid.
[76] 'The Extension of Martial Law in Ireland and the Consequent Naval and Military Measures', Report of Cabinet Irish Situation Committee, 27 May 1921. C.P. 2983, CAB.24 123.
[77] Cabinet, 2 June 1921. C.47(21), CAB.23 26.
[78] Cabinet, 2 June 1921. Jones, *Whitehall Diary*, iii. 73.
[79] Ibid.
[80] Sturgis diary, 4 June 1921. P.R.O. 30 59/4.
[81] Report of Cabinet Irish Situation, Cttee., 27 May 1921. C.P. 2983, CAB.24 123.

These reprisals had certainly always been disliked by the Government, and the whole matter was now getting out of hand, with the rebels burning loyalists' mansions as reprisals for reprisals. Macready apparently told Chamberlain that he would regard the enforcement of the death penalty for carrying arms as a substitute for reprisals, but that he 'had felt it difficult to enforce this while martial law was only partially applicable'.[82] His reasoning at this stage is hard to follow. He had taken a rather different line in explaining to the new Viceroy, Lord Fitzalan, that the Army 'hated reprisals' and that the real reason for them was 'the indiscipline of the Black and Tans'.[83] When Greenwood ordered on 3 June that all reprisals should cease, Macready again protested that police discipline was too weak to be 'proof against' such a step.[84] But however much they disliked them now, it was the military who had initiated official reprisals. It is noteworthy that Macready and Strickland did not attempt to maintain the argument on which they had originally based the policy, namely that reprisals were an effective way of putting pressure on the rebels.

The order to cease reprisals on 3 June, long before the planned extension of martial law, was significant. Although C. J. C. Street, in describing the May–June discussions, said that the Government had at last accepted the necessity of treating Ireland as a 'zone of battle' (in other words abandoning the 'murder gang' theory and recognizing the wide hostility of the population),[85] it seems clear that few members of the Cabinet or the Irish Government were really prepared for another round of coercion on this basis. Indeed, Sturgis remarked on 24 June that if it went ahead, there was a chance of Anderson and Cope 'asking leave to haul down their flags'.[86]

The military balance
Militarily there was hardly a glint at the end of the tunnel. The weekly totals of I.R.A. operations now exceeded even the remarkable peak of September 1920, and, though many of these were trifling,[87] the period from the beginning of May to the Truce on 11 July accounted for well over a quarter of all the Crown casualties suffered in the whole two-and-a-half-year conflict.[88] Military losses also rose in proportion to those of the police. In another field, that of sabotage, hitherto neglected by the rebels, the burning of the ordnance store in the Dublin Shell

[82] Chamberlain's report to Cabinet, 2 June 1921. Jones, *Whitehall Diary*, iii. 72–3.
[83] Fitzalan to Midleton, 10 May 1921. Midleton papers, P.R.O. 30 67/44.
[84] Macready, *Annals*, ii. 563–4.
[85] Street, *Ireland in 1921* (London, 1922), p. 49.
[86] Sturgis diary, 24 June 1921. P.R.O. 30 59/4. Cf. also entries for 3, 4, and 21 June. The impression is that in Ireland only the police viewed the prospect with equanimity; they, of course, had nothing to gain from peace.
[87] Cf. Appendix V below, p. 214, especially the number of raids on mails.
[88] Ibid. Casualties in these 12 weeks were: police 114, military 48 (all fatal).

Factory on 4 June pointed to a type of action which could be repeated elsewhere with great effect. It destroyed £88,000 worth of stores, including 5 Peerless armoured cars and 35 other vehicles.[89] At Rathcoole, Co. Cork, on 16 June the I.R.A. showed that it had not altogether lost the ability to mount big attacks, for 130 rebels were assembled from five districts to ambush an A.D.R.I.C. supply convoy.[90]

It was commonly said after the truce, and is often accepted now, that the I.R.A. was reaching the end of its tether.[91] Such a conclusion, as the next chapter will suggest, seems exaggerated. There is no reason to doubt that, given time, strength, and public support, the British forces could have reduced rebel operations to negligible proportions. But these quintessential conditions were missing. While the I.R.A. survived, political pressure on the British Government increased, and though the balance was tantalizingly fine, the I.R.A. held out longer than the Government's nerve. That was what mattered.

Irish Command was heavily reinforced from early June onwards, but the military situation gave no reason to believe that coercion, whether or not in the form of full martial law, would succeed in the near future. Co-operation between the Crown forces remained disturbingly poor. The discipline issue still smouldered: on 6 June Sturgis recorded that the Deputy Inspector General of the R.I.C.,[92]

always difficult to understand, has been in to see me absolutely incoherent with rage against Umfreville who he says won't let him alone in any detail. . . . This incessant squabbling *is* such a bore—he threatens resignation.[93]

Even the simplest principles of joint command had not yet been widely accepted,[94] and there is no doubt that the military authorities often adopted a patronizing or arrogant attitude towards the police.[95] The result, as the Irish Situation Committee reported on 27 May, was that 'great care has to be exercised to avoid friction' between the two forces.[96] Between the Army and the Navy, on the other hand, the

[89] Ordnance Summary, 5th Div. and D.D. W.O. 35 182(1)/1.
[90] For a military analysis and map, see Add. 1 to 'The Irish Republican Army', Ch. V (Operations), G.H.Q. Ireland, June 1921. C.O. 904 168/2 June 1921.
[91] Cf. J. M. Curran, 'The Consolidation of the Irish Revolution', *University Review*, v, No. 1 (Dublin, 1968), p. 39.
[92] C. A. Walsh. The Inspector Generalship had been vacant since T. J. Smith's retirement in November 1920.
[93] Sturgis diary, 6 June 1921. P.R.O. 30 59/4.
[94] Cf. R.I.C. Circular Order by Deputy I.G., 17 June 1921. C.O. 904 178; Chief of Police to Commandant A.D.R.I.C., 1 July 1921. D.D. War Diary, W.O. 35 91.
[95] For instance, Jeudwine admitted that the Brigade Major of the Galway Brigade had 'shown some want of tact' in his communication with the R.I.C. D.C. for Galway, and that the latter's complaints were justified. G.O.C. 5th Div. to G.O.C.-in-C., 14 February 1921. Cf. also D.P.S. to Chief of Police to H.Q. D.D., 2 June 1921 (Jeudwine papers) (D.D. H.Q. File, W.O. 35 71); Sturgis diary, 24 June 1921. (P.R.O. 30 59/4.)
[96] C.P. 2983, CAB.24 123.

problem was one not of familiarity breeding contempt, but of near-absence of contact.

The course of military operations showed few triumphs over endemic problems. In June the Army resorted to closing all telegraph offices outside garrison towns, in the hope of hampering rebel communications (the telegraph service, like the rest of the post office, had long been too full of rebel sympathizers for the Crown Forces to use it for anything but routine matters).[97] Large-scale searches were tried everywhere,[98] most spectacularly in the north midlands, where 5th Division employed a cavalry column of no less than four regiments, reinforced by local infantry units, in a series of drives lasting from 27 May until 16 June and traversing eight counties (Map 8, p. 188). Thousands of men were rounded up, but few known rebels were identified.[99] The main difficulties were, as usual, those of sealing off the search areas and identifying wanted men. The impressive scope of the operation provided no guarantee of success. The same was true of two big drives mounted by 6th Division after the Rathcoole ambush. On 18 June no less than 1,850 troops, with police and air co-operation, converged on the Killarney–Rathmore area, whose inhabitants

professed never having seen a soldier or policeman before, and had naturally come to view the so-called Irish Republic as the ruling power.[100]

It is worth noting that, though they were now armed, the role of aircraft was limited to dropping messages at Brigade H.Q.s indicating the positions of the troops. On 23 June a similar drive was carried out in the area to the west, but the net haul of both did not exceed a few wanted men and a number of vehicles. One brigade commander observed that five of these

were discovered by pure chance. The advancing troops had actually passed the spot where they were hidden in a sunken boreen, one behind the other, and so completely hidden with gorse, etc., that a sick man whilst being escorted to the rear by a comrade, actually fell on top of one of them.[101]

It was also by chance that this commander prevented the release of several members of a rebel flying column, when he and his brigade intelligence officer arrived just as a crowd of rounded-up men were

[97] G.H.Q. Ireland, *Record*, i. 43.

[98] D.D. Orders, 25, 26 June 1921. D.D. H.Q. File, W.O. 35 71; D.D. War Diary, June 1921. W.O. 35 91.

[99] Hist. 5th Div., p. 97, and full operational report in App. XVIII. G.O.C.-in-C. W.S.R., 18 June 1921. C.P. 3071, CAB.24 124. It should be noted that 5th Division claimed that intelligence improved in July, and that the final drive that month was successful.

[100] G.O.C.-in-C. W.S.R., loc. cit.

[101] Remarks by O.C. Kerry Bde., attached to 'Points Regarding Carrying Out Drives and Searches', 6th Div. to 16th, 17th and 18th Bdes., 6 July 1921. Copy to D.D., W.O. 35 71.

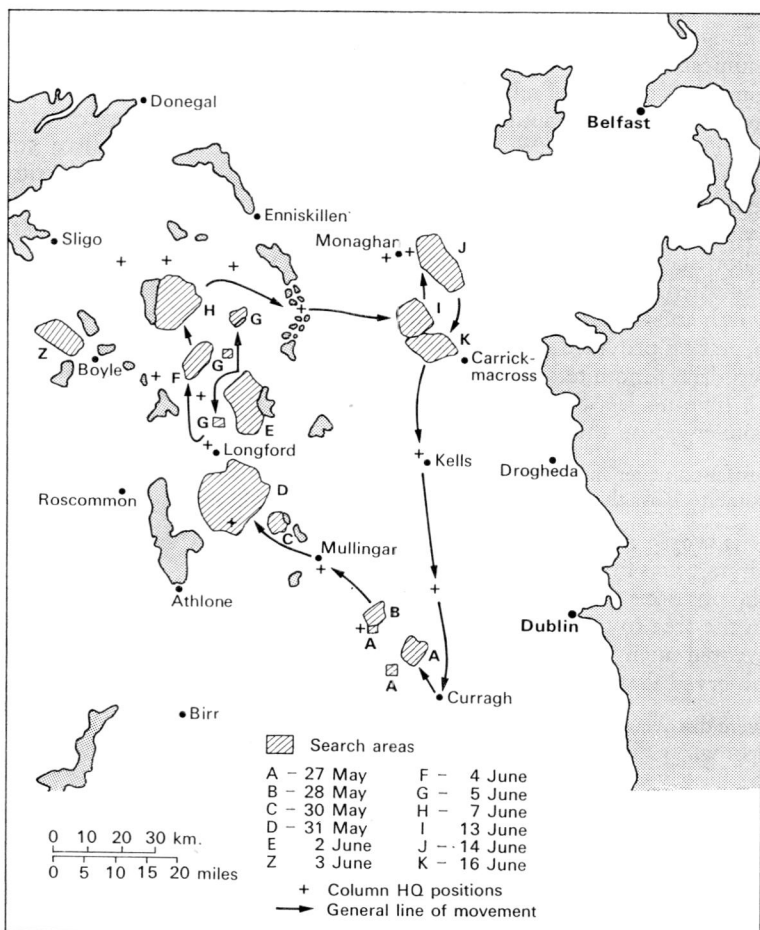

Map 8: Drive operations by 5th Division Mobile Columns, May–June 1921

about to be freed by search officers who had pronounced them 'only yokels'.[102]

It would be wrong to dismiss these big operations as entirely ineffectual. With improvements in technique, which would doubtless have come about in time, they would certainly have yielded results less disproportionate to the effort involved. But while intelligence remained faulty, and slackness among the ordinary officers and troops common, any promise of success lay in the indefinite future.

The military outlook

General Macready followed his cheerless appreciation of 24 May with another severe test of the Cabinet's determination. On 15 June he presented the Irish Situation Committee with his draft proclamation of full martial law. This declared not only the I.R.A. but also Dáil Eireann to be a treasonable organization, and included such measures as the suppression of hostile newspapers, the application of economic punishments and restrictions (isolation of areas, closure of ports, curtailment of exports, etc.), a system of passports and of identification cards, and the stoppage of any legal proceedings concerning the activities of the Crown Forces.[103] Macready disowned the idea of identity cards, which came from his generals: he himself thought that the I.R.A. would rapidly wreck such a scheme by shooting anyone who carried a card. But he expressed himself bitterly over the need to arrest Republican political as well as military leaders, and over the Sinn Féin boycott on British goods, saying that

He, personally, was losing his self-respect. For instance, it put him in an absurd position to be unable to buy English goods in Dublin, although he was C-in-C of the British Forces. He felt that he was losing the confidence of his men and he asked the Committee and the Government to bear in mind the personal feeling of the tools they were using. If they did not do so, those tools would break in their hands.[104]

He repeatedly stressed that the Government would have to be prepared for many shootings in Ireland, perhaps a hundred a week, and it would be no use if they began to howl once they discovered what martial law really involved. This, and the need to encourage the troops, was the reason for the proclamation's tone, which Balfour found 'unnecessarily terrifying'.[105]

Fundamentally, however, as Tom Jones wrote to Lloyd George after the committee, Macready 'made no concealment of his own

[102] Ibid.
[103] Cabinet Irish Situation Cttee., 9th meeting, 15 June 1921. S.I.C. 9th conclusions, CAB.27 107.
[104] Ibid.
[105] Ibid.

personal belief (shared by John Anderson) that the policy of coercion will not succeed'.[106] This gave an odd air to the discussion, in which the committee tried to tone down the provisions for the death penalty on members of the Dáil, and for economic blockade. Greenwood, 'who was clearly not in accord with Macready on several points', argued that he had not opposed the arrest of Dáil members, except de Valera. Chamberlain was obviously shaken by the extremity to which Government policy had been reduced. Balfour suggested transportation rather than death penalties. Only Shortt and Worthington-Evans seemed 'willing to go all the way with Macready'.[107]

A few days later, Worthington-Evans himself was confronted with another depressing military document, this time a letter to Sir Henry Wilson from Colonel Elles,[108] head of the tank corps, who had visited Ireland on 13 and 14 June. Wilson was so struck by this letter that he got Worthington-Evans to circulate it to the Cabinet.[109] It was the most chilling opinion that had yet been heard. Elles regarded the Army in Ireland as 'besieged', with its communications at a minimum:

To go from Dublin to Cork, one may fly, one may go by T.B.D. [destroyer] and be met by escort at the docks, or one may go—very slowly—by armed train. . . .

On the other hand, the population moves when, where and by whatever route it wishes. This is a curious situation for a force whose raison d'être in the country is to maintain order.[110]

The situation as a whole he found 'Gilbertian, with the humour left out': 'in a long experience of liaison work', he said, 'I have never before been left so bewildered'. The administrative system was confused and cumbersome, the controls on importation of arms were farcical, and as regards morale, a 'great listlessness' could be detected in all but the most senior people. The only solution, he said, was the vigorous exploitation of martial law, with identity controls, naval blockade, and block-houses on which to base drive operations. Even so the campaign would take two years, but

with anything short of these extreme measures the present situation might go on for such time that political pressure or political change will cause us to abandon the country, and we shall be beaten.[111]

[106] Jones to Prime Minister, 15 June 1921. Jones, *Whitehall Diary*, iii. 76.
[107] Ibid., 77.
[108] Hugh Jamieson Elles, 1880-1945. Temp. Maj.-Gen. Commanding Tank Corps, 1918; Col. Comd. Tank Corps Centre, 1919; K.C.M.G., 1919; Director Military Training, 1930; General, 1938.
[109] Note of conversation between Wilson and Worthington-Evans, 13 October 1920. Worthington-Evans papers.
[110] Memo by Col. Comd. Tank Corps Centre, circulated to Cabinet by Sec. of State for War, 24 June 1921. C.P. 3075, CAB.24 124.
[111] Ibid.

18. TRUCE (June–July 1921)

The pretext for peace
A political change occurred much more suddenly than Elles can have envisaged, and may well have been hastened by his own advice. In the House of Lords on 21 June, Birkenhead delivered a speech which at last admitted that 'a small war' was going on in Ireland, and which contained the still more striking declaration that

> the history of the last three months is the history of the failure of our military methods to keep pace with, and to overcome, the military methods which have been taken by our opponents.[112]

This was intended as a prologue to the redoubling of coercion, but it turned into an epitaph on the policy of force. On 22 June the Ulster issue was taken out of British politics, for the time being at least, as partition became a final reality. King George V opened the Northern parliament in Belfast, and his speech on this occasion has been widely regarded as the principal catalyst in the process of negotiations with the south. It was, of course, a catalyst only on the British side: as F. S. L. Lyons has remarked, the circumstances of the speech—made by the British king to his subjects, while consecrating the partition of Ireland—could hardly appeal to Sinn Féin.[113]

None the less, the speech was of great importance as a kite. It was the Government for whom the need to make peace was most pressing. The Southern parliament was due to assemble on 28 June, and nobody could imagine that it would do so. Crown Colony rule would ensue, with full martial law on 14 July.[114] The military situation indicated that this would be, to paraphrase Macready, merely another step into the mire.[115] It is not surprising that the enthusiastic British reaction to the King's speech[116] convinced Lloyd George that he could now open negotiations, with a semblance of magnanimity rather than of seeking terms with men who had been branded as murderers. On 24 June, after a highly secret Cabinet discussion, he sent invitations to both de Valera and Craig to take part in unconditional negotiations. The Cabinet was still cautious, with Lloyd George and Churchill speaking in terms of the moral value of having made such an invitation, if de Valera rejected it.[117] But although Birkenhead was 'not sanguine' about the chance of de Valera's accepting, only Balfour voiced a determination

[112] Speech of Lord Chancellor, 21 June 1921 (motion of Lord Donoughmore). 45 H.L. Deb. 5s, col. 690.
[113] Lyons, *Ireland Since the Famine*, p. 425.
[114] See Cabinet, 2 June 1921. Jones, *Whitehall Diary*, iii. 74.
[115] See his remarks to the Irish Situation Cttee.; Jones to Prime Minister, 15 June 1921. Ibid., 76.
[116] Boyce, *Englishmen and Irish Troubles*, p. 138.
[117] Cabinet, 24 June 1921. Jones, *Whitehall Diary*, iii. 80.

to go on pursuing 'murderers'. The rest of the Cabinet echoed Curzon's wholehearted approval of the invitation, and agreed that there must be a halting, or 'choking off', of the conflict during the talks.[118]

There was indeed some reason to doubt whether de Valera would accept the invitation. He had a highly, perhaps unduly, developed sensitivity to nuances in forms of words. This was to produce his famous sparring correspondence with Lloyd George in the summer of 1921, and was to help in 1922 to produce civil war in Ireland. At this preliminary stage, his main concern was the implicit recognition of Ulster's separation in the British invitation.[119] Like most nationalists he had strong hopes of forcing Irish unity, and he does not seem to have realized that inducing Britain to negotiate on terms other than the Government of Ireland Act was both the triumph and the limit of the Republican campaign. Republican success so far had been due to unerring psychological aim; the physical defeat and eviction of the British forces had never been a possibility. The Republic had succeeded by making the price of British military victory too high for British public opinion, and the final arbiter of its success was not its own strength or will, but that opinion. British opinion had turned against the Government's methods of coercion, but it would not support Republican intransigence against a fair constitutional offer—and its idea of fairness did not include the 'coercion of Ulster' into a united Ireland.

Pressures on the Republic

The Irish decision to negotiate turned less on an appreciation of the state of British opinion than on the state and prospects of the I.R.A. Fortunately for both sides, these were not conducive to prolonging the struggle. The balance, as was suggested above, was fine. It is significant that a rather unambitious rebel operation, the mining of a troop train carrying the King's escort of the 10th Hussars back from the opening of the Belfast parliament, was seen by C. J. C. Street as the final proof of the failure of British military policy.[120] The rebels retained their moral advantage. Whether their physical power was nearing its end remains a matter of some doubt. Michael Collins's oft-quoted remark, 'you had us dead beat. We could not have lasted another three weeks',[121] may be taken with a helping of salt. It was less an admission of military defeat than a boast of moral success. It was certainly an

---

[118] Ibid., p. 81.

[119] Macardle, *The Irish Republic*, p. 432.

[120] Street, *Ireland in 1921*, p. 80. The incident, in which 4 cavalry troopers were killed and 20 injured, occurred near the six-county border on 24 June.

[121] Made to Greenwood after the signing of the treaty. L. S. Amery, *My Political Life*, (London, 1953), ii. 230.

exaggeration, just as, at the other extreme, was Tom Barry's assertion to de Valera on 23 May that the West Cork flying column could 'keep the field' for five years.[122] The truth, as usual, must have lain somewhere in between. Most importantly, the limit of endurance would have varied from area to area and from unit to unit. An efficient formation such as the West Cork column could, as Barry suggested, reduce the pressure on itself by moving to a quieter area. Of relevance, too, from Collins's point of view, was the fact that the higher co-ordinating apparatus of the I.R.A. in Dublin, which was Collins's prime concern, was much more fragile than the local units. There is no doubt that Collins was convinced that a prolongation of the struggle would result in the breaking of the I.R.A., and that in any case it could not achieve anything more than had already been achieved. This was later to form one of his main lines of argument in favour of the Treaty, and in it he was supported by the I.R.A. Chief of Staff, Richard Mulcahy. But it is possible that their perspective was distorted by the difficulties they faced in running administrative offices in Dublin, where, as we have seen, British military operations were unusually effective. This can, however, only be a suggestion. It is necessary now to try to assess the impact of British military measures in terms of known facts.

Courts martial and internment

To begin with, the use of military courts had no apparently decisive effects, and did not live up to earlier expectations. Courts martial, working under the terms of R.O.I.A., continued to supply a large proportion of criminal justice throughout Ireland, but could not prevent the upsurge of rebel activities in 1921. The military courts in the Martial Law Area were differentiated from them, and suffered from several disabilities, one of which was noted in a G.H.Q. order of 21 June that in future

trial by Military Court will not be ordered as a rule in any case where there is no likelihood that a death sentence will be awarded and carried out. It is to be remembered that a man sentenced to penal servitude or imprisonment cannot serve his sentence in any prison outside the Martial Law Area, and it is desirable that prisoners should be sent to England so as to relieve congestion in the Irish prisons.[123]

This handicap derived from the fact that martial law tribunals had no status in law. Yet the corollary of this, that their acts could not be questioned in the civil courts, was, as we have seen, repeatedly flouted.

[122] Barry, *Guerrilla Days in Ireland*, p. 175. Barry points out that he was exaggerating intentionally, because he was unsure of de Valera's motive in asking for the estimate.
[123] Amendment to Circular Memorandum on Martial Law, 21 June 1921. General Routine Orders, W.O. 35 173/2.

An appeal was made in every case where military courts passed sentences of death: only 14 such sentences were actually executed in 1921.[124]

Eventually, on 8 July, an appeal for habeas corpus on the same grounds as those urged in the *King (Garde)* v. *Strickland*—that any use of military courts was now governed by R.O.I.A.—succeeded. The Court of Chancery in Dublin, ignoring all analogous decisions in the King's Bench, issued writs of habeas corpus for two appellants (Egan and Higgins), returnable for 29 July. When the military authorities did not surrender the men, the Master of the Rolls called this 'a deliberate contempt of court—a thing unprecedented in this court and in the whole history of British law', and issued writs of attachment against Macready and Strickland.[125] This was indefensible in law,[126] but it was politically critical. Although the Truce had by then been concluded, negotiations were still at a delicate primary stage. The Cabinet, notwithstanding the advice of a special committee that the decision would undermine the use of martial law in future,[127] decided that 'the movement for peace in Ireland would be gravely prejudiced if the Order of the High Court were flouted'.[128] Without consulting Macready, it released the two men; and all that Macready could do to mitigate the military humiliation was to circulate to the Army the face-saving statement made by Chamberlain in the House of Commons, that the men had been released 'solely on the basis of the existing circumstances in Ireland', and that 'civil courts have no power to overrule the decisions of military courts in the martial law area'.[129] To the Army Council, however, Macready wrote that a situation in which the Military Governor could be called to account by a judge, 'however distinguished and politically unbiased, makes the administration of martial law impossible, and if I may be permitted to use the expression, ridiculous'.[130]

The confusion surrounding martial law which underlay the Egan–Higgins crisis had undoubtedly reduced the effect of such executions as had been carried out, but there is no proof that even the strictest application of capital punishments could have succeeded in face of what H. A. L. Fisher called 'the tragic passion of the Irish race for

---

[124] Macready, *Annals*, ii. 518.

[125] Chancery Division, Ireland, 6, 7, 8, 26, 29 July 1921. *The Irish Reports*, 1921, i. 265f., 281.

[126] For an analysis of the decision see Keir and Lawson, *Cases in Constitutional Law* (London, 1967), pp. 232–6.

[127] Cabinet Committee on Military Law in Ireland, 1 August 1921. 1 (M.L.) 1st conclusions, CAB.27 155.

[128] Cabinet, 2 August 1921. C.62(21), CAB.23 26.

[129] 146 H.C. Deb. 5s, col. 437.

[130] Macready, *Annals*, ii. 590. (Macready mistakenly attributes the Commons statement to Bonar Law.)

martyrdom'.[131] In fact, as Fisher suggested, executions tended to achieve the opposite of the intended result, at least on the small scale on which they occurred, with massive public attention focused on individual cases. Whether Macready's hundred executions per week would have had a different effect must be a matter of conjecture.

As for the more regular proceedings of courts martial, the weekly totals of convictions reached a peak of 114 in late January, and then fell rather unevenly to an average of 45 in May and 54 in June.[132] In the latter months the R.I.C. recorded totals of 2,167 and 2,244 'non-agrarian' indictable offences, as against a January total of 1,209.[133] This seems to indicate that courts martial were exerting little braking effect on the Republican campaign. Internment without trial, which ran at 50 to 100 cases per week, also had little noticeable result. By the time of the Truce there were some 4,500 internees, a total nearly equal to the 'parade strength' of the I.R.A. in May 1921.[134] But there was no sign that the rebel forces were threatened by manpower shortage, and it is hard to see that they ever could have been, unless the policy of arrests had been conceived and executed on a far greater scale.

Military operations and reinforcements
More damaging to the Republic's fighting capacity were the big captures of arms and ammunition made from March 1921 onwards. In the six months from December 1920, according to Irish Office statistics, 300 rifles, 554 shotguns, 731 pistols (including automatics), and 45,593 rounds of ammunition were captured.[135] A further 1,271 rifles, 4,931 shotguns, 1,924 pistols, and 188,579 rounds of ammunition had been surrendered (these figures are, however, slightly suspect;[136] and of course a large proportion came from loyalists, so were not direct rebel losses). It is evident that the moral and material effects of arms captures were greatest in Dublin.[137] In the provinces there are no figures for rebel arms losses except in combat; but the reduction in supplies from Dublin must have been important, and, if the British had been able to mount a proper naval blockade, it might well have been decisive. In the event, however, the Army was convinced that the rebels were bringing in replacement arms from abroad.[138]

The final military factor bearing on the end of the war was numerical

---

[131] Memo by President of the Board of Education, February 1921. C.P. 2656, CAB.24 120.
[132] C.S.I. Weekly Surveys, January–July 1921. CAB.24 123–4.
[133] Returns of Persons Protected and Indictable Offences, 1919–21. C.O. 904 108–16.
[134] For internment figures see Appendix XII below, p. 223.
[135] Loughnane to Hemming, 7 July 1921. Hemming papers.
[136] Cf. the case of apparently bogus arms surrenders reported by the ambitious R.I.C. D.C. in Galway, Sturgis diary, 10 February 1921. P.R.O. 30 59/3.
[137] Cf. Dalton, *With the Dublin Brigade*, p. 142.
[138] G.H.Q. Ireland, *Record*, i. 44.

strength. Between 14 June and 7 July, Irish Command was reinforced by 17 infantry battalions:[139] Dublin District and 5th Division received 5 each, and 6th Division 7, as well as an R.A.M.R. brigade (two Mounted Rifle regiments formed from divisional artillery units).[140] The dispatch of further cavalry, marine, and tank corps forces was planned for later in July. Military strength thus increased by about one-third in less than a month, and at last began to approach a level at which a firm grip might have been taken on the rural areas. Whether or not these reinforcements would have had their full effect during the vital summer of 1921 is a different question. As Macready had stressed in his 24 May memorandum, new units were to be eased gently into Irish conditions; and experience indicated that full adjustment might take at least six months, perhaps even more than twelve.[141]

It seems likely that the immediate effect of the reinforcement was more psychological than physical. Although the British Government was still afflicted with uncertainty, it seems for once to have conveyed the opposite impression to its opponents. The phraseology commonly used of the Anglo-Irish settlement—'peace by ordeal', 'negotiation at gunpoint'—suggests a belief that the British threat of imminent, over-whelming force, was a real one. The famous scene in December 1921, when Lloyd George told the Irish delegates to sign his draft of the Treaty at once, or face 'war, and war within three days', turned entirely on how far this belief was held by the delegates, amongst whom was Collins. It could thus be argued that the military situation in the summer of 1921 exercised an influence not only on the decision to enter on negotiations but also on their outcome. The reinforcements had, belatedly, made it clear to the rebels that the military balance had turned against the Republic.

The cessation of hostilities

In this climate, with doubts on both sides, events followed quickly on Lloyd George's invitation. On 28 June Dublin Castle ordered the Crown Forces to suspend raids 'on premises occupied or frequented by persons of political importance'.[142] At the same time, without consult-ing Macready, the Government released Griffith and other 'moderate' leaders from Mountjoy gaol.[143] De Valera (who had himself been arrested on 22 June and hastily released on the orders of the Govern-

---

[139] 'G' War Diary, G.H.Q. Ireland, 14, 15, 16, 17, 28 June, 2, 5, 6, 7 July 1921. W.O. 35 93(1)/1.
[140] G.H.Q. Ireland, *Record*, i. 46.
[141] This was most noticeably true of intelligence methods. See G.H.Q. Ireland, *Record*, ii. 33.
[142] U.S. to Chief of Police, 28 June 1921. Anderson papers, C.O. 904 188/2. The sus-pension date is given as 30 June by Macready (*Annals*, ii. 569) and G.H.Q. (*Record*, i. 54).
[143] G.O.C.-in-C. W.S.R., 2 July 1921. C.P. 3109, CAB.24 125.

ment)[144] did not directly accept the invitation to negotiate, but he called for a truce as a prelude to talks, and in the meantime he instructed that the American flag should be flown on 4 July to emphasize 'the principle for which we are fighting'.[145]

To the Government, the idea of negotiations and the idea of a truce were not equally attractive. The arguments against a truce at the time of the elections had been slightly modified. Balfour had then objected to the word itself, which, he said, 'implies they are belligerents whereas they are really murderers',[146] and Lloyd George had later agreed that the word 'truce' was 'rejected by everybody' in the Cabinet.[147] By 24 June, however, only Balfour held to his original objection. Churchill still disliked the idea of a formal truce, but thought that 'we should choke off our people and they theirs'.[148] Birkenhead reassured Balfour that a truce would not prevent the continued 'pursuit of murderers'. but agreed that 'neither party should strengthen his military position. If we go on pouring in troops', he added, 'de Valera might protest.'[149] On the other hand, there is no evidence that the Army had altered its view that a truce would cripple the intelligence services and allow the I.R.A. to recover and reorganize. From the military standpoint, an armistice during the summer season still represented the height of unwisdom.

A truce was not therefore a foregone conclusion when de Valera opened a Dáil conference at the Dublin Mansion House on 5 July. It seems to have been mainly due to the efforts of Lord Midleton, whose Southern Unionist group was now playing a central part in bringing the two sides together, that General Macready arrived at the conference three days later.[150] The general was somewhat surprised to be cheered by the crowds outside the Mansion House, and greeted like a long-lost brother by the Lord Mayor of Dublin.[151] At the conference, Midleton thought that de Valera agreed to Macready's terms in a very reasonable spirit, though noticeable differences emerged when the two sides came to publish the agreement. As printed in the *Irish Bulletin*, the terms of the truce were:

---

[144] The military authorities seem seriously to have proposed to prosecute him for high treason. For the documents captured with him, including I.R.A. operation reports, see C.O. 904 23/7.

[145] Macardle, *The Irish Republic*, p. 433.

[146] Cabinet, 27 April 1921. Jones, *Whitehall Diary*, iii. 61.

[147] Cabinet, 12 May 1921. Ibid., 65.

[148] Cabinet, 24 June 1921. Ibid., 81.

[149] Ibid.

[150] See P. Buckland, *Irish Unionism 1: The Anglo-Irish and the New Ireland 1885–1922* (Dublin, 1972), pp. 235–43. Midleton himself gave one of the best accounts of the conference in his book *Records and Reactions* (London, 1939), pp. 258–63.

[151] Macready, *Annals*, ii. 572f., includes a photograph of his arrival at the Mansion House, with an automatic pistol making a conspicuous bulge in his tunic pocket.

A. On behalf of the British Army it is agreed as follows:

1. No incoming troops, RIC and Auxiliary Police and munitions, and no movements for military purposes of troops and munitions, except maintenance drafts.

2. No provocative display of forces, armed or unarmed.

3. It is understood that all provisions of this truce apply to the martial law area equally with the rest of Ireland.

4. No pursuit of Irish officers or men or war material or military stores.

5. No secret agents, noting descriptions of movements, and no interference with the movements of Irish persons, military or civil, and no attempts to discover the haunts or habits of Irish officers and men.

NOTE: This supposes the abandonment of curfew restrictions.

6. No pursuit or observance of lines of communication or connection.

B. On behalf of the Irish Army it is agreed as follows:

(a) Attacks on Crown Forces and civilians to cease.

(b) No provocative displays of forces, armed or unarmed.

(c) No interference with Government or private property.

(d) To discountenance and prevent any action likely to cause disturbance of the peace which might necessitate military interference.[152]

In Macready's version the British terms were:

1. All raids and searches by Military or Police shall cease.

2. Military activity shall be restricted to support of Police in normal civil duties.

3. Curfew restrictions shall be removed.

4. Despatch of reinforcements from England shall be suspended.

5. The police functions in Dublin to be carried out by the DMP.[153]

In this version the Irish undertook not just to avoid 'provocative displays', but 'To prohibit the use of arms', and they also undertook 'To cease military manoeuvres of all kinds'. Both of these terms were obviously unacceptable to the I.R.A., and looking at point A.2 of the Irish version, it is equally improbable that Macready would have agreed to stop his troops from carrying arms.

The Truce came into effect at noon on Monday, 11 July, having been preceded by one of the bloodiest weekends of the conflict, with the I.R.A. killing some 20 people in 36 hours. The last shot was fired at a police patrol in Kingscourt, Co. Cavan, at 11.55 a.m.[154] The suddenness with which all serious outrage ceased was impressive testimony to the I.R.A.'s overall control, though few of the terms of the truce were so punctiliously observed. The I.R.A. went on drilling and training with arms, and embarked on a considerable recruitment drive. Irish Command reported that up to 10 September there were 128 breaches of the

[152] 'Arrangements Governing the Cessation of Active Operations in Ireland', 1921 Cmd. 1534 xxix 427.

[153] Ibid.; G.O.C.-in-C. W.S.R., 9 July 1921. C.P. 3134, CAB.24 125.

[154] C.S.I. Weekly Survey, 11 July 1921. C.P. 3130, CAB.24 125.

truce in the Martial Law Area alone, including 10 attacks on Crown Forces and 74 instances of 'interference with property', and that thereafter I.R.A. activities steadily increased.[155] On 1 October Macready angrily declared that

Advantage has been taken of the truce to convert the IRA, which was three months ago little more than a disorganized rabble, into a well-disciplined, well-organized and well-armed force.[156]

The Army's tendency to harp on the contrast between rebel weakness at the time of the truce and their renewed strength afterwards became so pronounced that on 13 October Worthington-Evans sharply reminded Wilson of the military pessimism which had prevailed in June, and asked why their opinion had 'so materially modified'. Wilson's reply was that the earlier assessment had simply been wrong— that the precariousness of the rebel position had not been realized.[157]

Whether this revised opinion of the situation in the early summer was correct, or whether it was conditioned by military resentment at the arrogance of the I.R.A. after the Truce, and widespread suggestions that the Army had been defeated, is an open question. It did less credit, however, to the political instincts of the military leaders than did their earlier pessimism. That pessimism had, perhaps, owed something to an overestimation of rebel power; but it had also been grounded on a realization that British political commitment to the repressive campaign was not sufficient to give it a chance of success. Still more fundamentally, those generals in Ireland who had thought deeply on the use of military force as a means to political settlement had never shared the Cabinet's apparent faith in its efficacy. Even apart from the style of violence employed by the police, which aroused their intense dislike, they believed that military rule in Ireland could only inflame age-old hatreds and impede the arrival of a lasting peace. Subsequent Irish history was to suggest both the humanity and the good sense of their analysis.

[155] App. B, C.I.G.S. to Sec. of State for War, 11 October 1921. Worthington-Evans papers.
[156] G.O.C.-in-C. W.S.R., 1 October 1921. C.P. 3377, CAB.24 127.
[157] Note of conversation between Sec. of State for War and C.I.G.S., 13 October 1921. Worthington-Evans papers. Worthington-Evans had drawn particular notice to Macready's 24 May memorandum and Elles's June letter.

VII

CONCLUSION

THE employment of military force in the attempt to achieve a settlement in Ireland raises two obvious questions—first, 'Why was it used?', and second, 'Why did it fail?'. The complexity of these questions will by now be evident, and no easy answer can be given to either of them. It may, however, be useful here to subsume the major political and military aspects of the conflict under these general headings.

Why was it used?: Political attitudes
The use of force resulted less from clear-cut decisions than from instinctive reactions on the part of the British Government, and indeed on the Republican side also. There was an important kind of truth, psychological rather than factual, in the Republican claim that in 1919 Britain was the aggressor against a lawfully and peacefully established Irish state. Although British rule in Ireland had existed in some form for over 800 years, and in its final form for over 100, it had never won the sort of loyalty that would have transformed government through power into government through authority. In the generation before the Great War, admittedly, a higher degree of consensus was reached than ever before; but during that war it rapidly collapsed under the dual pressure of Sinn Féin within and Britain without. When put to the proof, there was no doubt that the British administration was still external to Irish life—was still 'foreign'—and when an independent Irish parliament, Dáil Eireann, arose in 1919, it had little difficulty in assuming moral authority over most of the country. The British, for their part, had responded to the latent hostility of the Irish with a benign contempt. When Lloyd George declared that 'Irish temper is an uncertainty and dangerous forces like armies and navies are better under the control of the Imperial Parliament',[1] he was partly giving expression to the common British view of the Irish as a quaint, childlike race, often incompetent, and easily terrorized or led by extremists into violent behaviour. This opinion was always most apparent to foreign observers:[2] in 1921 it was a French Professor at University College, Dublin, who laid central importance on the fact that the Englishman

---

[1] In his Caernarvon speech in October 1920. See pp. 36–7 above.
[2] This is an aspect of Anglo-Irish relations which has not commended itself to study by the English. Cf. Curtis, *Anglo-Saxons and Celts*.

had for the Irishman 'un mépris doux, tranquille, bienveillant, établi, inconscient, inné'.[3]

The resultant tendency to lay down the law rather than to consult, to coerce public opinion rather than seek its consent—and thereby to exacerbate Irish opposition—was reinforced by the fact that the Union with Ireland was grounded on British strategic necessities. This was the other part of what Lloyd George was saying. The overall attitude thus generated could be clearly seen in men like Bonar Law, Balfour, Long, French, and Wilson, who looked upon the suppression of Irish separatism as a natural defence of British interests, and had few qualms about using the strongest methods to achieve it. In addition, the defensive reaction affected others in the Cabinet who were less naturally disposed towards the use of force, but who had no constructive ideas for solving the Irish problem. The principle of 'restoration of law and order' meant to some extent the acceptance of repression out of inertia. Other steps, such as granting Ireland more freedom than had ever been envisaged by Home Rule, or 'coercing Ulster' into a united Ireland, would have required bold decisions, whereas to lay down that any positive step must be contingent on the restoration of order was to buy time. During the Chief Secretaryship of Macpherson, when the distinctive lines of the military campaign emerged (the militarization of the police, and the dichotomy of the Crown Forces), this approach was very evident.

The Liberal wing of the Government showed markedly greater reluctance to use force against Sinn Féin, and markedly less repugnance towards the Republican claim to independence. While throughout 1919 and 1920 the general mood of the Cabinet was hostile to any concessions that went beyond what Lloyd George called 'the Gladstonian Home Rule that he grew up with', such men as H. A. L. Fisher, Shortt, Montagu, and Addison, later reinforced outside the Cabinet by Macready, Anderson, Warren Fisher, and the Castle group, were prepared to envisage something like Dominion status for Ireland, with control of income tax and customs. Most of them disliked coercion in principle, but they were placed in a dilemma by the identification of Sinn Féin with I.R.A. terrorism and violence. The increases in attacks on the Crown Forces, and the breakdown of constitutionalism and justice, compelled even the Liberals to accept the inevitability of a forcible response. For them the restoration of law and order was not just a convenient slogan behind which to temporize, but a moral priority. Unfortunately, in consenting to the militarization of the police, they participated in the creation of a force whose behaviour became as immoral as that of the terrorists.

It is not possible to describe the development of this force in terms of a process of political decisions. It is not even possible to identify a point

[3] 'S. Briollay' (R. Chauviré), *L'Irlande Insurgée* (Paris, 1921), pp. 120–1.

at which a clear decision was made in favour of a policy of force as against another policy. The nearest thing to such a decision was perhaps the Restoration of Order Act in August 1920, which followed a period of reduced coercion and of strong argument by the Irish Executive in favour of negotiation. Even here, however, the current of violence engendered by the expansion and militarization of the R.I.C.—a process which the Government failed to reverse in the reforms of May 1920—had already gained enough momentum to sweep the Government along with it; while the Act itself was a paradigm of the Government's reticent and confusing approach to military measures.

Why did it fail? : Military difficulties

In asking why such measures failed to bring about the restoration of order, a primary answer must be that the Republican guerrilla campaign proved too determined, too resilient, and too resourceful to be put down by the military force which was employed against it. In the relentlessness of its idealism, and still more in the efficiency with which it organized itself and mobilized the population in its support, the Republic of 1919–21 was outstanding in the history of Irish resistance movements.

The British administration by contrast displayed no comparable energy or fixity of purpose. The forces which it deployed lacked direction and definition. As the civil law broke down under the pressure of the Republican campaign, the Irish police became increasingly militarized, and by early 1920 they could operate only by methods which were characteristically military rather than civil. But at no time was an overall system of command and control established such as would normally be associated with armed forces in a theatre of war (or indeed any other theatre). The rearming and expansion of the R.I.C. was a 'military' measure, its tactical employment was on military lines, but it was never under formal military control or discipline. The violence of the Black and Tans, which made a mockery of the police force as an instrument of law and order, was due to this simple fact.

The independence of the police, even if it did not exercise such a crippling influence on the efficiency of the Crown Forces as the Army liked to maintain, had incalculable consequences in the alienation of public opinion, and must be seen as both a symptom and a cause of the failure of the policy of force. It was a product of the Government's uncertain response to the challenge of the Republic. The historian of 5th Division suggested in 1922 that

During the last two years it would appear that the Government never realized the true state of affairs in Ireland, at all events until it was too late. Consequently they never devised a suitable and clear policy, or made any attempt to convince the country of the need for putting one into force.[4]

Several tendencies can be seen to bear on this lack of determination. There was a natural political desire to play down the scale of the crisis, and a fear of the public reaction to the adoption of outright military rule in a part of the United Kingdom 'in time of peace'.[5] There was, moreover, a traditional ignorance of Irish affairs, most noticeable in the Cabinet of 1919, and the gigantic problems to be faced elsewhere did not encourage efforts to rectify it. Memories of Irish resistance attempts over the last century were not conducive to a realization of the revolutionary nature of Sinn Féin, and there was a constant tendency to underestimate the strength and determination of the new rebels, and to believe that they could be broken without recourse to extreme measures. By and large the Cabinet adhered to the 'murder gang' theory—the belief that the majority of the Irish people were not hostile but were terrorized by a small group of fanatics—and based on it a dual policy of 'crushing murder' while reconciling the 'moderates'. But no real attempt was made to assess the strength and outlook, or even to prove the existence, of this moderate group on which the whole policy hinged. The dual policy, summed up in Lloyd George's dictum 'We must be sternly just',[6] also faced the formidable difficulty, shown by all guerrilla experience, of rooting out extremists without injuring the ordinary population. In the case of Ireland, it could not be done.

To the Cabinet, the need to avoid measures which might alienate moderate opinion was often of greater importance than the need to adopt measures which would actually have a chance of success. The reinforcement of the R.I.C. rather than the Army, the prolonged hedging over outright military rule, both seem to have stemmed from such a preference. Admittedly, the adoption of martial law as the Army envisaged it was a difficult question, for the Commander-in-Chief himself was at first unenthusiastic about it. But even when the need for such a system of control became obvious, and the strength of the Army approached the level necessary to implement it, the Cabinet did not accept that the Irish emergency justified 'war' measures. Not until after the shocks of November 1920 was a—very limited—form of martial law declared; and not until June 1921 was it admitted that 'It is a small war that is going on in Ireland.'[7] Above all, the need for unified command, and for control of the R.I.C., was ignored. The Cabinet's policy over 'unauthorized' reprisals was particularly questionable, and

[4] Hist. 5th Div., p. 140.
[5] Cabinet Conference, 26 July 1920; see p. 137 above.
[6] Cabinet, 20 December 1920; see p. 140 above.
[7] Speech of Lord Chancellor, House of Lords, 21 June 1921. 45 H.L. Deb. 5s, col. 690; cf. p. 191 above.

while the idea that counter-terror could have a positive effect was also held by the Army, the Cabinet shied from the military proposal to bring reprisals under control and take public responsibility for them.

The failure to attain unity of command can certainly be blamed, in part, on Macready, who was offered, on his appointment as C-in-C in April 1920, the joint command of both Army and police. But even if a greater degree of theoretical co-ordination might have been achieved under such an arrangement, it is possible that, short of a complete absorption of the police system into that of the Army, there would still have been severe divergences (the failure of Colonel Winter in the intelligence sphere may be put down partly to the sheer incompatibility of the two systems); and in view of the Cabinet's antipathy to military rule, such an absorption would seem to have been unlikely. The real need was for a properly-structured system of co-ordination. As with Macready, some of the blame for the failure to develop this may be laid personally on Tudor, who showed a dogged determination to maintain the independence of the R.I.C., and an unfortunate tolerance of its indiscipline. The Army also played a part by failing to conceal its sense of superiority. The fundamental problem, however, was that the Government never defined the nature of the Irish conflict, or the respective roles and aims of the police and military forces.

After the breakdown of the R.I.C.'s normal police capacity, well advanced by late 1919, it was clear that great reliance would have to be placed on the Army. It would have been logical to reinforce Irish Command, involve it closely in the enforcement of the law, and make it acquire as rapidly as possible a capability for internal security duties, which it conspicuously lacked. Instead, it was the R.I.C. that was reinforced (with non-Irishmen of a type who tended to draw the force ever further away from a normal relationship with the community), while the Army was partially committed in January–April 1920, and withdrawn just as it was beginning to come to grips with the situation. Moreover, although the Irish administration was greatly strengthened with senior personnel in May, unity of command seemed if anything to recede further beyond the horizon.

The Army itself did not help matters by its very slow response to the challenge of guerrilla warfare. Until November 1920 it showed few signs of a professional approach, and even afterwards its tactical developments were not striking. As far as martial law was concerned, the efficacy of the measure itself could hardly be judged from its limited application in 1921. It was restricted to a quarter of the country, and even there military control was kept incomplete. This said, martial law was evidently no better than any other system of administration unless it was backed up by effective guerrilla warfare techniques, and 6th Division, which was responsible for the Martial Law Area, was not outstanding in the development of these. But at the same time it is necessary to remember that there was a general shortage of troops, and that most of those who were available were young and inexperienced. There was a particular dearth of capable officers, and the best men were constantly stripped away by drafts to overseas units. In these circumstances the establishment of effective military control over wide areas of country, through detachments, was impossible. Instead the Army relied on mobile patrols, which, in the absence of accurate intelligence information, operated more or less in the dark. Only in the final month of the conflict, June–July 1921, did enough reinforcements become available to raise the troop density to a level at which close control might have become possible. (Until then the 8-county Martial Law Area contained less than half the number of troops that were to be employed in Northern Ireland during the emergency of the 1970s.)

Neither the Army nor the police were able to build the essential foundation for success in guerrilla warfare, a dependable intelligence service. The attempt to unite the intelligence systems of the two forces was not pressed to completion, and neither benefited fully from the efforts of the other. In the sphere of raids on rebel arms stores, particularly in Dublin, there were noticeable improvements in intelligence from March 1921 onwards. But certain problems proved intractable. The difficulty of identifying wanted men remained a crippling handicap to operations until the end of the conflict; and only a tactical innovation—in fact an imitation of the I.R.A.'s flying column system—seemed to hold out any hope of disrupting the rebel forces. The ground-base for large-scale clearance operations simply did not exist. With the benefit of hindsight, Irish Command reached the conclusion that, in such a guerrilla situation, pacification must be approached through the creation of loyalist groups ('civil guards') and defended towns.[8] But at the time, no policy for involving loyalists was developed, and the use of civil guards, whether for intelligence or other purposes, was desultory. The Brigade Major of 17th Brigade in Cork frankly remarked after the conflict, 'I think I regarded all civilians as "Shinners", and I never had any dealings with any of them.'[9] Such an approach, though understandable, offered few roads to success in internal security work.

The effects of the conflict

A few days after the truce of 11 July 1921, General Macready wrote in his weekly report to the Cabinet,

[8] G.H.Q. Ireland, *Record*, i. 55.
[9] Montgomery to Percival, 14 October 1923. Percival papers. This is not to say that front-line units also ignored loyalists, for some certainly tried to use them as an intelligence source, but that no overall plan existed for involving them.

In my own mind I am quite clear that the present negotiations have only been made possible by the fact that the unceasing efforts of troops and police together with the arrival of reinforcing units from England have brought home to the Sinn Féin leaders the advisability of coming to some terms before the rebellion is openly and obviously crushed.[10]

Whether this eventuality was foreseeable even in July 1921 may be open to doubt, but the evidence suggests that the general proposition was correct. On the other hand, if the rebel leaders were beginning to smell military defeat, the British Government had already been forced to accept political and moral defeat. Only rapid military success could have averted public pressure in favour of a settlement, and without such success the Government was driven to compromise. The period of military confrontation had eroded the ground beneath both Republicans and Imperialists.

It may be accepted that, on the British side, some form of military struggle was inevitable before Irish demands would be taken seriously, and that from a military point of view the style of warfare adopted by the Republicans would inevitably have given the struggle a nightmarish quality. It must, however, be judged that the British response was brutal, and in many ways counter-productive. The terrorism practised by a section of the Crown Forces—significant out of all proportion to its size—both spread and stiffened opposition in Ireland, and left a legacy of bitterness which has not yet been eradicated from Anglo–Irish relations. It arose because these forces were placed in a false position, and were never controlled by a definite and realistic policy. It may be objected that military criticisms of the Government tended to ignore the complexities of the political situation; but it remains more important that the Government failed to meet the requirements of the military situation. The power of decision lay, after all, not with the Army but with the Government, and it chose to apply military force without reference to military logic. Military victory in Ireland, in so far as the term had any meaning, was only conceivable if the use of force was pressed to its limits along a defined course, and if it was fully backed by the Government and public opinion. Without such backing, force became a two-edged weapon when it encountered determined resistance; failing to cut through, it became isolated amidst opposition from both sides. Ultimately it was this isolation which left the greatest impression on the military mind after the Irish war, for, as one staff history put it, 'The Army is only the spear point; it is the shaft of the spear and the force behind it that drives the blow home.'[11]

[10] G.O.C.-in-C. W.S.R., 16 July 1921. C.P. 3155, CAB.24 125.
[11] Hist. 5th Div., p. 140.

APPENDICES

Appendix I

Royal Irish Constabulary: Recruitment, 1920[1]

	All R.I.C.	Regular R.I.C. only[2]	Non-Irishmen[3] No.	%	Wastage[4] No.	%
January	206	—	111	54	114	55
February	286	—	77	27	129	45
March	481	—	153	32	246	51
April	370	—	90	24	115	31
May	165	159	115	70	84	53
June	250	228	100	40	85	37
July	419	316	333	80	151	48
August	707	366	667	94	157	43
September	682	493	638	94	202	41
October	1,428	1,244	1,310	92	409	33
November	985	674	907	92	240	36
December	1,220	993	1,075	88	263	26

[1] Derived from R.I.C. General Register, H.O. 184 36–40. The categories and figures have been worked out by the author and are not official.

[2] Excluding 'Defence of Barracks Sergeants', 'Cadets', and 'Temporary Cadets' (A.D.R.I.C.), whose numbers became significant in May. Their numbers in July were: Defence of Barracks Sergeants—12; Cadets—28; Temporary Cadets—63. In September the A.D.R.I.C. ceased to appear in the General Register, but another special category, 'Temporary Constables', appeared.

[3] Based on country of birth. A considerable number of native Irishmen resident in Britain joined through non-traditional channels (Major Fleming or R.I.C. Recruiting Offices) but have been counted as Irish recruits. On the other hand a few non-Irishmen joined through traditional channels (recommendation by local D.I. R.I.C.) but have been counted as non-Irish. Percentage figures in this category apply to all R.I.C.

[4] Through death, discharge, dismissal or resignation. Figures apply to intake for that month, not to personnel wastage during the month. Percentage figures in this category apply to Regular R.I.C. only, as the Register does not have details of men in special categories.

Appendix II

Auxiliary Division R.I.C.: Strength, 1920[1]

Company	26.9.20	20.10.20	3.11.20	19.11.20	29.11.20
A	99	94	109	104	77[2]
B	92	86	102	98	72
C	103	102	116	115	115
D	104	102	111	106	110
E	105	104	108	100	63
F	54	108	102	79	78
G		93	109	107	103
H			60	83	84
I				88	89
J				26	73
K[3]					44
Depot	34	35	50	61	89
TOTAL	591	724	867	967	997

[1] Based on incomplete holograph tables in R.I.C. Auxiliary Division Register No. 1 which includes details of arrivals, transfers and wastage for each company in the period late September–early December 1920. All totals are derived from these.

[2] The tendency, about which the Army later complained (G.O.C.-in-C. to C.S.I., 7 June 1921. 'G' War Diary, G.H.Q. Ireland, W.O. 35 93(1)/1), to run down companies already in service so as to form new companies, is already clearly visible.

[3] The establishment of this company is of interest, because after the Cork burnings the military inquiry stated that it had been sent into action precipitately. Its total of 44 at the end of November was made up as follows:

22.11.20—3 T.C.s transferred from various coys.

26.11.20—16 T.C.s transferred, mainly from E Coy.

27.11.20—22 T.C.s ditto.

29.11.20—3 T.C.s transferred from C, G, and J Coys.

Thus while the company had only lately been formed when it was sent to Cork (a week later), much of its personnel came from comparatively well-established companies.

Appendix III

*Strength of the Police Forces, 1920–1921**

	4.7.20		11.7.20		18.7.20		25.7.20	
R.I.C.	10,110	−31	10,129	+19	10,114	−15	10,069	−46
A.D.R.I.C.								
D.M.P.	1,163	−9	1,166	+3	1,165	−1	1,164	−1

	4.8.20		8.8.20		15.8.20		22.8.20	
R.I.C.	10,030	−39	9,920	−110	9,903	−17	9,954	+51
A.D.R.I.C.								
D.M.P.	1,162	−2	1,159	−3	1,142	−17	1,141	−1

	29.8.20		5.9.20		12.9.20		19.9.20	
R.I.C.	9,987	+33	9,934	−53	9,913	−21	9,856	−57
A.D.R.I.C.					478	+73	563	+85
D.M.P.	1,138	−3	1,137	−1	1,137		1,139	+2

	26.9.20		3.10.20		10.10.20		17.10.20	
R.I.C.	10,002	+146	10,208	+206	10,463	+255	10,744	+311
A.D.R.I.C.	591	+28	614	+33	629	+15	683	+54
D.M.P.	1,141	+2	1,134	−7	1,133	−1	1,143	+10

	24.10.20		31.10.20		7.11.20		14.11.20	
R.I.C.	10,982	+208	11,194	+212	11,309	+115	11,569	+260
A.D.R.I.C.	770	+87	846	+76	884	+38	930	+46

	21.11.20		28.11.20		5.12.20		12.12.20	
R.I.C.	11,776	+197	11,853	+87	11,998	+145	12,258	+260
A.D.R.I.C.	969	+39	997	+28	1,014	+17	1,054	+40
D.M.P.	1,131	−5	1,129	−2	1.128	−1	1,129	+1

	19.12.20		26.12.20		4.1.21		12.1.21	
R.I.C.	12,500	+242	12,613	+113	12,755	+142	12,992	+167
A.D.R.I.C.	1,114	+60	1,154	+40	1,227	+73	1,262	+35
D.M.P.	1,130	+1	1,131	+1	1,127	−2	1,130	+3

	19.1.21		25.1.21		4.2.21		9.2.21	
R.I.C.	13,213	+291	13,468	+255	13,643	+175	13,737	+94
A.D.R.I.C.	1,326	+54	1,375	+49	1,375		1,387	+12
D.M.P.	1,134	+4	1,133	−1	1,131	−2	1,128	−3

* Compiled from C.S.I. Weekly Surveys of the State of Ireland, prepared for Cabinet Irish Situation Cttee. from 5 July 1920 (CAB.27 108), and circulated to Cabinet from 4 January 1921 (C.P. series, CAB.24 118–24). Totals, including discrepancies, are taken directly from these.

8

	18.2.21		25.2.21		5.3.21		10.3.21	
R.I.C.	13,843	+106	13,920	+77	13,999	+79	14,047	+48
A.D.R.I.C.	1,416	+29	1,445	+29	1,461	+16	1,472	+11
D.M.P.	1,127	−1	1,123	−4	1,121	−2	1,119	−2

	17.3.21		26.3.21		31.3.21		6.4.21	
R.I.C.	13,626	?	13,673	+57	13,595	?	13,660	+65
A.D.R.I.C.	1,479	+7	1,483	+4	1,483		1,487	+4
D.M.P.	1,117	−2	1,120	+3	1,131	+11	1,130	−1

	12.4.21		22.4.21		29.4.21		3.5.21	
R.I.C.	13,771	+111	13,822	+51	13,875	+53	13,906	+31
A.D.R.I.C.	1,478	−9	1,481	+3	1,474	−7	1,469	+5
D.M.P.	1,131	+1	1,130	−1	1,126	−4	1,126	

	10.5.21		17.5.21		24.5.21		28.5.21	
R.I.C.	13,911	+5	13,910	−1	13,948	+38	13,972	+24
A.D.R.I.C.	1,479	+10	1,507	+28	1,508	+1	1,505	−3
D.M.P.	1,125	−1	1,124	−1	1,127	+3	1,127	

	6.6.21		13.6.21		20.6.21		27.6.21	
R.I.C.	13,959	−13	13,983	+24	14,077	+94	14,212	+135
A.D.R.I.C.	1,510	+5	1,515	+5	1,522	+7	1,526	+4
D.M.P.	1,125	−2	1,126	+1	1,126		1,126	

Appendix IV

R.I.C. Statistics of Indictable Offences, 1919–1921*

		Agrarian	Non-Agrarian	Total
1919	January	29	169	198
	February	26	259	285
	March	32	136	168
	April	41	217	258
	May	37	219	256
	June	32	218	250
	July	55	243	298
	August	37	312	249
	September	24	322	346
	October	41	312	249
	November	35	312	347
	December	62	421	483
1920	January	60	540	600
	February	102	557	659
	March–April		records missing	
	May	237	1,163	1,400
	June	110	1,070	1,180
	July	64	1,696	1,760
	August	33	1,291	1,324
	September	17	2,166	2,183
	October	23	1,399	1,422
	November	23	1,312	1,335
	December	27	1,456	1,483
1921	January	25	1,209	1,234
	February	54	1,229	1,283
	March	34	1,664	1,698
	April	32	1,835	1,867
	May	21	2,167	2,188
	June	12	2,244	2,256
	July	25	2,115	2,140

* Source: R.I.C. Monthly Reports, C.O. 904 108–16.

APPENDIX V

*Irish Office Statistics of Outrages, 1919–1921**

Cumulative totals from 1 January 1919 to end of:

	June 1920	Sept. 1920	Dec. 1920	March 1921	June 1921	Truce
Courthouses destroyed	30	63	69	74	83	88
Vacated R.I.C. barracks destroyed	343	483	510	512	521	522
Vacated R.I.C. barracks damaged	104	114	119	120	121	121
Occupied R.I.C. barracks destroyed	12	19	23	24	25	25
Occupied R.I.C. barracks damaged	24	41	54	113	232	267
Raids on Mails	91	540	959	1,392	2,368	2,564
Raids on Rate Collectors, etc.				51	121	122
Raids on Coastguard Stations or Lighthouses	19	38	47	56	85	97
Raids for Arms	(760)†	2,645	2,973	3,087	3,210	3,218
Police killed	55	101	177	264	381	405
Police wounded	74	168	258	406	631	682
Military killed	5	16	54	98	139	150
Military wounded	(?)	60	121	206	320	345
Civilians killed	15	25	42	91	172	196
Civilians wounded	39	75	104	133	179	185
TOTAL		4,516	5,510	6,608	8,641	8,987

* Source: C.S.I. Weekly Surveys, (1920) Cabinet Irish Situation Cttee. papers II (Memoranda), CAB.27 108; (1921) Cabinet papers, C.P. series, CAB.24.
† Figure for August (none available for June).

APPENDIX VI

Tactical Motor Transport (Army), Summer 1920*

	Present Allotment				Total Required				Increase Required			
	5th Div.	6th Div.	D.D.	Total	5th Div.	6th Div.	D.D.	Total	5th Div.	6th Div.	D.D.	Total
3-ton lorries	32	24	30	86	60	50	43	153	28	26	13	67
15-cwt. box bodies	20	65	4	89	84	112	13	209	64	47	9	120
Ford vans			4	4	10		10	20	10		6	16
Motor cars	6	7	1	14	19	20	6	45	13	13	5	31
TOTAL	58	96	39	193	173	182	72	427	115	86	33	234

* Source: Military Requirements in Ireland, memo by Gen. Sir C. F. N. Macready; Appendix to Appendix II, C.29(20), 11 May 1920, CAB.23 21.

Appendix VII

Dublin District: Operational Strength, July 1920*

	Total strength (O.R.)	Total O.R. available for mobile operations
1st King's Own Regt.		
Richmond Barracks	741	474
1st Lancs. Fusiliers		
North Dublin Union	905	475
Ship St. Barracks	329	255
2nd Worcs. Regt.		
Portobello Barracks	932	589
1st Cheshire Regt.		
Rathdrum	155	123
Enniskerry	49	44
Kingstown	45	45
Newtownmountkennedy	140	39
Wicklow	40	40
Arklow	71	68
Shillelagh	25	25
	525	384
1st South Lancs. Regt.		
Wellington Barracks	567	262
2nd Welch Regt.		
Richmond Barracks	642	344
2nd Royal Berks. Regt.		
Portobello Barracks	820	465
1st Wilts. Regt.		
Royal Barracks	1,003	595
1st West Riding Regt.		
Collinstown Barracks	481	330
Rathmooney Workhouse	30	30
1st S. Wales Borderers		
Drogheda	149	149
Swords	58	58
Gormanstown	142	142
Navan	35	35
Trim	25	25
Skerries	30	30
Marlborough Barracks	29	29
H.Q.	293	49
	761	517
TOTAL	7,726	4,270

* Adapted from D.D. Operation Strength Return, 2 July 1920. W.O. 35 179/1. Cf. proportions in Appendix VIII, especially of smaller detachments.

Appendix VIII

6th Division: Operational Strength, June 1920*

	1 Total O.R. including men absent	2 Total present but not 3†	3 Total available for mobile operations
16TH INFANTRY BRIGADE			
1st Buffs			
Fermoy	728	378	160
Kilworth	138	11	—
Lismore	48	47	—
Dungarvan	23	23	—
House nr. Dungarvan	10	10	—
1st Lincolnshire Regt.			
Tipperary	693	237	300
Killenaule	27	13	14
Cashel	27	13	14
Dundrum	26	13	13
Cappawhite	12	12	—
Emly	8	8	—
1st Devonshire Regt.			
Waterford	1,381	149	931
2nd Yorkshire Regt.			
Tipperary (April figures:	543	201	90)
1st Manchester Regt.			
Kilworth	534	48	402
Moore Park	211	7	164
Mitchelstown	46	18	28
17TH INFANTRY BRIGADE			
1st Essex Regt.			
Kinsale	424	35	195
Fort Charles	134	30	104
Bandon	118	23	95
Dunmanway	36	26	—
Timoleague	32	32	—
Clonakilty	69	34	35
Bantry	63	30	33
Skibbereen	35	35	—
Furious Pier	35	35	—

* Adapted from 6th Division Weekly Operation Strength Return No. 20, 21 June 1920. W.O. 35 179/1.

† The figures in this column show men unavailable for mobile operations either through inadequacy of training or requirements of defence.

2nd Cameron Highlanders

Queenstown	335	60	202
Ballincollig	158	2	92
Whitepoint	24	24	—
Crosshaven	4	4	—
Midleton	53	53	—
Killeagh	51	51	—
Ballycotton	7	7	—

1st Machine Gun Corps

Ballyvonaire	1,067	282	232

17th Lancers

Buttevant	178	26	51
Baelincollig	353	67	100

2nd East Lancs. Regt.

Tralee	392	67	256
Killarney	80	21	44
Listowel	76	19	46
Valentia Island	25	13	10
Cahirciveen	42	20	20
Ballyheigue	36	20	16
Castleisland	30	20	10
Browhead	9	9	—
Ballynagall	14	14	—
Dingle	14	14	—
Milltown	14	14	—
Glenbeigh	35	15	20
Fenit	13	13	—
Buttevant	27	5	21

2nd Hampshire Regt.

Cork	834	38	555
Youghal	231	31	200
Macroom	77	37	40
Mallow	42	42	—
Ballyvourney	38	38	—

2nd Oxon. and Bucks. L.I.

Cork	622	100	396

18TH INFANTRY BRIGADE

10th Hussars

Ennis	616	70	170

2nd Yorkshire Regt.

Newcastlewest	54	54	—

2nd Royal Welch Fusiliers

Limerick	627	75	369

1st Oxon. and Bucks. L.I.

Limerick	670	236	323
Ballyvonare	45	45	—

1st Northants. Regt.			
Templemore	507	186	187
Nenagh	112	56	56
Thurles	56	26	30
Birr	45	20	25
Castlefogerty	25	25	—
2nd Highland L.I.			
Ennistymon	197	30	127
Ennis	139	45	43
Scarriff	22	10	12
Gort	30	14	15
Kilrush	71	32	31
Kilmihil	60	25	22
Corofin	67	30	32
Lisdoonvarna	82	33	40
Milltownmalbay	33	15	14
Carrigaholt	21	10	11
B Coy. 1st Machine Gun Corps			
Bruff	27	—	27
Kilmallock	33	—	33
Pallas Green	31	—	31
Croom	24	—	24
Newport	30	—	30
Leinster Regt. (Depot)			
Birr	80	79	—

Appendix IX

*6th Division: Operational Strength, 1920–1921**

	April 1920	July 1921
16th Infantry Brigade (Fermoy)	1,995	3,899 +85 A.D.R.I.C.
17th Infantry Brigade (Cork)	2,997	4,259 +146 A.D.R.I.C.
18th Infantry Brigade (Limerick)	2,538	4,289 +173 A.D.R.I.C.
Kerry Infantry Brigade (Buttevant)	not formed	2,036 +133 A.D.R.I.C.
TOTAL	7,510	12,483 +537 A.D.R.I.C.

* Totals for April 1920 derived from 6th Div. Weekly Strength Return No. 10, 12 April 1920. W.O. 35 179/1. The figures given here are arrived at by totalling the categories A and B (men present and available for mobile operations, and men present and fit for mobile operations but required for defensive purposes), and excluding categories C, D, and E (men present but not available for mobile operations owing to

(a) lack of training or physical fitness	1,173
(b) absence in Ireland	460
(c) absence outside Ireland	587).

The grand total of infantry (other ranks) at this time was 9,730.

Totals for July 1921 derived from 6th Div. Composition and Dispositions for August 1921, Return to G.H.Q. Ireland, 23 July 1921. W.O. 35 179/4. The records for this later period do not specify the proportion of troops available for mobile operations but these totals certainly include men required for defensive purposes (old category B), and possibly also men partially trained (old category C).

Appendix X

Courts Martial 1917–1920*

Totals before August 1920
1917	137
1918	202
1919	138
Jan.–July 1920	94

Weekly totals after R.O.I.A., August 1920

Week ending	Arrests	Courts Martial	Convictions
14 Aug.	59	8	8
21 Aug.	37	2	2
28 Aug.	32	13	12
4 Sept.	49	16	15
11 Sept.	89	25	20
18 Sept.	47	39	33
25 Sept.	133	31	21
2 Oct.	64	72	50
9 Oct.	42	78	71
16 Oct.	71	44	36
23 Oct.	74	24	15
30 Oct.	84	77	70
6 Nov.	49	29	25
13 Nov.	110	52	41
20 Nov.	137	40	29
27 Nov.	189	39	25
4 Dec.	58	43	35
11 Dec.	130	70	60
18 Dec.	66	54	39
25 Dec.	66	53	48

* Source: Irish Office Statistics, C.O. 904 150 and C.O. 906 19; C.S.I. Weekly Surveys and G.O.C.-in-C. W.S.R.s, CAB.27 108; *Manchester Guardian*, 20 October 1920.

APPENDIX XI

Martial Law: Police Co-operation

G.H.Q. 2/33227 G.   6th Division   1st Div.
                      Police Adviser   5th Div.
                                        D.D.   / for information

1. From the date of the Proclamation of Martial Law, the police in the areas in which martial law takes effect will come under the orders of Military Governors of such areas.

2. Military Governors, although they are at liberty to make use of the police forces in their areas for operations, must ensure that the normal and necessary routine of police patrols and duty is interfered with as little as possible.

3. When a Military Governor wishes to issue orders to the police, he will (except in cases of emergency) do so through the highest police authority in his area.

4. Military Governors will hold Divisional Commissioners responsible for the discipline of police forces in their areas. The Divisional Commissioners concerned will continue to follow as far as possible the ordinary procedure of the force.

5. No Military Governor below the Divisional Military Governor has the power to alter the location of police detachments.

6. The police will continue to be disciplined and administered by their own officers.

11.12.20.

APPENDIX XII

Internment of I.R.A., 1921: Cumulative Statistics*

Week ending	Brigade Commandants	Brigade Staff	Battalion Commandants	Battalion Staff	Company Officers	Others	TOTAL
17 January	11	31	35	80	608	713	1,478
7 February	15	36	46	98	780	882	1,857
21 February	15	36	49	99	804	982	1,985
5 March	17	37	58	124	976	1,105	2,317
21 March	17	38	63	145	1,053	1,253	2,569
2 April	17	43	69	160	1,117	1,350	2,756
30 April	18	47	71	175	1,189	1,505	3,005
21 May	19	53	81	191	1,454	1,891	3,689
4 June	19	53	85	202	1,502	1,978	3,839
18 June	19	54	88	209	1,564	2,205	4,139
2 July	19	55	90	213	1,593	2,317	4,287
16 July	19	58	93	217	1,623	2,444	4,454

Analysis of Internment by Divisions

	1st Div.	5th Div.	6th Div.	Dublin Dist.	TOTAL
21 February	188	456	519	822	1,985
5 March	237	571	668	841	2,317
2 April	302	697	833	924	2,756
7 May	389	889	1,049	1,007	3,334

* Source: G.O.C.-in-C. W.S.Rs, January–July 1921. CAB.24 118-25.

SOURCES AND
BIBLIOGRAPHY

A. Unpublished Sources

i: *Official records, coded as referred to in the text notes*

CAB. Records of the Cabinet Office, in the Public Record Office, London.

    CAB. 1 Miscellaneous records.

    CAB. 21 Registered files.

    CAB. 23. Minutes and Conclusions of Cabinet meetings and conferences.

    CAB. 24 Cabinet papers, G.T. series (to 1919) and C.P. series (1919 onwards), including Cabinet memoranda; Committee reports, and conference minutes; C.S.I. Weekly Surveys of the State of Ireland and G.O.C.-in-C. Weekly Situation Reports from January 1921.

    CAB. 27 Committees: General series, including Irish Situation Cttee. minutes and memoranda, with C.S.I. Weekly Surveys and G.O.C.-in-C. W.S.R.s from July 1920 to January 1921.

C.O. Records now in the Colonial Office series in the Public Record Office, London.

    C.O. 761 Register of Parliamentary Questions.

    C.O. 903 C.S.O. Judicial Division records, including Intelligence Notes, 1915–19.

    C.O. 904 C.S.O. and R.I.C. records, including Military Intelligence Reports 1916–18; R.I.C. Reports (Monthly Confidential Reports of Inspector General and County Inspectors) 1916–21; Propaganda and counter-propaganda records; and the papers of Sir John Anderson as Joint Under Secretary, C.S.O.

    C.O. 906 Miscellaneous records, including Irish Office intelligence telegrams on disorders 1920–1.

Cork County Library: Malicious Injury Claim Files; personal testimonies.

C.S.O. Records of the Chief Secretary's Office, in the State Paper Office, Dublin.

    C.S.O. R.P. Registered papers, collected in files. Most of the material relevant to this study was removed to London in 1922; the bound volumes of R.P. Indexes remain.

    Register of Persons Arrested by R.I.C. and Military Authorities, 19 November 1920–1 July 1921.

H.O. Records of the Home Office, in the Public Record Office, London.

    H.O. 184 Police records, including R.I.C. Nominal Rolls and registers of intake of R.I.C. and Auxiliary Division R.I.C.

I.W.M. Records in the Imperial War Museum, London.

> H. D.F. K. 37957. 'A Side Show in Southern Ireland, 1920' (Anon.).
> *See also* Private Papers, Jeudwine and Percival.

W.O. Records of the War Office, in the Public Record Office, London.

> W.O. 32 Irish files, including notes on martial law and military opera-
> tions 1916; active service 1920.
>
> W.O. 35 Irish records, including Dublin District H.Q. File and War
> Diary 1920–1 with accompanying documents; fragments of G.H.Q.
> 'G' (Operations) War Diary and 5th Division War Diary; fragment-
> ary movement orders and location and strength returns; Proceedings
> of Military Courts of Inquiry in Lieu of Inquest on Civilians (not
> courts martial); claims for damages caused by military personnel
> and in official reprisals; G.H.Q. press cuttings series, with comments.
> About half the records in this group are under official closure of 100
> years.

ii: *Private records, listed as referred to in the text notes*

Anderson papers. Papers of Sir John Anderson (later Viscount Waverley) as
   Joint Under Secretary, C.S.O., 1920–1, especially series A (correspondence and
   memoranda) and B.1 (including a large correspondence with Sir Nevil
   Macready); in the Public Record Office, London.

Bonar Law papers. Papers of Andrew Bonar Law, especially correspondence
   with Sir Warren Fisher, Lord French, Walter Long, and Sir Hamar Greenwood; in the Beaverbrook Library, London.

Churchill papers. Papers of Winston Churchill as Secretary of State for War
   and Air, including correspondence with Lloyd George, Greenwood,
   Macready, and Trenchard. Copies in the possession of Mr. Martin Gilbert.

Fisher papers. Papers of H. A. L. Fisher as President of the Board of Education
   (mainly diaries); in the Bodleian Library, Oxford.

Hemming papers. Papers of Sir Francis Hemming as Private Secretary to Sir
   Hamar Greenwood. A small collection, mainly of speech notes, correspondence and memoranda; in the Library of Corpus Christi College, Oxford.

Jeudwine papers. Papers of Lieutenant-General Sir Hugh Jeudwine, including
   situation reports; correspondence concerning the declaration of martial law;
   200pp. typescript History of the 5th Division, and printed Record of the
   Rebellion by General Staff Irish Command (see General Staff histories); in
   the Imperial War Museum, London.

Lloyd George papers. Papers of David Lloyd George as Prime Minister (Series
   F), especially correspondence with Bonar Law, Sir Warren Fisher, Lord
   French, Sir Hamar Greenwood, Walter Long, and Sir Nevil Macready; in
   the Beaverbrook Library, London.

Midleton papers. Papers of the 1st Earl of Midleton, including notes of meetings
   with the Cabinet; correspondence and memoranda on the Irish situation; in
   the Public Record Office, London (P.R.O. 30).

Percival papers. Papers of Major (later General) A. E. Percival, including two
   lectures on guerrilla warfare based on experience in Ireland; notes and
   photographs; in the Imperial War Museum, London.

Strathcarron papers. Papers of Ian Macpherson (later Lord Strathcarron) as
   Chief Secretary for Ireland, including memoranda and correspondence on

security matters with Lord French, Bonar Law, and Long, and between Lt. Gen. Shaw and Brig. Gen. Byrne.

Sturgis diary. Typescript, with holograph corrections, of the diary of Mark Sturgis as Joint Assistant Under Secretary, C.S.O, 1920–1; in the Public Record Office, London (P.R.O. 30).

Wilson papers. The diaries of General Sir Henry Wilson as Chief of the Imperial General Staff, in the possession of Major C. J. Wilson.

Winter papers. Papers of Colonel Ormonde Winter. A very small collection concerning his appointment as Director of Intelligence; in the Public Record Office, London (C.O. 904).

Worthington-Evans papers. Papers of Sir Laming Worthington-Evans as Minister of Pensions and Secretary of State for War, including Cabinet Irish Situation Committee papers; in the Bodleian Library, Oxford.

iii: *General Staff Histories*

G.H.Q. Ireland (General Staff, Irish Command), *Record of the Rebellion in Ireland in 1920–21, and the Part played by the Army in dealing with it.* A. 2448–1: vol i (Operations), March 1922; A. 2448–2: vol. ii (Intelligence), May 1922. Jeudwine papers.

History of the 5th Division in Ireland, 1919–1922 (? General Staff, 5th Division, 1922), 200pp. typescript with appendices and maps. Jeudwine papers.

B. PUBLISHED SOURCES

i: *Parliamentary papers*

Parliamentary Debates, 5th series:
House of Commons, vols. 112–43.
House of Lords, vols. 33–45.

Reports.

1916 Cd. 8279 xi 171. Report of the Royal Commission on the Rebellion in Ireland.

1918 Cd. 9019 x 697. Report of the Proceedings of the Irish Convention. (Especially Appendix XV, Schedule A, Memorandum on the Question of Police Administration, by Brig. Gen. Byrne.)

1921 Cmd. 1220 xv 335. Report of Mallow Court of Enquiry.

1921 Cmd. 1534 xxix 427. Arrangements governing the Cessation of Active Operations in Ireland, which came into force on 11th July, 1921.

1922 Cmd. 1610 xii 611. General Annual Report on the British Army, 1919–20.

1922 Cmd. 1618 xvii 785. Royal Irish Constabulary Auxiliary Division. Outline of Terms on which Cadets were engaged and of Conditions on which at various times it was open to Cadets to re-engage for further Periods of Service.

1923 Cmd. 1941 xiv 665. General Annual Report on the British Army, 1920–21.

ii: *Books, articles*

Amery, L. S. *My Political Life.* vol. ii, *War and Peace 1914–1929.* Hutchinson, London, 1953.

Arthur, Sir G. *General Sir John Maxwell*. Murray, London, 1932.

Ash, B. *The Lost Dictator, A Biography of Field-Marshal Sir Henry Wilson, Bart., G.C.B., D.S.O., M.P.*, London, 1968.

Atkinson, C. T. *The South Wales Borderers, 24th Foot, 1689–1937*. Cambridge University Press, 1937.

Barry, T. *Guerilla Days in Ireland*. 1st edn. The Irish Press, Dublin, 1949; new edn. Anvil Books, Tralee, 1962.

Bell, J. Bowyer. 'The Thompson Submachine Gun in Ireland, 1921', *Irish Sword*, viii. No. 31 (1967).

Bennett, R. *The Black and Tans*. 1st edn. Hulton, London, 1959; new edn. New English Library, London, 1970.

Béaslaí, P. *Michael Collins and the Making of a New Ireland*. Harrap, London, 1926.

Birkenhead, Earl of. *F. E.: The Life of F. E. Smith, 1st Earl of Birkenhead*. Eyre and Spottiswoode, London, 1959.

Blake, R. *The Unknown Prime Minister*. Eyre and Spottiswoode, London, 1955.

Blight, Brig. G. *The History of the Royal Berkshire Regiment 1920–1947*. Staples Press, London, 1953.

Bowden, T. 'Bloody Sunday—A Reappraisal', *European Studies Review*, ii. No. 1 (1972).

Bowden, T. 'The Irish Underground and the War of Independence 1919–1921', *The Army Quarterly*, iii. No. 3, (1973).

Bowden, T. 'The Irish Underground and the War of Independence 1919–1921', *Journal of Contemporary History*, viii. No. 2 (1973).

Boyce, D. G. 'British Conservative Opinion, the Ulster Question, and the Partition of Ireland, 1919–21', *Irish Historical Studies*, xvii, No. 65 (1968).

Boyce, D. G. 'How to Settle the Irish Question: Lloyd George and Ireland 1916–21', in A. J. P. Taylor (ed.), *Lloyd George*.

Boyce, D. G. *Englishmen and Irish Troubles. British Public Opinion and the Making of Irish Policy 1918–22*. Jonathan Cape, London, 1972.

Breen, D. *My Fight for Irish Freedom*. Talbot Press, Dublin, 1924; new edn. Anvil Books, Tralee, 1964.

Briollay, S. (pseud. R. Chauviré). *L'Irlande Insurgée*. Plon-Nourrit, Paris, 1921.

Broeker, G. *Rural Disorder and Police Reform in Ireland 1812–36*. Routledge and Kegan Paul, London, 1970.

Buckland, P. *The Anglo-Irish and the New Ireland 1885–1922*. (*Irish Unionism* i). Gill and Macmillan, Dublin, 1972.

Butler, E. *Barry's Flying Column*. Leo Cooper, London, 1971.

Callwell, C. E. *Field-Marshal Sir Henry Wilson. His Life and Diaries*. 2 vols., Cassell, London, 1927.

Caulfield, M. *The Easter Rebellion*. Muller, London, 1964.

Chorley, K. C. *Armies and the Art of Revolution*. Faber, London, 1943.

Churchill, W. S. *The Aftermath. A Sequel to the World Crisis*. Macmillan, London, 1941.

Clarkson, J. D. *Labour and Nationalism in Ireland*. Columbia U. P., New York, 1925.

Clode, C. M. *Military and Martial Law*. Murray, London, 1872.

Corfe, T. *The Phoenix Park Murders*. Hodder and Stoughton, London, 1968.

Crane, C. P. *Memories of a Resident Magistrate 1880–1920*. T. and A. Constable, Edinburgh, 1938.

Crozier, F. P. *Impressions and Recollections*. Laurie, London, 1930.
Crozier, F. P. *A Word to Gandhi: The Lesson of Ireland*. Williams and Norgate, London, 1931.
Crozier, F. P. *Ireland for Ever*. Jonathan Cape, London, 1932.
Curran, J. M. 'The Consolidation of the Irish Revolution, 1921–1923', *University Review*, v, No. 1 (1968).
Curtis, L. P. *Coercion and Conciliation in Ireland 1880–1892*. Princeton University Press, Princeton, N.J. 1963.
Curtis, L. P. *Anglo-Saxons and Celts*. Conference on British Studies, Univ. of Bridgport, Connecticut, 1968.
Dáil Eireann. *The Constructive Work of Dáil Eireann*. 3 vols., Talbot Press, Dublin, 1921.
Dalton, C. *With the Dublin Brigade 1917–1921*. Peter Davies, London, 1929.
Daniell, D. S. *Cap of Honour. The Story of the Gloucestershire Regiment 1694–1950*. Harrap, London, 1951.
Darling, Sir W. Y. *So It Looks to Me*. Odhams, London, 1953.
Dawson, R. *Red Terror and Green*. Murray, London, 1920.
Desmond, S. *The Drama of Sinn Féin*. Collins, London, 1923.
Dicey, A. V. *Introduction to the Study of the Law of the Constitution*. Macmillan, London, 1885.
Dublin's Fighting Story 1916–21. The Kerryman, Tralee, 1949.
Duff, D. V. *Sword for Hire*. Murray, London, 1934.
Duggan, G. C. ('Periscope'). 'The Last Days of Dublin Castle', *Blackwood's Magazine*, mcclxxxii (1922).
Farrell, B. *The Founding of Dáil Éireann = Parliament and Nation-Building*. Gill and Macmillan, Dublin 1971.
Figgis, D. *Recollections of the Irish War*. Ernest Benn, London, 1927.
Finlason, W. F. *A Treatise on Martial Law*. Stevens, London, 1866.
Finlason, W. F. *Commentaries upon Martial Law*. Stevens, London, 1867.
Finlason, W. F. *Martial Law*. Butterworth, 1872.
Fisher, H. A. L. *An Unfinished Autobiography*. Oxford University Press, London, 1940.
Forester, M. *Michael Collins—The Lost Leader*. Sidgwick and Jackson, London, 1971.
French, Hon. E. G. F. *The Life of Field-Marshal Sir John French*. Cassell, London, 1931.
Gallagher, F. (Introd. T. P. O'Neill.) *The Anglo-Irish Treaty*. Hutchinson, London, 1965.
Gilbert, M. *Winston S. Churchill*. Vol. iii, Heinemann, London, 1971.
Gleeson, J. *Bloody Sunday*. Peter Davies, London, 1962.
Gough, Gen. Sir H. 'The Situation in Ireland', *Review of Reviews*, lxiii (Feb. 1921).
Graubard, S. R. 'Military Demobilization in Great Britain following the First World War', *Journal of Modern History*, xix (1947).
Greaves, C. D. *Liam Mellows and the Irish Revolution*. Lawrence and Wishart, London, 1971.
Guevara, Che. *Guerrilla Warfare*. Penguin Books, Harmondsworth, 1969.
Hally, Col. P. J. 'The Easter 1916 Rising in Dublin: the Military Aspects', *Irish Sword*, vii–viii. Nos. 29–30 (1966–7).

Hancock, Sir W. K. *Problems of Nationality 1918–1936* (Survey of British Commonwealth Affairs, vol. i). R.I.I.A., Oxford University Press, London, 1937.

Hawkins, R. 'Dublin Castle and the Royal Irish Constabulary', in T. D. Williams (ed.), *The Irish Struggle*. Routledge and Kegan Paul, London, 1966.

Hobsbawm, E. J. *Bandits*. Penguin Books, Harmondsworth, 1972.

Hobson, B. *Ireland Yesterday and Tomorrow*. Anvil Books, Tralee, 1968.

Hogan, D. (pseud. F. Gallagher). *The Four Glorious Years*. Irish Press, Dublin, 1953.

Higham, R. *Armed Forces in Peacetime*. Foulis, London, 1962.

Holt, E. *Protest in Arms. The Irish Troubles 1916–1923*. Putnam, London, 1960.

Jones, T. *Lloyd George*. Oxford University Press, London, 1951.

Jones, T. (ed. K. Middlemas.) *Whitehall Diary*. Vols. i, iii, Oxford University Press, London, 1969, 1971.

Kee, R. *The Green Flag. A History of Irish Nationalism*. Weidenfeld and Nicolson, London, 1972.

Keir and Lawson. *Cases in Constitutional Law*. 5th ed., Oxford University Press, London, 1972.

Kemp, Lt. Cdr. P. K. *The Middlesex Regiment 1919–1952*. Gale and Polden, Aldershot, 1956.

Kendle, J. E. 'The Round Table Movement and "Home Rule All Round"', *Historical Journal*, xi. 2 (1968).

Kendle, J. E. 'Federalism and the Irish Problem in 1918', *History*, 56, No. 187 (1971).

Kerryman, The. *Kerry's Fighting Story 1916–21*. Compiled by The Kerryman, Tralee, 1949.

Kerryman, The. *With the IRA in the Fight for Freedom*. Tralee, 1955.

Kitson, Brig. F. E. *Low Intensity Operations. Subversion, Insurgency and Peace-keeping*. Faber, London, 1971.

Labour Party. *Report of the Labour Commission to Ireland*. London, 1921.

Liddell Hart, Capt. Sir Basil, 'Lessons from Resistance Movements—Guerrilla and Non-violent', in A. Roberts (ed.), *The Strategy of Civilian Defence. Non-violent Resistance to Aggression*, Faber, London, 1967, pp. 195–211.

Long, Viscount. *Memories*. Hutchinson, London, 1923.

Longford, Earl of, and T. P. O'Neill, *Eamon de Valera*. Hutchinson, London, 1970.

Lyons, F. S. L. *Ireland Since the Famine*. Weidenfeld and Nicolson, London, 1971.

Macardle, D. *The Irish Republic 1911–1925*. Gollancz, London, 1937; new edn. Corgi Books, London, 1968.

MacCarthy, Col. J. M. (ed.) *Limerick's Fighting Story 1916–21*. The Kerryman, Tralee, 1949; new edn. Anvil Books, Tralee (n.d.).

McCartney, D. 'The Political Use of History in the Work of Arthur Griffith', *Journal of Contemporary History*, viii. No. 1 (Jan. 1973).

McCracken, J. I. *Representative Government in Ireland. A Study of Dáil Eireann, 1919–1948*. Oxford University Press, London, 1958.

McDonald, Rev. W. *Some Ethical Questions of Peace and War*. Burns and Oates, London, 1919.

McDonnell, Kathleen. *There is a Bridge at Bandon. A Personal Account of the Irish War of Independence.* Mercier, Cork, 1972.

McDowell, R. B. *The Irish Convention 1917–1918.* Routledge and Kegan Paul, London, 1970.

McEwen, J. M. 'The Liberal Party and the Irish Question during the First World War' *Journal of British Studies,* xii, 1972.

MacFarlane, L. J. 'Hands Off Russia: British Labour and the Russo-Polish War 1920', *Past and Present,* 38 (1967).

Mac Giolla Choille, B. *Intelligence Notes 1913–1916.* Oifig an Soláthair, Dublin, 1966.

Macready, Gen. Sir C. F. N. *Annals of an Active Life.* 2 vols., Hutchinson, London, 1924.

Mansergh, N. *The Irish Question 1840–1921.* Allen and Unwin, London, 1965.

Markievicz, Countess. *Prison Letters.* Longmans, London, 1934.

Martin, F. X. (ed.) *The Irish Volunteers 1913–1915.* James Duffy, Dublin, 1963.

Martin, F. X. (ed.) *Leaders and Men of the Easter Rising: Dublin 1916.* Methuen, London, 1967.

Martin, H. *Ireland in Insurrection.* Daniel O'Connor, London, 1921.

Midleton, Earl of. *Records and Reactions 1856–1939.* Murray, London, 1939.

Miller, D.W. *Church, State and Nation in Ireland 1898–1921.* Gill & Macmillan, Dublin 1973.

Morgan, K. O. 'Lloyd George's Premiership: A Study in "Prime Ministerial Government".' *Historical Journal,* xiii (1970).

Mowat, C. L. *Britain between the Wars.* Methuen, London, 1955.

Mullaly, Col. B. R. *The South Lancashire Regiment, the Prince of Wales's Volunteers.* White Swan Press, Bristol, 1955.

Neeson, E. *The Life and Death of Michael Collins.* Mercier, Cork, 1968.

Nevinson, H. W. 'The Anglo-Irish War', *Contemporary Review,* No. 667 (July 1921).

Nevinson, H. W. *Last Changes, Last Chances.* Nisbet, London, 1928.

Nicolson, H. *King George V.* Constable, London, 1952.

O Broin, L. *Dublin Castle and the 1916 Rising.* Sidgwick and Jackson, London, 1970.

O'Connor, Sir James. *A History of Ireland 1798–1924.* 2 vols., Arnold, London, 1925.

O'Donoghue, F. *No Other Law.* Irish Press, Dublin, 1954.

O'Donoghue, F. 'Guerrilla Warfare in Ireland'. *An Cosantóir,* xxiii (May 1963).

Officer's Wife. *see* Woodcock, Mrs.

O'Hegarty, P. S. *The Victory of Sinn Féin. How It Won It, and How It Used It.* Talbot Press, Dublin, 1924.

O Lúing, S. *I Die in a Good Cause. A Study of Thomas Ashe, Idealist and Revolutionary.* Anvil Books, Tralee, 1970.

O'Malley, E. *On Another Man's Wound.* Rich and Cowan, London, 1936. American edition: *Army Without Banners.* Houghton Mifflin, Boston, Mass., 1937.

O'Suilleabhain, M. *Where Mountainy Men Have Sown.* Anvil Books, Tralee, 1965.

Pakenham, F. (Earl of Longford) *Peace by Ordeal.* Jonathan Cape, London, 1935. New edition: Sidgwick and Jackson, London, 1972.

Petrie, Sir Charles. *The Life and Letters of the Rt. Hon. Sir Austen Chamberlain.* 2 vols., Cassell, London, 1940.

'Periscope', *see* Duggan, G. C.

Phillips, W. Alison. *The Revolution in Ireland.* Longmans, London, 1923.

Pope-Hennessy, R. *The Irish Dominion. A Method of Approach to a Settlement.* Nisbet, London, 1920.

Rhodes James, R. *Churchill. A Study in Failure 1900–1939.* Weidenfeld and Nicolson, London, 1970.

R.I.C. *Tales of the RIC.* Blackwood, Edinburgh, 1921.

Riddell, G. A. *Lord Riddell's War Diary.* Nicolson and Watson, London, 1933.

Riddell, G. A. *Lord Riddell's Intimate Diary of the Peace Conference and After.* Gollancz, London, 1933.

Roberts, A. (ed.) *Civilian Resistance as a National Defence.* Penguin Books, Harmondsworth, 1969.

Robinson, L. (ed.) *Lady Gregory's Journals 1916–1930.* Putnam, London, 1946.

Roskill, Capt. S. W. *Hankey. Man of Secrets.* Vol. 2, *1919–1931.* Collins, London, 1970.

Ryan, D. *Seán Treacy and the 3rd Tipperary Brigade.* Alliance Press, London, 1945.

Savage, D. W. '"The Parnell of Wales has become the Chamberlain of England": Lloyd George and the Irish Question', *Journal of British Studies,* xii (1972).

Street, C. J. C. ('I.O.') *The Administration of Ireland 1920.* Philip Allan, London, 1921.

Street, C. J. C. *Ireland in 1921.* Philip Allan, London, 1922.

Taber, R. *The War of the Flea. A Study of Guerrilla Warfare Theory and Practice.* Paladin, London, 1970.

Taylor, A. J. P. (ed.) *Lloyd George: Twelve Essays.* Hamish Hamilton, London, 1971.

Taylor, A. J. P. (ed.) *Lloyd George. A Diary by Frances Stevenson.* Hutchinson, London, 1971.

Taylor, R. *Michael Collins.* Hutchinson, London, 1958.

Ward, A. J. *Ireland and Anglo-American Relations 1899–1921.* Weidenfeld and Nicolson, L.S.E. London, 1969.

Ward, A. J. 'Lloyd George and the 1918 Irish Conscription Crisis', *Historical Journal,* xvii (1974).

War Office. *Manual of Military Law.* H.M.S.O., 1914.

Wheeler-Bennett, Sir J. W. *John Anderson, Viscount Waverley,* Macmillan, London, 1962.

Williams, D. (ed.) *The Irish Struggle 1916–1926.* Routledge and Kegan Paul, London, 1966.

Williams, T. D. (ed.) *Secret Societies in Ireland.* Gill and Macmillan, Dublin, 1973.

Wilson, T. (ed.) *The Political Diaries of C. P. Scott.* Collins, London, 1970.

Winter, Brig. O. de l'E. *Winter's Tale.* Richards Press, London, 1955.

'Woman of No Importance, A.' (? Mrs. A. C. Stuart Menzies) *As Others See Us.* Herbert Jenkins, London, 1924.

Woodcock, Mrs. *Experiences of an Officer's Wife in Ireland.* Blackwood, Edinburgh, 1921. (Published anonymously.)

Wylly, Col. H. C. *History of the Manchester Regiment.* vol. ii, *1883–1925.* Forster Groom, London, 1925.

Younger, C. *Ireland's Civil War.* Muller, London, 1968.

Younger, C. *A State of Disunion. Arthur Griffith, Michael Collins, James Craig, Eamon de Valera.* Muller, London, 1972.

INDEX

(references marked B in personal entries indicate biographical footnote)

Shortt, Edward: Chief Secretary for Ireland (1918–19), 9B; clashes with Lord French, 13; Home Secretary (1919), 20; doubts over proscription of Sinn Féin, 25, 26, 210; influence bewailed by Macpherson, 49; accepts 'full' martial law (June 1921), 190

Sinn Féin ('Ourselves'): Irish nationalist organization, founded by Griffith, 1; Convention in Dublin (1917), 7; proclaimed a Dangerous Association (1918), 10; illegal (1919), 27; victory in 1918 general election, 14; Executive plans public welcome for de Valera, 15; Lord French advocates crushing movement in its entirety, 23, 24, 25, 39, 97, 119–20; strength in summer 1920, 72; proscription of, 26, 31, 32, 79, 100; and elections of 1921, 179, 181; boycott of British goods, 189

Smith, T. J.: Deputy Inspector General, RIC; Walter Long argues should head RIC (May 1919), 25; replaces Byrne as Inspector General, 45, 75, 79, 82; fears breakdown of RIC, 92

Smyth, Colonel: RIC Divisional Commissioner, Cork, 97B

Soloheadbeg, Co. Tipperary: first fatal police casualties in rebel attack (January 1919), 16

Spa Conference, 100, 111n.

Special Military Areas, see Defence of the Realm Act

Stack, Austin: Dáil Minister of Justice, 15

Stevenson, Frances, 99, 179

Stokes mortars. use of in clearing road blocks, 87

Street, Maj. C. J. C. Irish Office publicity officer, 61–2, 65, 72, 185; list of reprisals, 119; on failure of military police, 192

Strickland, Maj. Gen. Sir Peter. GOC 6th Division, and Military Governor of Martial Law Area (December 1920), 44B; on army-police cooperation, 57, 83, 142, 165; expels ADRIC from Cork (December 1920), 139; and martial law, 140, 150, 176; official reprisals, 150–1, 185; Writ of Attachment against, 194

'Strickland Report': blames police for burnings in Cork, 139

Sturgis, Mark: Assistant Under Secretary, Dublin Castle, appointed July 1920, 80B, 98, 103, 108, 109, 113, 116, 118, 124, 135, 139, 161, 162, 169, 174, 185, 186; responsible for British railway policy (1920), 124–5; on need for unity of control in Ireland, 113, 162, 165

Swanzy, District Inspector, RIC: 96

Sykes, Maj. Gen. Sir Frederick: Chief of Air Staff, 170

Taylor, Sir John: Assistant Under Secretary, Dublin Castle: greed for work causing administrative bottleneck, 13B; favoured by Macpherson, 47; policy, 48; and re-creation of RIC Divisional Commissioners, 56; goes on leave and is replaced (April 1920), 76

Thomas, J. H.: General Secretary, National Union of Railwaymen, 71

Thomson, Sir Basil: Director of Intelligence, Home Office, 91, 179

Thomson, Brig. Gen. C. B.: military adviser, Labour Commission to Ireland, 159 and n.

Thurles, Co. Tipperary: first daylight assassination of police officer (June 1919), 20; effect of attack, 26

Tipperary: military reprisal at, 96

Tralee, Co. Kerry: 'blockaded' by RIC, 125

Treacy, Seán: Commandant, 3rd Tipperary Volunteers; carries out Soloheadbeg ambush, 16; Knocklong attack, 20; and 'Fernside' affray, 128; killed in Dublin, 122

Trenchard, Maj. Gen. Sir Hugh: Chief of Air Staff, 170

Trim. Co. Meath: looting of shop by Auxiliaries (February 1921), 163

Truce, Anglo-Irish: discussed by Cabinet, 178–9, 191–2; negotiation and terms, 197–9

Tuam, Co. Galway: military reprisal at, 96

Tudor, Maj. Gen. H. H.: Police Adviser, later Chief of Police, Ireland; selected by Churchill, 81; reorganization of RIC, 56, 92–5; Black and Tan recruitment, 46, 94; Auxiliary Division, 102, 110; policy, 97, 101, 102, 124; relations with civil and military authorities, 81–2, 141–2, 204; and reprisals, 95, 100, 116; Cork burnings, 139; police indiscipline, 142–3, 160, 163, 204; Sturgis on character of, 162; Lloyd George and Churchill's support of, 82, 163, 184

Ulster; constitutional problem, 35–6; separate administration (September 1920), 124

Umfreville, Col. R.: placed on RIC staff, 165, 186

Walsh, C. A.: Deputy Inspector General, RIC, 186 and n.